THE COMPLETE GUIDE TO
CONTESTED AUCTIONS

BY MIKE LAWRENCE

A world champion explains all the weapons
and the judgement necessary to win when the
enemy interferes with your opening bid.

LAWRENCE & LEONG PUBLISHING

Printed in the United States of America

Lawrence & Leong Publishing
10430 Greenview Drive
Oakland, California 94605

Library of Congress Catalog Card Number: 92-090023

ISBN 1-877908-04-5

CONTENTS

Chapter One

CONTESTED AUCTIONS

BRIDGE IS NOT PLAYED BY TWO PEOPLE. It is played by four people. You can study your system for months. You can discuss all the conventions in the world. You can create rules to cover every imaginable situation. And then you sit down to play.

Three rounds into the session, you take out your cards from the board, noting as you do that your partner is the dealer and that no one is vulnerable.

"One Diamond," says your partner. You look at your hand and find:

♠ 92　♡ AJ104　◇ Q7　♣ AKJ83

A nice hand. Not only is it a nice hand, but because of your system discussions, you know that your correct response is 2♣. This is almost game forcing in your methods. You intend to bid hearts later, which will tell partner that you have an honest forcing–to–game hand. From this point on, you will look for the best game contract and if the auction suggests it, you will be willing to look for a slam. All very nice.

"One Spade," interrupts your right hand opponent. What should you do? Should you go ahead with your 2♣ bid and expect the bidding to go the same way? Or should you make a Negative Double?

There are obvious dangers to either bid. If you bid 2♣, there is a fair chance that the opponents will raise spades. It might be awkward for you to show your heart suit. Let's say that you make a Negative Double instead. If partner bids hearts, you will be well placed. But if he rebids 2 ◊, you won't be able to show your clubs AND your strength.

At this moment, I don't intend to discuss the right bid. It is sufficient to show that an overcall can create problems for you. Your Two Over One system is one of the most powerful methods around but for all of its strengths, it is vulnerable in some competitive situations. On some sequences which do not include a two over one bid you will be on weaker ground yet.

WHEN THE OPPONENTS GET INTO YOUR AUCTION

This can happen in one of two ways. One of them forces you to make large changes in your bidding rules. The other one does relatively little. It is important to recognize the differences between the two.

Case One

You open the bidding and your LHO bids something (double, a one level overcall, a two level overcall, a preemptive overcall, a Michaels Cue Bid, an Unusual Notrump, or even a strong notrump overcall).

Case Two

You open with a one bid and your partner makes a response. Your RHO comes in with a bid of some sort.

NOTE the difference. In CASE ONE, your partner had to contend with a bid by your LHO. Your partner was under pressure and his bid is often skewed a little. Here's what I mean.

None Vulnerable
As East you hold ♠ 74   ♡ K94   ◇ AQJ86   ♣ 984

WEST	NORTH	EAST	SOUTH
1♠	2♣	?	

What should East bid? Should he pass? This might cost a partscore, a game, or even a slam. Should East make a Negative Double without four hearts? How about bidding 2◇? 2◇ could work, but it isn't the right bid if you play it as game forcing. What is the right bid?

The right bid isn't known yet. For now, I am busy presenting problems. The solutions will come up in the appropriate section.

Compare CASE ONE with CASE TWO. In CASE TWO, your side gets to open AND make a response before the opponents start to compete. For instance:

WEST	NORTH	EAST	SOUTH
1♠	Pass	2◇	2♡

In this auction, West bid 1♠ and East made a two over one response of 2◇. South now got in with a 2♡ bid but it came after East–West established the strength of their auction. West knows that East has real values. 2◇ shows a good hand and the 2♡ overcall can't take away anything from this fact.

What I will do in this book is look at both cases and see how the Two Over One structure is affected by the interference.

Chapter Two

THEY OVERCALL AT THE ONE LEVEL

IT IS SO IMPORTANT TO FIND A FIT that responder should try hard to get his suits in while it is still possible to do so. There are a couple of circumstances which need elaborating.

I am going to assume that your partnership is using Negative Doubles. If you are using them, many of your one level bids can be better defined than if you are not using them. If you are not using them, I recommend you do so. Opponents have learned how effective it is to compete and they do so much more freely nowadays than they did a few years ago. You will need the Negative Double to protect your equity in the hand.

RESPONDER BIDS A NEW SUIT AT THE ONE LEVEL

WEST	NORTH	EAST	SOUTH
1♣	1♢	1♡	

Questions

1. What is the weakest hand East can have?
2. What is the strongest hand East can have?
3. What is the weakest suit East can have?

Answers

1. What is the weakest hand East can have?

The weakest hand East can have ranges from a shapely five count up to a wretched seven count. The important considerations are the quality of the few points you have, the quality of the suit you are bidding, and the shape of your hand.

WEST	NORTH	EAST	SOUTH
1♣	1♢	1♡	

You hold ♠ 1072 ♡ AJ865 ♢ 73 ♣ 983

1♡ is acceptable. You have good concentration of values and you have a five card suit. If you want a further excuse, you can claim that you have a mild fit for partner's clubs. Also, you can pass if partner rebids 1♠. With bad hands you have to plan ahead to see if the auction can turn into an embarrassment.

You hold ♠ Q6 ♡ Q763 ♢ Q732 ♣ 752

Pass looks acceptable. If partner rebids 1NT or 2♣, you are reasonably happy. But if he rebids 1♠ or 2♡, you will be uncomfortable. I don't really criticize 1♡. But I would be happier if I had the 108 of hearts and the nine or ten of diamonds.

You hold ♠ 83 ♡ 8642 ♢ KQ63 ♣ Q62

Well? I would want to bid something. I think I would bid 1♡. I might pass. I might bid 1NT. Why give you a hand that I can't answer? Just to show you that problems can arise in the simplest of situations.

2. What is the strongest hand East can have?

There is no limit to the strength that East can have. I mention this point because I see things like this.

WEST	NORTH	EAST	SOUTH
1♣	1♦	?	

You hold ♠ AJ9 ♡ AKJ64 ◇ Q2 ♣ QJ3

Who knows where this hand is going? Bid 1♡ and hear what partner has to say. The bid that I hate is a 2◇ cue bid. This hand has lots of points but nothing else. In a later section, I will discuss what the cue bid should mean. For now, I will say that responder should not cue—bid just because he has a good hand. Bid naturally, find a fit, and then do your cue—bidding if called for.

3. What is the weakest suit East can have?

The weakest suit East can have is 5432. You can bid 1♡ over the 1◇ overcall because you can't make a Negative Double with only one major suit.

You hold ♠ A6 ♡ 7652 ◇ 9742 ♣ KJ7

WEST	NORTH	EAST	SOUTH
1♣	1◇	?	

You have to bid 1♡ if you want to show the suit. A Negative Double shows four cards in both majors. You can't double 1◇ with this hand. 1♡, 7652 not withstanding, is your only bid. If your major suits were reversed, you would have to bid 1♠ on your 7652.

Compare the above discussion with the following.

You hold ♠ 7652 ♡ A73 ◇ J108 ♣ K104

WEST	NORTH	EAST	SOUTH
1♣	1♡	?	

Assuming you are using the Negative Double, you can

double with this hand, which guarantees exactly four spades. Notice that East does not have four diamonds. All that he promises is four spades and enough points to be in the bidding. More on this later when we get to the Negative Double.

You hold ♠ AJ862   ♡ J2   ◇ KJ32   ♣ 93

Bid 1♠. The important feature of this bid is responder promises five or more spades. If responder had only four, he would double.

Some players make a different distinction with their Negative Doubles after a 1♡ overcall. They play that double denies four spades and implies four or more cards in the unbid minor. If they bid 1♠, it promises only four spades. I recommend against this style, but there are a lot of good players using it, so it obviously has merit. The reason I prefer double to promise four spades is that I like the ability to differentiate between four spades and five spades. I don't feel very strongly about this issue.

The Effects On Opener's Rebids

In this case, there are almost no changes in opener's rebids. Opener may have some difficulties if he wished to rebid 1NT but can't do it for lack of a stopper in the overcalled suit. Other than this, the bidding will proceed more or less as if there had not been an overcall.

RESPONDER BIDS A NEW SUIT
AT THE TWO LEVEL

Of all the sections in this book, this one is possibly the most important. The reason for this is that the partnership has to decide whether to retain the game forcing meaning of a two over one response or whether to revert to a more limited style of bidding. I showed this hand earlier. What should responder do when partner opens 1♠ and RHO overcalls 2♣?

You hold ♠ 74 ♡ K94 ◇ AQJ86 ♣ 984

If you play 2◇ as game forcing or at least game invitational, you can't bid 2◇. If you use Negative Doubles, you can't fall back on them for fear that partner will bid too many hearts. And finally, if you pass, you may not be able to show these values later. It's possible that the hand will get passed out in 2♣. That would be bad. (More on partner's reopening obligations later.)

The approach that I recommend in my book on Two Over One bidding is that when there is an overcall, a new suit at the two level does not show much. It is still forcing, of course, but it does not promise another bid. It certainly is not forcing to game.

WHY DO I RECOMMEND THIS STYLE? Why give up the strengths of playing a two over one as game forcing? There are many reasons.

1. The strengths of Two Over One bidding lie in game and slam bidding. When there is an overcall there is a modest presumption of strength in the overcaller's hand. The chance of slam has been decreased dramatically by the overcall. Even the chance of game is lessened. If games and slams aren't as likely as they would be in a noncompetitive auction it means that

partscores are relatively more important than normal. I believe that you have to cater more to partscores once there has been an overcall.

2. When there is no intervention over the opening bid, opener's partner has lots of available tools. He has one over one responses and the forcing notrump which can be used on the partscore hands.

   After an overcall, responder loses some of the one over one responses and he loses the forcing notrump response entirely. It is true that you gain the Negative Double but it is a partial replacement at best. My thinking is that you still need a way to show some of your ten or eleven point hands. If you can't make a Negative Double, the alternatives may be a light two over one response or a pass. The result is to play a 'free' two over one response as less than game forcing.

3. The third reason is less a reason than a reaffirmation of the value of a partscore. Partscores are valuable! If you are playing matchpoints and the opponents make 110 when you could have made 110 yourself or could have pushed them higher where you might have beat them, your matchpoint score will suffer. −110 will get you two or three matchpoints. +110 would have been worth eight or nine points. The average swing is six or seven matchpoints. Playing IMPS, losing 110 when you could have made 110 costs you six IMPS. Regardless of what you are playing for, the price for losing a partscore is very expensive. I'm not proud. If I can't make a game or slam, I will be quite willing to make a partscore if I can find a way to bid it.

Going back to:

♠ 74   ♡ K94   ◇ AQJ86   ♣ 984

I would bid 2◇ after 1♠–2♣–? It is forcing but it does not promise another bid.

This is not a new theory at all. It is exactly the same style of bidding that was popular from 1930 to 1975. "Bid what you have and bid what you think you can make." Believe me. It's not a bad style at all. The only problem with it is that when it was in vogue, bridge players used it exclusively. There was little method available for use with this style. What I am suggesting here is that you use the freewheeling style only when the bidding precludes your getting good results from your normal methods.

Here is a selection of hands illustrating this carte blanche style of responding.

WEST	NORTH	EAST	SOUTH
—	1♣	1♠	?

What do you bid in the South seat on these hands?

1. ♠ 5   ♡ AJ8532   ◇ KQ93   ♣ 82
2. ♠ K3   ♡ 853   ◇ QJ10753 ♣ Q3
3. ♠ 753   ♡ 43   ◇ AKQ1073 ♣ 74
4. ♠ 542   ♡ 632   ◇ AKQJ   ♣ J82
5. ♠ 7   ♡ J753   ◇ AKJ1074 ♣ Q3
6. ♠ 964   ♡ A9   ◇ KQJ108   ♣ 862

Answers

1. Bid 2♡. It is forcing for one round only. The problem with making a Negative Double is that when partner bids 1NT or 2♣, you still want to show your hearts. How many hearts should you bid? If you bid 2♡ over partner's 2♣ rebid, you will feel as though you have

extra values. I like bidding 2♡ right away since it gets my suit and strength into the bidding. Something else might happen if you make a Negative Double. The opponents might raise spades. If they bid 2♠, you can bid 3♡, but if they bid to 3♠ or 4♠, your hearts will be lost.

2. Pass. In a later section, I will introduce the 'Jump Shift in Competition'. At this moment, I just want to emphasize that 2◊ would show more. Even in my style of bidding, this hand is too weak to bid. If both of my minor suit queens were kings, giving me ten decent points instead of the eight I have, I would bid 2◊.

3. 2◊ is clear. You hope partner can bid notrump. Imagine how difficult this auction would be if you had to pass this hand. Partner would never expect you to have six winners. Your side might still be able to buy the hand, but 3NT won't be the contract.

4. Bid 2◊. A sad hand that would bother anyone. I would bid 2◊ expecting to pass as soon as possible. 2◊ is not a great bid by anyone's standards, but it does keep partner from bidding hearts. That is why I wouldn't make a Negative Double. If I double, partner will bid hearts and this hand won't be suitable at all.

5. Double. Finally a hand that can make a Negative Double. You have the points to bid 2◊ but you also have hearts, which might be lost if you fail to double.

6. 2◊. This is one of the more common hand types that you have to cater to. You have ten points and a good five card suit. Not enough to force to game, but good enough that you can expect to make something. If you don't bid with this hand, you have to find a suitable bid when the bidding continues in one of these ways:

WEST	NORTH	EAST	SOUTH
—	1♣	1♠	Pass
Pass	2♣	Pass	?

WEST	NORTH	EAST	SOUTH
—	1♣	1♠	Pass
Pass	Double	Pass	?

WEST	NORTH	EAST	SOUTH
—	1♣	1♠	Pass
2♠	Pass	Pass	?

WEST	NORTH	EAST	SOUTH
—	1♣	1♠	Pass
2♠	Double	3♠	?

Personally, I don't know what I should do in these situations to convince partner that I have this fine a hand. This brings up an important question.

WHEN CAN THE PARTNERSHIP STOP SHORT OF GAME?

The answer is that the partnership can stop short of game in many cases and in practice, does so. I would hazard a guess that in competition, a two over one response is made on a 'light' hand more than half of the time. You will still get to game about 70% of the time. If opener has a good opening bid, he won't let responder off the hook.

When Can Opener Pass Short Of Game?

Here are some auctions that allow opener to stop short of game after partner has made a two over one response in competition.

1. Opener can pass when he bids and rebids his suit and responder raises it.

WEST	NORTH	EAST	SOUTH
—	1♡	1♠	2♣
Pass	2♡	Pass	3♡
Pass	Pass	Pass	

2. Opener can pass when responder bids 2NT on the second round (unless opener has reversed).

WEST	NORTH	EAST	SOUTH
—	1♢	1♡	2♣
Pass	2♢	Pass	2NT
Pass	Pass	Pass	

3. Opener can pass when responder rebids his suit.

WEST	NORTH	EAST	SOUTH
—	1♡	1♠	2♣
Pass	2♢	Pass	3♣
Pass	Pass	Pass	

4. Opener can pass when responder takes a preference for opener's first suit.

WEST	NORTH	EAST	SOUTH
—	1♡	1♠	2♣
Pass	2♢	Pass	2♡
Pass	Pass	Pass	

NOTE that if responder raises opener's SECOND SUIT, it is forcing.

WEST	NORTH	EAST	SOUTH
—	1♡	1♠	2♣
Pass	2♢	Pass	3♢
Pass	?		

Opener can't pass. If responder had a hand that wasn't

interested in forcing, he would have bid 2♣ and then 3♣ or he would have made a Negative Double the first time.

When Can Responder Pass Short Of Game?

Here are four auctions that allow responder to stop short of game. NOTE that responder's two over one bid can be made over a one level overcall OR a two level overcall. This section is aimed at situations starting with a one level overcall, but the points made here are valid after a two level overcall too.

1. Responder can pass when the opponents compete and opener doesn't rebid.

WEST	NORTH	EAST	SOUTH
—	1♣	1♠	2♦
2♠	Pass	Pass	Pass

2. Responder can pass when opener rebids 2NT.

WEST	NORTH	EAST	SOUTH
—	1♡	1♠	2♦
Pass	2NT	Pass	Pass
Pass			

3. Responder can pass when opener raises responder's suit.

WEST	NORTH	EAST	SOUTH
—	1♣	1♠	2♦
Pass	3♦	Pass	Pass
Pass			

4. Responder can pass when opener rebids his suit.

WEST	NORTH	EAST	SOUTH
—	1♥	1♠	2◇
Pass	2♥	Pass	Pass
Pass			

WEST	NORTH	EAST	SOUTH
—	1◇	1♠	2♥
Pass	3◇	Pass	Pass
Pass			

How Does Responder Show When He Has Made A Light Two Over One Response?

Since responder can make light two over ones in competition, he has to have a way to show that he doesn't have full strength. The following rebids by responder after making a two over over one response in competition show limited hands. Opener can pass many sequences which would be forcing had there been no competition.

1. Opener can pass if responder gives a preference to opener's first suit.

South's Hand ♠ 542   ♥ J8   ◇ AJ3   ♣ KQ986

WEST	NORTH	EAST	SOUTH
—	1♥	1♠	2♣
Pass	2◇	Pass	2♥
Pass	Pass	Pass	

NOTE that South does not have a clear heart preference. Nor does he have game forcing values. What South has is a decent hand that can't make a Negative Double (questionable shape), and is too good to pass. You have to get into the bidding with hands like these. The price

16

you pay is that you lose some of the strengths of your Two Over One system. Your slam bidding, for instance, will suffer a little because you lose some of your nice Two Over One tools. Usually, though, you will have fewer slams when an opponent can make an overcall. In return for this, you will gain some partscores and you will even gain a few games when your light two over one bid reveal a super fit.

2. Opener can pass if responder bids 2NT.

South's hand ♠ Q102   ♡ 82   ◊ AK9753   ♣ Q5

WEST	NORTH	EAST	SOUTH
—	1♡	1♠	2◊
Pass	2♡	Pass	2NT
Pass	Pass	Pass	

South might have bid 2NT the first time, but it would give up on the diamond suit. If opener has a singleton spade, this hand could produce a game or slam in diamonds. I would give 2◊ 100 points and 2NT about 85.

3. Opener can pass if responder rebids his own suit.

South's hand ♠ A43   ♡ 3   ◊ KQJ863   ♣ 1096

WEST	NORTH	EAST	SOUTH
—	1♡	2♣	2◊
Pass	2♡	Pass	3◊
Pass	Pass	Pass	

This is the hand that would have bid 2◊ and then 3◊ even if East hadn't overcalled. In my version of Two Over One, I play that when responder bids and rebids his suit, it is not game forcing. The overcall doesn't change the method here.

NOTE that in a later section, I will introduce the 'Jump Shift in Competition'. It will help you define your hands when you do bid and rebid your suit as opposed to jumping in immediately after the overcall.

South's hand ♠ J ♡ A1076532 ◇ 92 ♣ KJ3

WEST	NORTH	EAST	SOUTH
—	1◇	1♠	2♡
Pass	2NT	Pass	3♡
Pass	Pass	Pass	

Opener's 2NT bid doesn't promise a heart fit. The auction has cramped his bidding room so he may have been obliged to bid 2NT on a hand that normally wouldn't have wanted to bid notrump. Here is a possible hand for opener:

♠ K983 ♡ 8 ◇ AQJ63 ♣ Q106

These two hands will be happy to stop in 3♡.

4. Opener can pass if he rebids his original suit and responder raises.

South's hand ♠ 973 ♡ 1083 ◇ AKQ83 ♣ Q9

WEST	NORTH	EAST	SOUTH
—	1♡	1♠	2◇
Pass	2♡	Pass	3♡
Pass	Pass	Pass	

You might say that you would make a limit raise with the South hand, but I would object to that. Except in extreme cases, I do not make jump raises without four trump. If I were to do so, I would have very good support and no other way to show it. For instance:

♠ 973 ♡ AQ5 ◇ KJ63 ♣ J43

3♡ is acceptable since other alternatives don't exist. (Some players play that a Negative Double followed by

18

support shows the limit raise hand with only three card support. This works okay in general, but gets confusing if the opponents keep bidding. Sometimes the bidding is too high to show your support comfortably. More on this later.)

Also, I would hesitate to raise opener's 2♡ rebid to 3♡ without three card support. Opener may have only five hearts. His heart rebid does not promise six of them. It is much better for opener to rebid a five card suit now and then after a two over one response than to have to fabricate a bid he doesn't really want to make. (For more on this, read my Two Over One book, pages 12–21.)

Since responder can make light two over one responses after an overcall, opener will have to make strong rebids when he has extra values. Responder doesn't guarantee a rebid so if opener wishes to get to game, he has to make a strong rebid.

Here are a number of hands illustrating these points.

1.

	WEST	EAST	
	♠ 52	♠ K96	
	♡ AQ654	♡ 8	
	◇ AQ8	◇ KJ10954	
	♣ 1076	♣ QJ4	

WEST	NORTH	EAST	SOUTH
1♡	1♠	2◇	Pass
3◇	Pass	Pass	Pass

On West's second bid, he has to be aware that East is likely to pass. West's choices are 2♡ and 3◇. I like the raise because it follows the guideline that says you should show a fit when you can. West therefore raises to 3◇. East has a minimum hand and passes 3◇ as he is permitted to do.

2.

WEST		EAST	
♠ A3		♠ K6	
♡ 754		♡ Q83	
◇ AKJ63		◇ Q2	
♣ AQ7		♣ KJ10954	

WEST	NORTH	EAST	SOUTH
1◇	1♡	2♣	Pass
2♡	Pass	2NT	Pass
3♣	Pass	3NT	Pass
Pass	Pass		

The important part of this auction is how West handles the bidding when East bids 2♣ in competition. East's free 2♣ bid doesn't show too much so West has to make a bid that East can't pass. In this case, West wants to show a good hand with club support. The way he does it is to make a cue bid. This is tentatively an artificial bid telling East that West has a good raise for partner. The cue bid is forcing to game, or if you wish, to 4♣.

3.

WEST		EAST	
♠ 862		♠ J43	
♡ AQ732		♡ K5	
◇ AQ53		◇ J72	
♣ 8		♣ KQJ73	

WEST	NORTH	EAST	SOUTH
1♡	1♠	2♣	Pass
2◇	Pass	2♡	Pass
Pass	Pass		

When West rebids 2◇, it is a new suit and is therefore forcing. East can't pass yet. East preferences to 2♡ on a hand that is miles from what he would have if the auction had been an uncontested two over one sequence.

4.

	WEST	EAST
♠	K106	♠ J7
♡	J6	♡ AQ843
◇	KJ1084	◇ Q92
♣	A108	♣ Q72

WEST	NORTH	EAST	SOUTH
1◇	1♠	2♡	Pass
2NT	Pass	Pass	Pass

East is allowed to pass 2NT and he does. West should have a minimum for this bid. If West has even a little bit extra such that he would want to play in 3NT opposite an eleven count, he should bid 3NT.

5.

	WEST	EAST
♠	KQ8	♠ 6
♡	K10	♡ A9875
◇	AJ843	◇ K106
♣	J105	♣ A842

WEST	NORTH	EAST	SOUTH
1◇	1♠	2♡	Pass
3NT	Pass	Pass	Pass

East has one of those minimum hands that might pass a 2NT rebid by opener. West has only fourteen points but they include a heart fit and they include a double spade stopper. West should bid 3NT to ensure getting to game.

This style of bidding plays hob with your slam bidding. This is a big price to pay, in theory. At the table, though, it seems to work. Remember. The overcall takes away your favorite tools so you have to use whatever is second best. Some versions of Two Over One bidding like to play that a two over one is forcing to game even in competition. I agree that this understanding is the best one possible if you are going to have lots of game forcing hands. If you are like me, though, you usually have medium hands which aren't good enough to make forcing two over one bids. I try to use a method that caters to the hands that I have, not the ones some other author has.

6.

	WEST		EAST
	♠ AK3		♠ 1084
	♡ KQ862		♡ J4
	◇ J3		◇ AKQ74
	♣ 975		♣ J106

WEST	NORTH	EAST	SOUTH
1♡	1♠	2◇	Pass
2♡	Pass	Pass	Pass

No contract is too good here so stopping in a partscore is reasonable. The important thing is to recognize that West can rebid a five card suit and that East can pass with a small doubleton. It is unlikely that East will ever pass 2♡ with a singleton. If East has a singleton heart, he will usually have a six card suit to rebid and will do so.

7.

	WEST		EAST
	♠ A73		♠ J92
	♡ AK10863		♡ J4
	◇ Q3		◇ K74
	♣ K4		♣ AQ1085

WEST	NORTH	EAST	SOUTH
1♡	1♠	2♣	Pass
3♡	Pass	4♡	Pass
Pass	Pass		

The point of this hand is that West can't afford to rebid only 2♡. It is passable. West's 3♡ bid isn't up to normal Two Over One standards, which require a solid suit, but it is necessary under the circumstances.

8.

	WEST		EAST	
	♠ 983		♠ 107	
	♡ KJ6		♡ A87	
	◇ A973		◇ QJ2	
	♣ AQ8		♣ KJ1064	

WEST	NORTH	EAST	SOUTH
1◇	1♠	2♣	2♠
3♣	Pass	3◇	Pass
3♡	Pass	4♣	Pass
Pass	Pass		

Lots of stuff going on here. The specific addressable points are:

a) West's bid of 3♣ is forcing. West didn't have room to show a weak raise to 3♣ and a strong raise to 3♣. South's 2♠ bid got in the way. This raises a question your partnership has to answer. Should you keep opener's raise as weak when both opponents are bidding or should you say that it shows extra values? My view is that opener's raise should be forcing for one round. If opener has a weakish raise, too bad. If opener has a strong raise, he is assured of another bid from partner.

b) East rebids 3◇. He has to do something since West's raise is forcing.

c) West has a choice of bids. He can bid 3♡ showing a heart stopper. Or he can bid 3♠ asking for a spade stopper. Whatever your partnership tends to do in these situations is fine.

d) East has a minimum without a spade stopper so he goes back to 4♣. I think this should show a minimum hand and that opener should be allowed to pass. If responder had more, he would have to show it now.

9.

	WEST		EAST
	♠ 972		♠ 1083
	♡ AQ864		♡ J95
	◇ AQJ5		◇ K7
	♣ 9		♣ AQJ62

WEST	NORTH	EAST	SOUTH
1♡	1♠	2♣	Pass
2◇	Pass	3♡	Pass
4♡	Pass	Pass	Pass

If this makes, your opponents aren't going to be happy. The reason I include this hand is that it represents one of the problems that you may have. East has only three trumps and they aren't good enough for a limit raise. East starts with 2♣. When West rebids 2◇, East has to choose from an underbid of 2♡ and an overbid of 3♡. I would make the overbid because of the quality of the points. We will be in a bad game, but I think somewhat unavoidably. In a way, this hand doesn't fit too well. If opener had one less spade and one more club, 4♡ would be a better spot.

10.

	WEST		EAST
	♠ 972		♠ Q83
	♡ AQ864		♡ 753
	◇ AQJ5		◇ 94
	♣ 9		♣ AKQ107

WEST	NORTH	EAST	SOUTH
1♡	1♠	2♣	Pass
2◇	Pass	2♡	Pass
Pass	Pass		

This hand has similar values as the previous one. On Hand 9, my approach got us too high. On this hand, my approach allowed us to stop in a sensible partscore.

11.

WEST		EAST	
♠ A75		♠ 963	
♡ QJ72		♡ AK1083	
◇ AQJ92		◇ K8	
♣ 7		♣ J82	

WEST	NORTH	EAST	SOUTH
1◇	2♣	2♡	Pass
4♣*	Pass	4◇	Pass
4NT	Pass	5♡**	Pass
6♡	Pass	Pass	Pass

* Shows a heart raise and a singleton club.
** Key Card response showing two key cards.

This is a good slam to reach. East–West have 24 working points and a couple of wasted extras. The key to it is to get the heart fit established early enough to have a sensible cue bidding auction. If East is not allowed to bid 2♡ because he needs a better hand, the auction is likely to bog down in a game or even a partscore. You can tell me that you would bid it anyway, and I am prepared to believe you. You can believe me that there are many pairs who would miss this one if East couldn't bid 2♡ over 2♣.

12.

WEST		EAST	
♠ AQ872		♠ 103	
♡ 3		♡ AQJ872	
◇ K3		◇ 742	
♣ QJ763		♣ K4	

WEST	NORTH	EAST	SOUTH
1♠	2◇	2♡	Pass
2♠	Pass	Pass	Pass

West can't bid 3♣. Bidding a new suit at the three level shows a good hand regardless of whether East's two over one was in competition or not.

13.

WEST	EAST
♠ AKJ54	♠ 102
♡ 3	♡ AQJ872
◇ A3	◇ 742
♣ A10763	♣ K4

WEST	NORTH	EAST	SOUTH
1♠	2◇	2♡	Pass
3♣	Pass	3♡	Pass
?			

It is not clear what West should do now. With his aces and kings, a raise to 4♡ makes some sense. Also possible is 3NT. I lean towards 4♡ and regret that the singleton heart is not more substantial. It is important to see that West has to do something. West's 3♣ bid showed a good hand since he went to the three level. It created a forcing auction which is forcing to at least 4♣. This means that East's 3♡ bid can not end the auction. Compare the considerations for this hand with the prior hand where West had a weak opening bid.

RESPONDER MAKES A JUMP SHIFT TO THE TWO LEVEL

What do you do when you have a hand that you know should be bidding but which will be a disappointment to partner if he plays the hand himself? For instance:

None Vulnerable
As South you hold ♠ Q107643   ♡ J72   ◇ J103   ♣ 6

WEST	NORTH	EAST	SOUTH
—	1♣	1◇	?

What do you bid?

Everyone I know does something. Six card spade suits are hard to suppress. But can you get away with bidding them? If you bid 1♠, everything is wonderful if partner doesn't rebid too many clubs or if he doesn't insist on notrump. But he always does. Or maybe the bidding continues and partner doubles 3◇ hoping you have something.

There is an answer to hands like this. It is called the 'Weak Jump Shift in Competition' (WJSC). It works this way. If the opponents overcall at the one level and you have a hand with a six card suit but which doesn't have enough strength to bid at the one level, you can play that a jump to the two level shows the hand. There are three advantages to this.

1. You get to bid your suit. Yea!!!

2. You tell partner that you have less than six points.

3. You make life harder for your LHO, who may have a decent hand of his own.

Doesn't It Cost You Not To Have A Strong Jump Shift Available?

You have to weigh the pros and cons and balance them with their respective frequencies. Tell me. When is the last time that the bidding went 1♣ by your partner, 1◇ on your right, and you had a hand that wanted to make a strong jump shift? I have played a lot of hands and I can't recall having a suitable hand. I have had, however, a fair number of hands with 3–5 points that really wanted to bid but which could lead to disaster if partner got excited.

In terms of frequency, I believe you will have thirty or forty hands which can benefit from the WJSC before you will have one hand that might gain from being able to use the strong jump shift.

If it is agreed that the WJSC comes up often enough to justify using it, it is still necessary that the convention works well enough that you want to use it.

This isn't difficult to show. Properly used, the WJSC has all the benefits mentioned above. It allows you to show your suit, it doesn't mislead partner, and it makes life more difficult for the opponents. Its only drawback is that if you find partner with a poor hand, you may go for a number. It can happen. There are many reasons why you shouldn't worry about that. The first reason is that the opponents have to double you. Sometimes they have you set a bunch, but they can't judge this so they bid something and you escape. Or perhaps they just pass it out and you escape undoubled. The second reason is problematical. We both know that sooner or later, we are going to bid on one of these weak four point hands and sooner or later, we are going to get into trouble. Usually in the form of an irate partner who wants to know what we were bidding on. My feeling about this is that if I am going to bid on these bad hands, I might as well do it in a way that keeps partner informed and which has some definite tactical benefits.

What Should A WJSC Look Like?

There are two ways to play this bid. You can play it sensibly or you can play it with abandon. In both cases, you have to keep an eye on the vulnerability.

The Nonvulnerable WJSC
If You Play Them Sensibly

If you play the WJSC as it was originally intended to be played, you will have a range of 2–5 high card points and a six or seven card suit. Partner will expect you to have a six card suit, but a seven bagger is okay if you can't bring yourself to jump to three (see ensuing sections).

None Vulnerable

WEST	NORTH	EAST	SOUTH
—	1♣	1♡	?

1. ♠ QJ8642　♡ 863　♢ 42　♣ J7

Bid 2♠. This is the classic hand for this bid. You have the average number of points and a decent six card suit.

2. ♠ J98642　♡ 8642　♢ K2　♣ 4

Bid 2♠. The suit is weaker, but the playing strength is quite good. No one who has used the WJSC would overlook this one.

3. ♠ 1097652　♡ J42　♢ 7　♣ Q106

You can bid 2♠ or you can pass. I see nothing wrong with 2♠. You have minimum points, but you have nice shape and you have a fitting card in clubs. If you don't bid 2♠, won't you feel that you possibly should have? As this auction goes on, I know that I would be having second thoughts.

　　Let's say that West bids 1NT and it is passed back to me. I can still bid 2♠. That part is true. There is a huge and important difference. If I had bid 2♠ the first time, West might not have known what to do. Having passed, West has been able to bid 1NT, which tells East all kinds of things and which also carries lots of negative inferences. By passing, I have allowed the opponents to have free bidding room which they have used to advantage. By waiting and then bidding 2♠ (assuming I choose to do so) I have lost the element of surprise. West won't be nearly as bothered as he would have been had I bid 2♠ earlier. Remember that even if 2♠ is a wretched contract, the opponents won't always be able to double it.

There is another fear which I hear expressed. Some of my students say that they hate to bid such a bad suit because partner will lead it. This is a thinking objection but it isn't a major one as long as you are playing with an understanding partner. If your jump to 2♠ shows 3–5 points, you can't have a good suit. Your average suit will be something like Q107532. Hardly a lead directing effort.

I don't think you are abusing the convention to bid 2♠ on this hand. In practice, if you are not vulnerable, any six card suit is worth bidding with if the hand has suitable points.

4. ♠ J109853   ♡ 2   ◇ 862   ♣ J94

With your partner's blessing, this is still an acceptable 2♠ bid IF THE OPPONENTS ARE VULNERABLE. If they are not vulnerable, I would stick to the 3–5 point range. Note that the two points you have are working. You have good spots in your suit and the two jacks should be useful.

5. ♠ 975432   ♡ Q4   ◇ 863   ♣ 52

Whatever the vulnerability is, this is not a 2♠ bid. You have the worst possible six card suit, no shape, and a wasted two points. If your queen was the queen of diamonds, you could hope it was worth something. If it was the queen of clubs you could count on it. But it is the queen of hearts, the opponent's suit, which means it is the least useful of queens. It will be worth an average of 1⁻ of a point in the long run whereas the queen of clubs would be worth about 3^+ points. If you are going to make a WJSC with minimum high cards, at least let them be working high cards.

6. ♠ K108743   ♡ 86   ◊ Q32   ♣ 104

Bid 2♠. This is about as good a hand as you will have when not vulnerable.

7. ♠ AJ10863   ♡ 843   ◊ 10   ♣ 954

Bid 1♠ or 2♠. Your partnership can decide whether this is too good or whether it is just a maximum.

8. ♠ KJ8654   ♡ 63   ◊ J82   ♣ Q2

Bid 1♠. Do not abuse the high card requirements of the WJSC. If you bid 2♠, your partner won't try for 3NT when he has 18–19 balanced points. He will expect you to have a queen less. A convention is only as good as it can be when it is followed correctly. It may feel like fun to jump to 2♠ with only one point. You may feel like you are showing good judgment when you jump to 2♠ with seven points ("they were bad points, partner"). But all you will be doing is losing partner's faith. Take the benefits that come from using a convention properly rather than try to push it to the limit.

9. ♠ J986532   ♡ Q6   ◊ J2   ♣ 107

Bid 2♠. A seven card suit is unlikely, but possible. In the next two chapters, I will discuss jumps to the three level. This is such a bad hand that it isn't logical that you would want to be at the three level but it is good enough that you want to bid. 2♠ is a fair compromise that tells partner you have a six card suit but not enough points to bid 1♠. Your seventh spade will be a surprise, but the general nature of your hand is as expected. If you are not happy with bidding 2♠, think how happy you would be if you bid 1♠ and partner reversed to 2◊.

10. ♠ 82   ♡ 9763   ◇ AJ9863   ♣ 4

This hand is just a reminder that the previous discussion applies only to jump responses at the two level. If the suit you want to bid requires you jump to the three level, you have to refer to one of the next two chapters.

The Nonvulnerable WJSC
If You Play Them With Abandon

There are some hands which feel as if they should be bidding but which don't fit into the normal definition of the WJSC. There are two types of hands. A hand with a poor six card suit and fewer than 3–5 points. Hands with a pretty good five card suit and 3–5 points. I will show and discuss both of these styles with examples.

Let me start this section with a disclaimer. I don't recommend you go to the extremes shown here. I include them because a number of players do make bids like these. I imagine you know some of them. For the most part, the best thing I can say about the bids illustrated here is that they can work.

In an effort to show how well a WJSC will work with one of the following hands, I have graded them on the ABCDF scale that was in use when I dropped out of college. An A means I approve of the bid assuming you are using pushy Weak Jump Shifts in Competition. An F means I wouldn't make the bid myself, but that I have seen others do so.

None Vulnerable

WEST	NORTH	EAST	SOUTH
—	1♣	1◇	?

1. ♠ 73   ♡ J86532   ◇ Q62   ♣ 82

Should you bid 2♡? You have the required three points, but the queen of diamonds is wasted and you don't have any heart spots. The only reason I can think of for bidding 2♡ is that it stops West from bidding 1♠. An axiom of bridge is that it is harder to bid against busy bidders than passive bidders. If you bid 2♡ on this hand, you will certainly qualify as a busy bidder. WITHIN THE FRAMEWORK of bidding WJSC with abandon, 2♡ gets a C–.

2. ♠ 976432   ♡ 76   ◇ 3   ♣ Q853

Should you bid 2♠? Your shape says it is okay and your fit in clubs gives you some safety. Within the framework of bidding WJSC with abandon, 2♠ gets a B.

3. ♠ 62   ♡ KQ1073   ◇ 862   ♣ 843

Should you bid 2♡? Making a WJSC with a five card suit is one of your realistic options. It has some merit. On the positive side is the fact that if you are jumping with a five card suit, you will have a good enough suit that you will actually like it if partner leads your suit. If you make this bid with a five card suit and partner has a singleton for you, your contract won't be any fun. You should have a goodish five card suit. After all, you have to have something good to say about your hand if you bid with bad hands. WITHIN THE FRAMEWORK of bidding WJSC with abandon, 2♡ gets an A.

4. ♠ 7542   ♡ A10963   ◇ 63   ♣ 96

Should you bid 2♡? Perhaps. You have a good suit, but it is not the kind of suit that needs partner to lead it. You will get your ace sooner or later. One problem with 2♡ is that you have four spades. Spades could be your spot. This hand would be better for 2♡ if you had almost any other shape that didn't include those spades. WITHIN THE FRAMEWORK of bidding WJSC with abandon, 2♡ gets a

C–. BUT, if you had 3–5–2–3 or similar shape, I would give 2♡ a B–.

5. ♠ QJ1073   ♡ 72   ◇ 1062   ♣ J53

Should you bid 2♠? Not a bad bid! 2♠ is very preemptive and will give West serious difficulties. I like this bid. At least, I like it in theory. Note that you have a good spade suit and you have mini help in clubs. It is important with five card suits not to have anything wasted. WITHIN THE FRAMEWORK of bidding WJSC with abandon, 2♠ gets a B+.

6. ♠ Q9642   ♡ J52   ◇ Q52   ♣ 73

Should you bid 2♠? No. You have a bad suit and red suit high cards which may be worthless. The combination of both of these flaws says to pass. WITHIN THE FRAMEWORK of bidding WJSC with abandon, 2♠ gets an F.

7. ♠ AJ1095   ♡ 74   ◇ 982   ♣ 873

Should you bid 2♠? I think yes. You have a good suit and good high cards (given what you are supposed to have). WITHIN THE FRAMEWORK of bidding WJSC with abandon, 2♠ gets an A–.

8. ♠ J72   ♡ KJ1083   ◇ J62   ♣ 106

Should you bid 2♡? No. Do not make a WJSC with these high card points. It is confusing enough to partner to have you making WJSC with five card suits. If you also do it with too many points, your partnership will be at odds. WITHIN THE FRAMEWORK of bidding WJSC with abandon, 2♡ gets an F.

The Vulnerable WJSC

If you are vulnerable, you have to be careful with your WJSC. The opponents can get rich by beating you two tricks undoubled and –200 may be a zero. If you do get doubled and partner has a poor hand (translate this to mean no fit for you), you can go for –200 for down just one, up to –800 and more. Vulnerable, you need some tighter definitions in your bidding.

Vulnerable, you don't have the room for freedom of expression that you had when you were not vulnerable. For this reason, I will present one discussion of the WJSC. If you insist on varying from these guidelines, do so at your own risk.

A vulnerable WJSC at the two level should show these qualities.

1. A decent six or seven card suit. Don't do this vulnerable with five card suits. In the prior section, I suggested that you might make a WJSC with five card suits, but the circumstances were specified and recommended rather tentatively.

2. Have 4–6$^+$ points. The lower range is moved to four GOOD points. The upper range is also moved up. Vulnerable, you are allowed to make a WJSC with a hand that could conceivably bid at the one level. This is allowed because the lower range is moved up. You still have a small 2$^+$ point range.

EXAMPLES: Vulnerable

WEST	NORTH	EAST	SOUTH
—	1♣	1♦	?

1. ♠ KQ10875   ♡ 762   ◇ Q2   ♣ 93

Bid 2♠. You have seven high card points, but you can demote the queen of diamonds a little. 2♠ shows 4–6⁺ points and a decent suit. That is what you have. Note that this hand would be too good for a nonvulnerable 2♠ bid. Vulnerable, your range moves up to protect you from yourself.

2. ♠ 65   ♡ QJ87542   ◇ K2   ♣ 82

Bid 2♡ or even 3♡ if your methods permit. It is much better to bid 2♡ with this hand than to bid 1♡. 1♡ could show:

♠ AK3   ♡ 10874   ◇ A643   ♣ K3

Since you can closely define your hand on what may become a competitive auction, you should do so. Partner will be able to judge well after a 2♡ bid. If you bid 1♡, you will have to spend the rest of the auction telling him you have lots of hearts and poor points. Why not tell it all in one bid?

3. ♠ Q86532   ♡ K102   ◇ Q10   ♣ 93

Bid 1♠. You can demote this hand to get it into the range for a WJSC but no amount of wishing will turn this spade suit into a decent six card suit. Bid 1♠ and then rebid 2♠ if appropriate.

4. ♠ J109852   ♡ 73   ◇ A107   ♣ 109

Bid 2♠. Your spade suit has top losers, but it is solid otherwise. You should be able to hold your losers to three even opposite a singleton. By comparison, on the previous hand, you could lose four tricks opposite a doubleton. In addition, this hand has good points. Your two high cards are each worth a trick.

Vulnerable

WEST	NORTH	EAST	SOUTH
—	1♣	1◇	?

5. ♠ KJ10653   ♡ KJ4   ◇ 82   ♣ 62

Bid 1♠. The reason this hand is in here is to offer you the possibility of changing your ranges for WJSC when vulnerable. I like the 4–6$^+$ point range I have been talking about but I realize that some players won't feel good about it. It makes sense to find a range you are happy with. Getting a six card suit off your chest in one bid puts your partnership in control of the auction. If you don't like my range, I suggest raising it up to 5–8 points when vulnerable. This will allow you to jump to 2♠ with this hand. I think you will give up some good opportunities. But you will still net something valuable if your alternative is to wait endlessly for a strong jump shift. Whatever range you choose, you must stick to it. If your agreed range is the 4–6$^+$ point range I recommend, you can't suddenly decide to do it with some eight point hand. Partner will misjudge the hand and it will be your fault.

6. ♠ 103   ♡ KQJ97   ◇ 8632   ♣ 96

Bid 1♡. Five card suits may be okay when not vulnerable.

7. ♠ A1096   ♡ K109874   ◇ 4   ♣ 75

Bid 1♡. Don't bid 2♡ and jeopardize your possible spade fit. Remember. Just because the opponents have overcalled, it is not necessarily their hand. If the hand belongs to you, you want to get to the best spot.

8. ♠ A109753   ♡ 10873   ◇ 5   ♣ Q4

I don't know. You could bid 2♠, going for the most

descriptive bid, or you could bid 1♠ hoping somehow to get hearts into the game. The trouble with 1♠ is that you are not going to find the heart suit unless something unusual happens. For instance, if you bid 1♠ and North rebids 1NT, will you show the hearts or will you rebid 2♠? Likewise, if partner rebids 2♣, will you have the courage to bid 2♡, which will be forcing? I wouldn't have the nerve. In the real world, this hand doesn't have a way to bid the hearts. Actually, you might get away with a Negative Double. It feels alien to me.

9. ♠ K10863   ♡ AQJ   ◇ KQ   ♣ KJ3

Even if I had a strong jump shift, I wouldn't want to make one. I would rather bid 1♠ and see what partner wanted to do. This hand is shown here to emphasize how rare a true jump shift is after an overcall. How often will your partner open the bidding, your opponent have the ten or more points (give or take) for an overcall, and you in turn have the points for a strong jump shift? Even if you have the points, it is not likely that you will have the right kind of hand for the jump.

How Does Opener Rebid After Responder Makes A Two Level Weak Jump Shift?

When responder makes a WJSC, opener usually passes. Occasionally, opener competes. What does opener do if he has a good hand?

The situation won't come up often enough to require much discussion, but it is necessary to have some understandings. A simple one is to play whatever method you use after your weak two bids. I will give a couple of examples using 2NT asking for a feature. You can adapt any other structure in similar fashion.

1. None Vulnerable

WEST	EAST
♠ A4	♠ Q107652
♡ 8643	♡ J
◇ AJ	◇ 8532
♣ AKQ63	♣ J8

WEST	NORTH	EAST	SOUTH
1♣	1♡	2♠	Pass
2NT	Pass	3♠	Pass
Pass	Pass		

West has a lot of tricks and he has adequate spade support. Using 2NT to ask for a feature, West asks East to evaluate his hand. East has only shown 3–5 high card points, so East will evaluate his hand in this light. If East has a minimum, he will sign off in 3♠. If East has more, he will bid the closest thing to a stopper that he has. I don't think it likely that West will ever bid 2NT without a fit for partner so East should be allowed to jump to 4♠ if he feels like it.

On this hand, East has a minimum. His jack of hearts doesn't count for much so he has a three count with good shape. East shows his minimum by bidding 3♠ and West passes.

2. Opponents Vulnerable

WEST	EAST
♠ J43	♠ K109852
♡ 5	♡ 863
◇ AKQJ4	◇ 72
♣ A863	♣ Q10

WEST	NORTH	EAST	SOUTH
1◇	1♡	2♠	Pass
2NT	Pass	3♣	Pass
4♠	Pass	Pass	Pass

West can envision a game. He might even bid it directly over East's 2♠ bid. If East can be trusted to have a six card suit, 4♠ is a good risk. This is the most suspicious of vulnerabilities, though. We are not vulnerable. They are. If it is possible that East can have one of those horrors that I showed as an example of free speech in the preceding section, West should ask East for an opinion as he does here. In this case, East sees five high card points and a good spade suit. He can bid 3♣ which is supposed to show a 'feature'. Since East's range is 3–5 points, he is unlikely to have an ace or a king on the side so a queen will have to do. Once West finds out that East has something reasonable, he goes to game.

Since there has been an overcall, there is a good chance that the opponents will be bidding. When this happens, opener has to use his judgment. It shouldn't be too difficult to do this because partner has a very narrow range of possible values. I suggest that you use opener's raise as a preemptive bid regardless of whether the opponents are bidding over the WJSC. If opener can bid 2NT he uses that bid as his invitational bid and if there is competition, opener just guesses. For example.

3. None Vulnerable

WEST	EAST
♠ A72	♠ KJ8653
♡ 872	♡ J6
◇ 72	◇ 1093
♣ AKJ92	♣ 104

WEST	NORTH	EAST	SOUTH
1♣	1◇	2♠	3◇
3♠	?		

West knows that there is no game. West also knows that the opponents may have a game of their own. West's raise to 3♠ is competitive. West would bid 3♠ whether South raised to 3 ◇ or passed. Looking at the East–West hands, it looks like the opponents can make from 2♡ to 4♡ depending on how many spade and club losers they have.

East is not invited to bid when West raises to 3♠. West's decision is final. NOTE the question mark in the bidding box. West's 3♠ bid has taken away important bidding room from North. North rates to have a good hand. Perhaps he was about to bid 3♡. Perhaps he wanted to bid 3♠ to ask for a spade stopper. Whatever North's intentions, he will have to make his decisions at the four level.

4. Both Vulnerable

	WEST	EAST
♠	Q95	K107642
♡	862	105
◇	AKJ652	74
♣	A	Q94

WEST	NORTH	EAST	SOUTH
1◇	1♡	2♠	3♡
4♠	Pass	Pass	Pass

West has no room to do any asking so he makes a decision. West knows there are only one or two heart losers so the hand fits well. The opponents did bid up to 3♡ vulnerable. They will have eight hearts and usually will have nine. Therefore 4♠ should be playable.

5. Opponents Vulnerable

	WEST	EAST
♠	4	A98632
♡	Q72	93
◇	K82	1064
♣	AKQ1072	84

WEST	NORTH	EAST	SOUTH
1♣	1♡	2♠	Pass
Pass	Pass		

West should pass 2♠. However good or bad the contract is, West should accept it. It's not even clear that clubs is better than spades. Spades is a level lower than clubs, which is a plus. Also, West's club suit will take tricks for East in spades. East's spades will probably be useless for West if he plays in clubs.

Now, a different question. If West does bid 3♣, is it clearly a sign–off bid or is it forcing? I think you can do anything you want but you must agree. I don't think I have discussed this one with any of my partners so you may be forgiven if you don't have an agreement on this issue.

And a final question. What if West bids a new suit after East makes a WJSC? For instance:

WEST	NORTH	EAST	SOUTH
1◇	1♡	2♠	Pass
3♣			

What does 3♣ mean? Again, I don't have agreements on this, but I would surely think partner had a good hand. I would bid again whatever I had for my weak jump response. Spend twenty seconds on this with partner, remember your agreement, and you won't have to worry about it. One thing I promise you. If you have an agreement, the problem will never come up. If you don't have an agreement, you will pick up:

♠ None   ♡ 32   ◇ AKJ873   ♣ AQ1096

and the bidding will go:

WEST	NORTH	EAST	SOUTH
1◇	1♡	2♠	Pass
?			

and you will wonder whether 3♣ by you is forcing or passable. It will happen tomorrow. I promise.

RESPONDER MAKES
A THREE LEVEL JUMP SHIFT

This section is a variation of the last one. This time, you have to decide how you want to play your jump shifts to the three level.

For most of the reasons that I used to justify the WJSC at the two level, I would also recommend the WJSC at the three level. If you are thinking in terms of strong jump shifts, I suggest you look elsewhere. Their frequency is so low that you will wait forever before one will come up. Conversely, if you are using a jump shift to show some sort of fit for partner's suit, then you are probably doing something good. But, if your methods don't provide you with a meaning for a three level jump shift after an overcall, then I think the treatment here should be adopted.

The only difference between a two level WJSC and a three level WJSC is that if responder wants to show his suit, he has to do so at the three level. Obviously, you can't bid at the three level on hands that barely were worth bidding at the two level so it is necessary to find a different definition for the WJSC at the three level.

The first point is that at the three level, you have to have a six or seven card suit. At the two level, you were supposed to have a six card suit, but there were times where you could try it on five. Three level jump shifts need six or seven card suits. No exceptions. Also, since you are a trick higher, you need a better suit and a better hand to justify bidding at the three level.

I suggest a working range of about 7–10 points not vulnerable and about 8–11 when you are vulnerable. You are entitled to use your judgment as you see fit. Good spots in your suit give you reason to be more aggressive. Wasted cards in the opponent's suit give you reason to be careful. Very few bids can be described in terms of exact points. Your experience will be worth a lot more than a stray jack.

What Does A Three Level WJSC Look Like?

In the discussion on WJSC at the two level, I suggested that you could play the bid correctly or you could use an aggressive style in order to give the opponents more problems. Three level WJSC have to be treated in normal fashion. At the three level, there isn't room to experiment. If you try to push the opponents around, sooner or later they get backed into a corner. When this happens, when you deprive them of easy things to bid, they start reacting like wounded animals. They lash out and double you. They may not know that they are doing the right thing, but if you are out of line, it is likely that their double will be good for them and bad for you.

EXAMPLES: Not Vulnerable

WEST	NORTH	EAST	SOUTH
—	1♦	1♠	?

1. You hold ♠ 63   ♡ A5   ◇ 872   ♣ KQ10953

This is the ideal 3♣ bid. Not vulnerable, you are nearly maximum. Vulnerable, you are about average. At the table, you won't see many hands as suitable as this. The hands you actually have will almost always be imperfect one way or another.

Not Vulnerable

WEST	NORTH	EAST	SOUTH
—	1♢	1♠	?

2. You hold ♠ K54 ♡ 1032 ♢ 2 ♣ KJ8743

3♣ again. This is a minimum hand that can go for a number if partner has only one little club. You don't win at bridge, however, by worrying that partner will have a singleton or void in your suit. It is much more rewarding to hope that he will have two or more of them. Q6 would be a very nice holding.

There is an important rule about preempts that no one teaches you. I will mention it. The usual caution about preempting is that the opponents will double you when you bid too much. If that were true, you would be careful. But the opponents don't do that. They double you sometimes, of course. But unless the trumps are in one hand AND that hand gets to double you, you usually escape. Have you always doubled the opponents when they preempted against you and you could beat them four or five tricks? I can remember watching my opponent in a World Championship go down six tricks in 3♡. He opened 3♡ on thirteen bad cards, only six hearts, and a wealth of gall. Neither of us could double. A double would have been for takeout. We both had balanced hands with about thirteen points each. I promise to you that if you preempt wisely but also with optimism, you will leave a long string of frustrated opponents in your wake. There will be a few Cheshire grins when you get caught, but the net will be in your favor.

3. You hold ♠ QJ3 ♡ K106532 ♢ 8 ♣ Q53

Pass or make a Negative Double. This hand has many of the things that make a hand bad. The spade strength isn't bad but it is subject to being ruffed off if West has a

45

singleton or doubleton spade. The heart suit is missing important spots. Adding the nine and eight of hearts would help this hand a lot. The singleton diamond is also a minus. Partner has diamond strength. But it may not be useful. If partner has the KQJxx of diamonds, the defenders may cash their tricks before you can use your diamond tricks. And finally, the queen of clubs is an okay value, but it isn't dynamic. There is little about this hand that is known to be good.

As noted, you can fall back on the Negative Double if you wish. If you double, the auction may allow you to bid 2♥ later in the auction. Definitely a possible approach with this hand. By bidding in this fashion, you get to show your heart suit without overstating your values or the quality of your suit.

Not Vulnerable

WEST	NORTH	EAST	SOUTH
—	1◇	1♠	?

4. You hold ♠ AJ63   ♡ J109653   ◇ J10   ♣ 4

Bid 3♥. Good spots can make up for missing high cards. Let's say that your partner puts down the singleton queen of hearts. Even if the hearts divide 4–2, you can hold your trump losers to two. In the previous hand, declarer had ♡ K106532. If partner has the singleton queen declarer will lose two tricks always, and will probably lose three when trumps divide 4–2. The difference between these two heart suits is the nine of hearts, which turns out to be an important filler.

The rest of the hand has quality points. The ♠ AJ63 are pretty good. With a spade lead, declarer should be able to hold the spade losers to one. The ◇ J10 will help partner's diamond suit and the singleton club is an obvious plus value. Nothing wrong with 3♥ on this hand.

Not Vulnerable

WEST	NORTH	EAST	SOUTH
—	1◊	1♠	?

5. You hold ♠ 963 ♡ 72 ◊ 92 ♣ AKJ1074

Bid 3♣. This is another good hand for a WJSC. When you
have a suit this good, you should try hard to get it into
the auction. Note how much more comfortable it is to bid
3♣, getting the hand described in one bid, than it is to
bid 2♣. If you bid 2♣, you will worry the rest of the
auction that something bad may happen.

THE WJSC AT THE THREE LEVEL GIVES YOU SOME
STRONG INFERENCES. Take Hand 5 above. What would
you do without the WJSC? You have two choices. You could
pass, which means your club suit will never be adequately
expressed. Or you can bid 2♣, which will show your club
suit, but which will also mislead your partner about your
strength. If 3♣ is available in your system, you can
say it all with one bid. Also, you may have inconvenienced
West.

In addition to the tactical strengths of the bid, it will
help your system on hands where you do not use the
convention. For instance.

WEST	NORTH	EAST	SOUTH
—	1♡	1♠	2♣
2♠	Pass	Pass	3♣

In my version of Two Over One, the 3♣ bid is not forcing
and this discussion will be made in light of this fact. This
sequence did not include a WJSC but the convention still
helps the N–S sequence. When South bids 2♣, it is not
known yet whether South has a real club suit or whether
he is making some kind of temporizing bid. When South
later bids 3♣, he is showing a good rebiddable club suit
and because the bid is not forcing, it must show eleven
or twelve points. Between the WJSC which shows seven

to ten points, and the 2♣–3♣ sequence which shows eleven points, responder is able to define his hand nicely.

6. You hold ♠ 83 ♡ K2 ◊ 72 ♣ AQJ10853

WEST	NORTH	EAST	SOUTH
—	1◊	1♠	?

Bid 2♣. You will rebid 3♣, which is highly invitational. Opener can pass it but he should try not to. If opener has a misfit and a minimum hand, he is entitled to give up. If he has anything in clubs, he should appreciate that South is making an encouraging bid.

Vulnerable

WEST	NORTH	EAST	SOUTH
—	1♣	1♠	?

You hold ♠ 8652 ♡ AJ10863 ◊ QJ ♣ 6

Vulnerable, you could bid 3♡ at matchpoints. Another possibility is to make a Negative Double hoping to bid 2♡ later. Neither approach is perfect. The one important point about this hand is that the suit is pretty good. You need something like this suit for a vulnerable three level jump.

You hold ♠ 1063 ♡ 1095 ◊ AKQ985 ♣ 7

A reasonable 3◊ bid. Your alternative is to bid 2◊ and then to rebid 3◊. I think it is a close decision.

You hold ♠ 74 ♡ AQ7 ◊ Q106532 ♣ 86

A hard hand. You are clearly too weak to bid 2◊. 3◊ is a possibility, but partner will expect a better suit. Another possible bid is a Negative Double. But you only have three hearts. You could also pass at risk of losing a partscore hand. I would double. Hopefully, the three excellent hearts will be enough if partner bids them.

You hold ♠ 742   ♡ QJ8753   ◇ 73   ♣ AQ

I would bid 3♡ even when vulnerable. The suit isn't up to full vulnerable standards, but it isn't a bad suit either. There is a good chance West will bid 2♠ if I pass or make a Negative Double. If I bid 3♡, I get my two cents in before West can speak. This hand represents a little judgment. You have good high card points and you have a minimal suit. Compromise.

You hold ♠ 4   ♡ AJ7632   ◇ KQ3   ♣ Q52

Just bid 2♡. 3♡ overstates the suit and it understates the strength. The WJSC is very descriptive. Don't abuse its range.

RESPONDER MAKES A DOUBLE JUMP SHIFT TO THE THREE LEVEL

This bid is easy to discuss.

WEST	NORTH	EAST	SOUTH
—	1♣	1♡	3♠

Responder has a weak hand which can't bid 1♠ and he has a seven card suit. It is a hand that might open with a 3♠ preempt.

None Vulnerable

WEST	NORTH	EAST	SOUTH
—	1♣	1◇	?

You hold ♠ QJ108532   ♡ 52   ◇ 4   ♣ J82

Bid 3♠. You have too much playing strength to bid only 2♠. 3♠ does two things. It gives West a big headache and it also tells North what kind of hand South has. North could have a hand that will bid 4♠ over a 3♠ bid but which would pass a 2♠ bid.

49

You hold ♠ KQ107642 ♡ 63 ◇ 83 ♣ K10

Bid 1♠. This hand is too good for a preemptive bid.

Both Vulnerable

WEST	NORTH	EAST	SOUTH
—	1♣	1◇	?

You hold ♠ KQ107642 ♡ 63 ◇ 83 ♣ K10

This hand is the same one as above. Vulnerable, it is sensible to play a jump to 3♠ shows a better hand. You don't want to overdo this, though. I would accept either 1♠ or 3♠ with this hand. You should discuss the range for this sequence with your partner.

You hold ♠ QJ109853 ♡ 43 ◇ 5 ♣ Q103

This is a minimum 3♠ bid vulnerable. It has solid spades, a club fit, and a singleton in the opponent's suit. Take away any of its features and this hand should bid only 2♠.

RESPONDER BIDS 1NT

This topic will be short. The only reason I included it was to remind you that your ranges for 1NT are a tiny bit different after an overcall than after a pass.

Some examples and explanations.

With None Vulnerable, you are South in the following hands.

WEST	NORTH	EAST	SOUTH
—	1♣	1♡	?

You hold ♠ J8 ♡ Q1073 ◇ A1096 ♣ 1095

1NT. You should not bid 1NT freely on less than this. Your

effective range for a free 1NT bid is a good seven to a so–so ten that doesn't lend itself to anything else. NOTE that if you had four spades, you would tend to show them one way or another.

You hold ♠ J875   ♡ Q873   ◇ A109   ♣ 109

Double. Show your four spades. You have a heart stopper, but it is a poor one and you do have four spades. With ♡ Q1096, 1NT would be a reasonable choice. I promise that 1♠ and 1NT will both work often enough that you won't be able to 'prove' the correctness of one choice or the other.

You hold ♠ Q6   ♡ KQJ8   ◇ 97642   ♣ Q7

1NT. This is an awkward ten that has no alternative.

You hold ♠ K72   ♡ 10652   ◇ 104   ♣ KJ82

Raise to 2♣. Partner will bid notrump whenever it's right. If it's right to compete in clubs, North will like knowing that you have a club fit.

You hold ♠ K5   ♡ 7643   ◇ AQ63   ♣ 432

Pass. Some nine point hands can't be bid. This is one. Actually, I wouldn't object to a 2♣ bid, but I know that will feel alien to many.

You hold ♠ 8542   ♡ KJ84   ◇ KJ3   ♣ J6

With four spades, you are supposed to make a Negative Double or bid 1♠ according to your partnership agreements. I think you could be forgiven for bidding 1NT. If you double, and partner doesn't have four spades to bid, he will probably have to bid 2♣. It is unlikely that he can bid 1NT given your heart strength.

RESPONDER BIDS 2NT

What does this show in your partnership? There are two schools of thought here. One school says this is a forcing bid in which case the bidding continues more or less as if there had been no overcall. The second school of thought says that the jump to 2NT shows 10^+–12^- points and is not forcing on opener. I play that a jump 2NT is not forcing in competition, but I don't feel strongly about it. One reason for liking it is that most of my partners want to play it that way. If you use the jump as game forcing, continue to do so.

The following discussion will focus only on the nonforcing variation. If you play 2NT is still game forcing, don't bother reading this section.

Assuming you play 2NT as nonforcing, you will have to answer these questions too. What do these auctions mean in your methods?

WEST	NORTH	EAST	SOUTH
—	1♡	1♠	2NT*
Pass	3♣		

*Nonforcing (10^+–12)

WEST	NORTH	EAST	SOUTH
—	1♡	1♠	2NT*
Pass	3♡		

*Nonforcing (10^+–12)

In the first sequence, opener rebids a new suit after South's jump to 2NT. Is 3♣ forcing or can South pass it? In the second sequence, opener rebids his original suit after South's jump to 2NT. Is 3♡ forcing or can South pass it?

While you are thinking about your answers, I will give you some hands to help you get your thoughts in order. Here is the first sequence again.

WEST	NORTH	EAST	SOUTH
—	1♡	1♠	2NT*
Pass	?		

*Nonforcing (10⁺–12)

What should North do with these two hands?

1. ♠ 8   ♡ AQ1075   ◇ 92   ♣ KQ1064
2. ♠ 8   ♡ AKJ82   ◇ KJ3   ♣ AQJ6

On Hand One, North wants to bid 3♣ and have it be nonforcing. On Hand Two, North wants to bid 3♣ and have it be forcing.

Here is the second sequence.

WEST	NORTH	EAST	SOUTH
—	1♡	1♠	2NT*
Pass	?		

*Nonforcing (10⁺–12)

What should North do with these hands?

3. ♠ 4   ♡ Q1096532 ◇ AQJ   ♣ Q5
4. ♠ 42   ♡ A108753   ◇ AKJ   ♣ K4

On Hand Three, North would like to bid 3♡ and have it end the auction. On Hand Four, North would like to bid 3♡ and have it be forcing.

If you play the jump to 2NT as competitive in competition, you have to have agreements on these questions. I suggest, somewhat indifferently, that you play any rebid by opener as forcing. The only way opener can sign off is to pass 2NT. Don't feel, though, that this suggestion is the right answer.

Here are some examples. Assume None Vulnerable.

1.
	WEST	EAST
	♠ 42	♠ J963
	♡ AJ10963	♡ Q8
	♢ Q7	♢ AK64
	♣ AK6	♣ J109

WEST	NORTH	EAST	SOUTH
1♡	1♠	2NT*	Pass
3♡	Pass	4♡	Pass
Pass	Pass		

*Nonforcing (10^+–12)

East has too much to bid 1NT so he has to find a stronger bid. If 2NT isn't forcing, it is the right bid. (If 2NT is forcing, East has to bid something else. Probably, East will make a Negative Double hoping to follow up with a 2NT bid.)

If you follow my suggestion, West can bid 3♡, forcing. East with a heart honor, soft spade stoppers, and a totally unstopped club suit, raises to 4♡.

2.
	WEST	EAST
	♠ 7	♠ AJ83
	♡ AQJ6	♡ 1073
	♢ KJ10764	♢ A3
	♣ 97	♣ Q652

WEST	NORTH	EAST	SOUTH
1♢	1♠	2NT*	Pass
?			

*Nonforcing (10^+–12)

East's 2NT invitational bid leaves West with a hard problem. What would you do? Whatever bid you choose, you have to remember that it will be forcing. You can not bid 3♢ and play it there. If you bid 3♢, East will have to bid something.

He might bid 3NT. He might raise your diamonds. But he won't pass. Your choices therefore are to pass 2NT or to bid 3◇, which will get you to a poor 3NT or a poor 5◇. NOTE that partner's 2NT bid denies four hearts. If East had four hearts, he would make a Negative Double and then would follow up with 2NT if West couldn't bid hearts. Since 3◇ is the right contract you might be tempted to say that 3◇ by West should be sign–off. (See next hand)

	WEST	EAST	
	♠ AJ2	♠ 1084	
	♡ 6	♡ KQJ4	
	◇ AQ107642	◇ J85	
	♣ AQ	♣ KJ10	

WEST	NORTH	EAST	SOUTH
1◇	1♡	2NT*	Pass
3◇	Pass	3NT	Pass
Pass	Pass		

*Nonforcing (10$^+$–12)

This is the kind of hand that West should have to bid 3◇. Anytime anyone looks for a minor suit game, there is the presumption of a possible slam. After all, if you can take eleven tricks, you are close to twelve. If 3◇ by West wasn't forcing, he would have to guess what to bid. He could guess to bid 3NT and then discover that 6◇ was cold. Or West could jump to 6◇ only to find that 3NT is high enough. Because 3◇ is forcing, West can bid it. East has nothing useful to suggest diamonds is a good spot so he signs off in 3NT. An easy sequence as long as your understandings are firm.

WEST		EAST	
♠ A52		♠ K106	
♡ QJ10874		♡ 93	
◊ KJ4		◊ Q875	
♣ 4		♣ AQ76	

WEST	NORTH	EAST	SOUTH
1♡	1♠	2NT*	Pass
4♡	Pass	Pass	Pass

*Nonforcing (10⁺–12)

*Nonforcing (10^+–12)

West would like to bid 3♡, nonforcing. When your system won't let you do what is right, you have to take the best of the alternatives. When East bids 2NT, West knows that 3♡ is the right spot. Since you can't get to 3♡, West has to decide if he would rather be in 3NT or 4♡, or whether he should pass 2NT. With West's good shape and good heart spots, 4♡ looks to be the better chance. West bids it and prays.

RESPONDER MAKES A SIMPLE RAISE

What do you show when your RHO overcalls and you make a simple raise? Are you making a 'free bid' or are you showing the usual 6–9 points? I suggest that if you do not wish to feel like a doormat, you should raise on most hands that would normally raise. The exceptions will be a composite of poor qualities.

None Vulnerable

WEST	NORTH	EAST	SOUTH
—	1◊	1♠	?

You hold ♠ Q873   ♡ Q83   ◊ J763   ♣ J3

Pass this. You don't have enough for 1NT and your hand is too poor to raise to 2◊. It is not that you don't have the values for a raise. It is just that you don't have one decent feature for partner.

You hold ♠ 9863   ♡ KJ4   ◇ Q1053   ♣ 73

Raise to 2◇. You have minimum points but they are all quality points. This hand has nothing wasted in spades as the previous hand did. If you raise to 2◇ and partner competes to 3◇ or higher, it will be okay with you.

None Vulnerable

WEST	NORTH	EAST	SOUTH
—	1♡	1♠	?

You hold ♠ QJ83   ♡ 953   ◇ Q83   ♣ Q43

Pass. Even with seven points, I don't like a heart raise. You do not want to hear partner going higher in hearts. If you put this dummy down in a heart contract, there isn't one thing you can be proud of.

You hold ♠ 2   ♡ K632   ◇ 10653   ♣ J954

Raise to 2♡. In support of hearts, this is a good hand. The only bad thing that can happen is for partner to double some number of spades. Even then, if your partner has good judgment, you should survive. NOTE that if you pass 1♠, LHO will raise to 2♠ like clockwork. Will you be happy passing this hand out in 2♠? I would hate it. By comparison, I wouldn't mind defending against a spade contract with the previous hand.

Do not pay much attention to the concept of 'free' bids. You will avoid getting too high but you will pay a big price for sitting quietly. Lose a few partscores and an occasional game and your score will show it.

RESPONDER MAKES
A LIMIT RAISE IN A MINOR

When your side is competing in a minor suit, it is easy for the opponents to outbid you. You don't want to make stretchy limit raises in a minor because your partner will be doubling the opponents or will be taking a save too often to suit you. An additional reason for mild caution is that your partner will often take a stab at 3NT. In 3NT your distribution will be worthless. The only thing partner will enjoy are your high card points. A minor suit limit raise implies BUT DOES NOT PROMISE five card support. If responder has the values for a limit raise but has only four card support, a limit raise may be the compromise. When you manufacture a bid before getting around to raising partner, many strange things can happen before you get to show support.

None Vulnerable

WEST	NORTH	EAST	SOUTH
—	1♣	1♡	?

You hold ♠ J43   ♡ 3   ◇ KJ63   ♣ Q10873

This adds up to a lot of points. But it doesn't have tricks on defense and it doesn't have tricks for notrump. 2♣ is probably enough.

You hold ♠ A73   ♡ 43   ◇ 43   ♣ K108652

You can risk 3♣ with this. You have a sure defensive winner, and if partner tries 3NT, you have a source of tricks for him.

You hold ♠ 82   ♡ A8   ◇ K10962   ♣ QJ93

Bid 3♣. Partner will expect a fifth trump. True. But he will also expect 11–12 support points for clubs and he will know you don't have four spades. If you start with a 2◇

bid, you may have to show your club support at the four level. Conversely, if you decide to raise to 2♣ only, your partner will misjudge your values by a king or so. 3♣ has only one little flaw. Any other approach comes with two or three flaws.

RESPONDER MAKES A LIMIT RAISE IN A MAJOR

When you hold a major suit, you are semisafe against competition and you don't have to worry that partner is going to bid 3NT. For this reason, you can count all your distributional values when you make a limit raise in a major suit.

Both Vulnerable
You hold ♠ 1032   ♡ K875   ◇ KJ732   ♣ 4

WEST	NORTH	EAST	SOUTH
—	1♡	1♠	?

3♡ or even 4♡ is acceptable. On this specific auction, the opponents own the higher ranking spade suit so they may outbid you. If the opponents are bidding a minor suit, though, you rate to own the hand. NOTE that your singleton club will be an asset to North because he will never play in notrump. The final contract will be hearts by your side or something by their side.

Vulnerable
You hold ♠ K82   ♡ Q93   ◇ 72   ♣ AJ1073

WEST	NORTH	EAST	SOUTH
—	1♡	2◇	?

Note that the overcall was 2◇. It is a little out of place in this chapter, but the following points are true whether the overcall is at the one level or at the two level.

This hand may bid 3♡. This is the only time I consider giving a limit raise with only three card support. If East passed instead of overcalling, I would not raise hearts directly. A possible alternative, discussed in other places in this book, is to make a Negative Double and then raise hearts. Not a bad idea. Bad in practice, though, if the opponents can jam the bidding. You should not make this error.

None Vulnerable

WEST	NORTH	EAST	SOUTH
—	1♡	1♠	?

You hold ♠ Q95   ♡ Q1032   ◇ Q87   ♣ KJ3

This is a 2♡ bid. It is not a limit raise. Aceless hands and 4–3–3–3 hands are worth less than their point count suggests. Even with four trumps, this is not close to a limit raise.

You hold ♠ AJ2   ♡ 863   ◇ KQ3   ♣ 10653

If you decide to raise hearts, 2♡ is adequate. You have good points but you have three small trump and you are still 4–3–3–3. Balanced hands with four trump tend to play awkwardly. Balanced hands with only three trump are worse yet. It is not as if you have a bad hand. You don't. All I am suggesting is that you exercise a little caution when your hand has obvious warning signs.

RESPONDER JUMPS TO FOUR OF OPENER'S MINOR

An odd bird, this one. A jump to four of partner's minor over an overcall is surely weak. It shows five or six trumps in a very distributional hand. Keep in mind that your jump gets beyond 3NT. If you have a hand that remotely looks like 3NT could be right, you should not jump to the four level.

WEST	NORTH	EAST	SOUTH
—	1♣	1♠	?

You hold ♠ 8652   ♡ None   ◇ J42   ♣ Q106532

4♣ is reasonable. As long as you have the weak hand you are supposed to have, you will come out ahead in the long run. For all you know, the opponents can make a game in hearts. Maybe they can make 3NT. Who knows? It is also possible you can make six clubs. Anytime you leap about like this, the auction is reduced to a guessing game. Your side will do better in this game than the opponents because your partner has a decent idea what you have.

If West bids 4♡ and your partner doubles, you should pass. When you have told partner what you have, you should accept his decision. If North wants to double 4♡ knowing you have a weak hand, that's fine. It is likely that they will go down two or more tricks. It is also likely that you will go down the same in 5♣.

If West bids 4♡ and your partner passes, you should also pass. North's pass is a strong statement. He heard your 4♣ bid and he chose not to bid over 4♡. This is consistent with most preemptive situations. When you preempt, you should be quiet for the rest of the auction unless asked by partner to do something. On this sequence and the last sequence, partner did not ask you a question. He told you that he thought it was best not to get to 5♣. Ignore that kind of opinion, and you are guilty of masterminding. After all. Your partner knows what his thirteen cards are and he has an idea what your thirteen are. You don't have a clue to what North has. Don't argue with him.

You hold ♠ 92   ♡ 102   ◇ J4   ♣ AQ87542

This hand is suitable for notrump if North wants to bid
it. Raise to 3♣ and see what he wants to do. You owe him
a point or two, but you have two extra clubs which will
be tricks. If he bids 3NT, this hand will be good enough.

RESPONDER JUMPS
TO FOUR OF OPENER'S MAJOR

This bid means the same thing whether RHO overcalls or
passes. It shows a shape hand with four or more trumps
and not much defense.

You hold ♠ J9763   ♡ KQ632   ◇ J   ♣ 32

WEST	NORTH	EAST	SOUTH
—	1♡	1♠	?

4♡ should work out all right. If they wish to keep bidding
spades, you won't mind. What you don't want is to hear
the opponents discover a fit in clubs or diamonds. Any
bid other than 4♡ gives the opponents room to work out
their potential. It is necessary that your partner doesn't
play you for a big hand. This jump is a weak bid and must
be understood as such.

You hold ♠ 7   ♡ KJ8753   ◇ AQ72   ♣ 82

Whatever you do, don't bid 4♡. If you play splinter raises
(see the next section), you can bid 3♠. Maybe a 2♠ cue
bid is right. Tough hand. What is wrong, for sure, is a
jump to 4♡. LHO will often bid 4♠ and your partner
won't know what to do because he won't know what you
have. You won't know what to do either because whatever
partner does over 4♠ will be uninformed.

CUE–BIDDING THE OPPONENTS' SUIT

When an opponent overcalls, it takes away some of your bids. You lose the forcing notrump response and you lose most of your one level responses. These are big losses. In partial compensation, you now have Negative Doubles and cue bids. These are useful conventions, but all in all, bridge would be easier if the opponents would be quiet when we open.

In this section, I will discuss the simple cue bid and the jump cue bid. The Negative Double will be next. (NOTE. At the end of this section, I will discuss some optional conventions you might like to play.)

THE SIMPLE CUE BID

WEST	NORTH	EAST	SOUTH
—	1♡	1♠	2♠

What does South's cue bid of 2♠ mean? There is more than one way to play this cue bid. One thing which is in common with all the variations is that the cue bid promises support for the opener's suit. The only question is how many points the cue bid shows. Here are the two most common treatments.

1. A jump raise in competition is preemptive. A cue bid shows a limit raise OR BETTER.

2. A jump raise in competition is a limit raise. A cue bid shows a balanced, game forcing raise.

Both of these treatments have merit. I happen to use the second treatment and will discuss it in detail. You can use the first treatment if you wish, but you will have to change the values a little bit so as to suit your definition.

Why do I prefer the second treatment over the first? The reason for my preference is that I do not like to have a bid be either invitational OR forcing. If I open and they overcall and my partner makes a cue bid, I don't want the ambiguity of his strength affecting my judgment. Yes, I may be able to find out what I want, but if the opponents are able to compete, I will lose valuable bidding room trying to find out whether partner has 10–11 points or 12–15 points. I prefer a defined structure so that I know my goal immediately.

Here is the structure I recommend when the opponents overcall at the one level. This discussion pertains to one level overcalls only. There are some differences when the overcall is at the two level or higher. I'll discuss cue bids again in the section on two level overcalls.

WEST	NORTH	EAST	SOUTH
—	1♣	1♡	2♡

South's 2♡ bid shows a variety of features.

1. It shows club support. Because the opening bid is a minor suit, South probably has five clubs.

2. It shows game forcing values. Responder will have a minimum of twelve points and may have a very good hand which will look for a slam. If responder has a big hand with support for clubs, it is a good technique to tell partner about the support and then to catch up with the extra points.

3. It denies a four card major. South would always introduce a major suit if he had one.

4. It shows a balanced hand. It is possible that exceptions exist to this rule. See the last hand in the ensuing examples of jump cue bids.

5. IMPORTANT. It says nothing about the holding in the opponent's suit. South may have the ♡ 532 or ♡ AQJ.

If South has a genuine control in hearts, he can show it later if prudent. At this moment in the bidding North has no idea what South has in hearts.

THE JUMP CUE BID

WEST	NORTH	EAST	SOUTH
—	1♣	1♡	3♡

This is what a jump cue bid shows.

1. It shows club support. Because the opening bid is a minor suit, South probably has five clubs.

2. It shows game forcing values. Responder will have a minimum of twelve points and may have a very good hand which will look for a slam. If responder has a big hand with support for clubs, it is a good technique to tell partner about the support and then to catch up with the extra points.

3. It denies a four card major. South would always introduce a major suit if he had one. The first three requirements are the same as for the simple cue bid. It is the fourth requirement that is changed.

4. It shows a singleton or void (rare) in the opponent's suit.

The advantage to having two cue bids is enormous. Opener knows if responder is balanced or has shape and that helps opener's judgment. Games and slams will be easier to bid. Also, if the opponents compete further, opener will know whether to double or bid. Here are some examples showing limit raises in conjunction with the two cue bids.

None Vulnerable. You are South.

WEST	NORTH	EAST	SOUTH
—	1♣	1♡	?

You hold ♠ AK2   ♡ 862   ◇ K2   ♣ QJ872

Bid 2♡. It shows a balanced, game forcing club raise. It starts at thirteen points and has no upper limit.

You hold ♠ 72   ♡ AK62   ◇ J103   ♣ AQJ7

Bid 2♡. This time South has stoppers in hearts. This is a coincidence. Notice that South doesn't rush to bid notrump. That will wait. By cue–bidding first, South shows club support. If South wishes, he can cue–bid hearts later or he can bid notrump later, according to how the auction is going. Notice also that South has only four clubs. The cue bid implies five card support for a minor, but it is acceptable to cue–bid with only four when they are good ones and when you have good points.

You hold ♠ Q62   ♡ KJ3   ◇ K7   ♣ KJ652

Bid 2NT if it is forcing in your system. Otherwise, bid 3NT. With soft high cards, there is no reason to give a club raise. You have all suits stopped and you have a suitable notrump hand. Make the more descriptive bid.

You hold ♠ J642   ♡ A3   ◇ 73   ♣ AK1063

Start with a Negative Double. If you bid 2♡, you won't be able to find a 4–4 spade fit. Say North has four spades. KQ98 for example. If North bids 2♠ over your 2♡, it will not show four spades. It will show a feature. Usually, when you make your cue bid, the partnership starts looking for 3NT. 2♠ by North is a step in that direction. Remember. Your 2♡ cue bid didn't promise anything in hearts. From partner's point of view, hearts may be unstopped. Because opener won't be able to bid spades naturally, responder has to introduce them whenever he has four.

You hold ♠ AJ ♡ 72 ◇ J87 ♣ K87542

Bid 3♣. A limit raise. South's sixth club makes up for his lack of points.

You hold ♠ 72 ♡ A3 ◇ AQJ82 ♣ Q1063

WEST	NORTH	EAST	SOUTH
—	1♣	1♠	?

Bid 2◇. With mild club support and with a good diamond suit, it is better to start with a natural bid. If you choose to cue–bid 2♠, I have only mild objections.

You hold ♠ 872 ♡ A ◇ AQ108 ♣ AQ1072

WEST	NORTH	EAST	SOUTH
—	1◇	1♠	?

Bid 2♠. This is such a good hand that you will try hard for slam. Partner assumes at this moment that you have 13–15 balanced points. You will come out of the weeds later in the auction.

You hold ♠ 8 ♡ KJ4 ◇ J104 ♣ AQ10652

WEST	NORTH	EAST	SOUTH
—	1♣	1♠	?

Bid 3♠. The jump cue bid shows GAME FORCING values, support, no other suit worth showing, and a singleton or void in the opponent's suit. The nice thing about this splinter (singleton or void) raise is that whenever opener bids 3NT, responder can pass comfortably.

You hold ♠ 8 ♡ K1073 ◇ AJ762 ♣ 872

WEST	NORTH	EAST	SOUTH
—	1♡	1♠	?

Bid 3 ♡ showing a limit raise. 3♠ would show a singleton spade but it also shows game forcing values. You aren't strong enough for that. If you wish, you could jump to 4♡.

You hold ♠ None   ♡ AKJ72   ◇ Q762   ♣ J932

WEST	NORTH	EAST	SOUTH
—	1♡	1♠	?

Bid 3♠. This nominally shows a singleton spade with game forcing strength and support. The void is acceptable. Partner won't expect it, though. What else can you bid that makes sense? 3 ♡ is too weak. 4 ♡ is misdescriptive. Partner will expect much less. And anything else you bid doesn't show heart support. You know the opponents are going to bid some more spades. It is necessary to get a general description of your hand into the auction before it becomes impossible to do so.

You hold ♠ 862   ♡ KJ2   ◇ 72   ♣ AQ653

WEST	NORTH	EAST	SOUTH
—	1♡	1♠	?

You have an awkward hand. Everything you might do violates a rule of one kind or another. 3 ♡ shows a limit raise but it promises four trumps. You might survive bidding 2♣ but the bidding may not allow you to show your hand. A possible solution is to make a Negative Double with the intention of showing heart support later. That is a popular way to show a limit raise with only three trumps. If the opponents can compete to 3♠, though, you may not get to show your support. I'll tell you what I do with these hands. I just make a limit raise. It is the one time that I make a jump raise without four trump. Specifically, the opponents overcall my partner's one of a major opening bid and I jump raise to the three level or make a fit–showing cue bid. The Negative Double route can also work but it is at the mercy of the opponents' bidding. If your trump suit is spades, you can use the Negative Double approach with less fear than with other suits.

You hold ♠ Q10652   ♡ J8752   ◇ QJ   ♣ 7

WEST	NORTH	EAST	SOUTH
—	1♡	1♠	?

Bid 4♡. This is preemptive. You aren't worried about the spade suit, but either minor suit could be a bother if the opponents find it.

You hold ♠ 97642   ♡ AJ8   ◇ AK3   ♣ J3

WEST	NORTH	EAST	SOUTH
—	1♡	1♠	?

Bid 2♠. You ostensibly have four card heart support. Unfortunately, you don't have them. You might consider a Negative Double. If you do make a cue bid with only three card support for hearts, you will have good hearts and good points. This hand qualifies on all counts. A much worse approach to this hand would be to bid 2◇. I hate bidding suits I don't have. Partner will expect me to have a five card suit and will bid accordingly.

You hold ♠ 75   ♡ KJ52   ◇ 5   ♣ A108653

WEST	NORTH	EAST	SOUTH
—	1♣	1◇	?

Bid 1♡. Responder should show the major suit.

You hold ♠ A63   ♡ AJ4   ◇ K109732   ♣ J

WEST	NORTH	EAST	SOUTH
—	1◇	1♠	?

Bid 2♠. There is no good way to show a forcing raise with

an unbid singleton. If you had a singleton spade, you could show that. All you can do here is cue–bid 2♠ implying a balanced hand. Perhaps you will be able to clear things up later.

In fact, you can show the singleton club if you want. You can use 4♣ to show a splinter in clubs with good diamond support. 4♣ may solve your problems, but it may also get you beyond 3NT. If 3NT is the right contract, 4♣ will create a problem rather than solve one. Using 4♣ as a splinter is something that you and your partner will have to discuss. I would never try this bid without the comfort of a firm understanding.

RESPONDER MAKES
A NEGATIVE DOUBLE

Much has been said about Negative Doubles so I don't intend to spend much time on them. Whatever you do is probably fine. If your side opens the bidding and the opponents overcall at the one level, a Negative Double by you PROMISES at least four cards in all unbid majors.

WEST	NORTH	EAST	SOUTH
—	1♣	1◇	Double

South promises four hearts and four spades. If South has only one major suit, he bids it, no matter how poor the suit is. For instance:

You hold ♠ 10762   ♡ AJ   ◇ 8532   ♣ QJ3

Bid 1♠. You can't double without both majors. Any four card suit is biddable under these circumstances.

You hold ♠ K872   ♡ Q1062   ◇ 32   ♣ J62

Double. You have both majors so the Negative Double is

70

appropriate. NOTE that you can double with a pretty light hand. Partner can bid a major at the one level so your double is not pushing up the auction.

You hold ♠ AJ104   ♡ 9843   ◇ 832   ♣ K5

WEST	NORTH	EAST	SOUTH
—	1◇	1♡	?

Double. This shows exactly four spades unless you have agreements to the contrary. If you bid 1♠, you would show five of them. On this auction, there is only ONE unbid major so when you bid 1♠, you can distinguish between a four and five card suit. NOTE that the emphasis is on the unbid major suit. You don't have to have the unbid minor.

You hold ♠ K32   ♡ A10652   ◇ J83   ♣ 92

WEST	NORTH	EAST	SOUTH
—	1♣	1♠	?

Double. You can't bid hearts at the two level without a better hand. Therefore, you double.

This shows:

1. Four hearts with seven or more points;

2. OR five or more hearts with too few points to bid 2♡ and probably too poor a suit to make a WJSC.

NOTE. Even hands with 22 points can make a Negative Double if it is inconvenient to bid a suit. There is no such thing as a 'limited' Negative Double.

I will discuss how opener should rebid when an overcall is passed back to him at the end of the next section.

RESPONDER PASSES

There are three reasons why opener's partner would pass after the opponent's overcall.

1. Responder has a bad hand that just doesn't want to bid. It happens.

2. Responder has a fair hand that doesn't have a way to express itself.

3. Responder has a hand that wants to penalize the opponent's overcall.

Some examples.

1. Responder passes because he doesn't want to bid.

This is self–explanatory. If you have a bad hand, the time–honored way to show it is to pass. I'm not going to bother giving examples of bad hands. We've all seen them. They're depressing. What I am going to show you is a few hands which are poor enough that passing them is a consideration. You are South with no one vulnerable.

You hold ♠ QJ862 ♡ 8 ◇ 872 ♣ J1074

WEST	NORTH	EAST	SOUTH
—	1♣	1◇	?

You should bid 1♠. If partner raises spades, you are happy with it. If partner bids notrump, you can usually escape to some number of clubs. You can bid 1♠ because you have a guaranteed home available. Additionally, 1♠ is a good bid because it stops the opponents from bidding 1♡.

None Vulnerable
You hold ♠ J53 ♡ Q72 ◇ Q652 ♣ Q52

WEST	NORTH	EAST	SOUTH
—	1♣	1◇	?

Pass. There are two poor bids you can make but neither has much going for it. You can bid 1NT or 2♣. The objections to each of these are obvious.

None Vulnerable
You hold ♠ 8752   ♡ J872   ◇ 62   ♣ AJ2

WEST	NORTH	EAST	SOUTH
—	1♣	1◇	?

Make a Negative Double. The ability to give partner two or three choices gives you more license to make a pushy bid.

None Vulnerable
You hold ♠ 8632   ♡ KQ   ◇ J542   ♣ 1042

WEST	NORTH	EAST	SOUTH
—	1♣	1◇	?

Pass. It is okay to bid 1♠ on this suit, but doing so requires you have something of value somewhere.

None Vulnerable
You hold ♠ 1087542   ♡ 42   ◇ K5   ♣ J82

WEST	NORTH	EAST	SOUTH
—	1◇	1♡	?

Jump to 2♠. Don't forget the WJSC.

None Vulnerable
You hold ♠ 762   ♡ 32   ◇ 8   ♣ KJ87542

WEST	NORTH	EAST	SOUTH
—	1♡	1♠	?

Not good enough for a WJSC at the three level. You should pass and possibly reenter the auction later.

2. Responder has a fair hand but no good bid.

This happens more frequently than you would expect. Partner opens and RHO overcalls at the one level. What should responder do with the following hands?

None Vulnerable
You hold ♠ 7652   ♡ Q   ◇ 962   ♣ AQ1064

WEST	NORTH	EAST	SOUTH
—	1♡	1♠	?

You should pass or make a risky Negative Double. The reason double is risky is that you don't want partner to bid 2◇. Nor do you want him to bid 3◇ if the auction gets competitive. Under no circumstances should you bid 1NT. If you had ◇ AQ1064, you could double and correct 2♣ to 2◇. Anticipate the auction and be sure you can survive partner's most likely bids. If some of them will get you into an inescapable mess, you should probably pass.

None Vulnerable
You hold ♠ 872   ♡ 7632   ◇ AK10   ♣ K53

WEST	NORTH	EAST	SOUTH
—	1♣	1♡	?

Well? Your choices are:

1. To pass, which feels wrong with ten good points.

2. To make a Negative Double with only three little spades.

3. To raise to 2♣ with only three trumps.

All three of these bids have major objections. I don't like passing with ten good points and will not do so if I can find any alternative at all. I hate to make a Negative Double with ♠ 872 because partner will bid spades when he can. This is the worst kind of dummy for a spade contract. The defenders will lead hearts, forcing partner

74

to ruff. Spades will not play well for us. The bid which I hate least is the raise to 2♣. The bad things that can happen are minimal and there are a lot of good things that can come of it. If the opponents bid again, I will double. If partner wants to bid again, my high cards will be appreciated. Perhaps 3NT is our spot. If so, 2♣ will help us get there better than if I pass.

None Vulnerable
You hold ♠ 852   ♡ J52   ◇ AKQ82   ♣ 92

WEST	NORTH	EAST	SOUTH
—	1♣	1♠	?

A nasty hand. I hate doubling with only three hearts and I hate bidding 2◇ which forces the bidding more than I want to. I can't even fall back on a club raise. Partner may be forgiving of KJ but not of the 92. My final choice? I would pass with intense misgivings.

None Vulnerable
You hold ♠ J3   ♡ KJ7   ◇ J104   ♣ A9852

WEST	NORTH	EAST	SOUTH
—	1◇	1♠	?

Finally a hand that can make a Negative Double with only three cards in the unbid major. There are three important reasons why you can do this.

1. You have three good hearts. Not the 843.

2. You have more than a minimum Negative Double. The extra points are necessary when your shape isn't correct.

3. You have short spades. If North bids hearts, the opponents can't make your partner ruff spades. Your doubleton spade will keep the opponents from using that defense. As on the prior hand, raising diamonds would be acceptable with only three trumps.

75

3. Responder wants to make a penalty double.

This area doesn't need elaboration. If you want to double the opponents for business you have to pass and let partner reopen with a double (assuming you are using Negative Doubles).

What Are Opener's Obligations If An Overcall Is Passed Around To Him?

When you open the bidding and LHO overcalls, are you required to reopen the bidding? No. Opener is allowed to pass it out. The criterion is fairly simple. Opener asks himself the following question. "Is it likely that my partner is making a penalty pass?" If opener determines that it is likely, he reopens. If opener determines that it is unlikely, he is allowed to pass.

When opener thinks it is likely that responder is making a penalty pass, he doubles when he is willing to defend and he bids something if he has a hand that does not want to defend.

Additionally, opener may have a hand that is so good that it wants to reopen even if responder has a poor hand.

None Vulnerable
You hold ♠ K62   ♡ 82   ◇ AJ7   ♣ KQ762

WEST	NORTH	EAST	SOUTH
—	—	—	1♣
1♡	Pass	Pass	?

Reopen with a double. Your doubleton heart plus East's silence suggest that North has a good hand with a heart stack. Your double does not promise a big hand.

None Vulnerable
You hold ♠ 92   ♡ KQ82   ◇ Q1085   ♣ AK9

WEST	NORTH	EAST	SOUTH
—	—	—	1◇
1♡	Pass	Pass	?

Pass. Something strange is going on here. You have four good hearts so North isn't waiting for a double. What is happening is that the opponents have a spade fit and they haven't found it yet. If you double, there are three bad things that can happen. It will be bad if West bids spades and finds a fit. It will be bad if your partner bids spades because you don't have support. And it will be bad if East bids spades because that will be their fit. They are in a contract you like. Don't give them a chance to go to a contract that you like less. IMPORTANT. If you chose to reopen with 1NT, your partner will play you for 18–19 points. If you chose to double intending to bid 1NT if partner bid spades, your partner would play you for more than 18–19 points.

None Vulnerable
You hold ♠ None   ♡ A8   ◇ KJ87   ♣ AJ87542

WEST	NORTH	EAST	SOUTH
—	—	—	1♣
1♠	Pass	Pass	?

Bid 2♣. The usual result of this is for partner to jump to 3NT. He was hoping you would double but you didn't have the hand for it. Don't reopen with a double if you have a void unless you have extra high cards or unless it is your only option.

None Vulnerable
You hold ♠ None ♡ K7642 ◇ A1085 ♣ KQ83

WEST	NORTH	EAST	SOUTH
—	—	—	1♡
1♠	Pass	Pass	?

You more or less have to double with this hand. Passing violates your partner's confidence.

None Vulnerable
You hold ♠ None ♡ AQJ863 ◇ K3 ♣ AK762

WEST	NORTH	EAST	SOUTH
—	—	—	1♡
1♠	Pass	Pass	?

Bid 3♣. This is a jump shift but is not game forcing. You didn't open with 2♣ so you can't create a game force opposite a partner who ostensibly has nothing. Do not double with this hand. The last thing you want is to play in 1♠ doubled.

None Vulnerable
You hold ♠ AQ ♡ 5 ◇ K43 ♣ AKQJ865

WEST	NORTH	EAST	SOUTH
—	—	—	1♣
1♡	Pass	Pass	?

Bid 2♡. The inference is that you have some kind of huge hand that doesn't want to double and doesn't have a suitable bid to make. This hand is a sensible interpretation. 3♣ would be too weak.

None Vulnerable
You hold ♠ 4 ♡ A ◇ A106542 ♣ KJ764

WEST	NORTH	EAST	SOUTH
—	—	—	1◇
1♠	Pass	Pass	?

Bid 2♣. You don't have a defensive hand and you don't want to hear partner bid 2♡. Both of these are good reasons for bidding 2♣. The greatest worry you have is not that partner will think you have anything. The greatest worry is that the opponents will find a heart fit. Against that, your distribution suggests your partner has a good hand. Even if they get to a heart contract, it won't play all that well for them. Their spades are splitting poorly for them and the heart suit will break poorly also.

None Vulnerable
You hold ♠ 6   ♡ KQJ10752   ◇ A   ♣ AJ109

WEST	NORTH	EAST	SOUTH
—	—	—	1♡
1♠	Pass	Pass	?

Reopen with 4♡. You are entitled to hope for as little as the queen of clubs. Don't worry that they will bid and make 4♠. If they could, they would be higher by now.

RESPONDER JUMPS TO THE FOUR LEVEL IN AN UNBID SUIT

WEST	NORTH	EAST	SOUTH
—	1♡	1♠	4♣

What does South's 4♣ bid mean in your methods? There are quite a few things it can be.

1. 4♣ can be a natural bid, probably preemptive.

2. 4♣ can be a splinter bid in support of opener's hearts, showing twelve or more points, four or more hearts, and a singleton club.

3. 4♣ can be a fit showing jump. The kind of hand

usually shown with this bid is something like:

♠ 83   ♡ KJ104   ◇ 73   ♣ AQ983

You can assign any range of points you want to this bid. The idea is to help your partner decide what to do if the opponents continue bidding. None of these meanings will come up very often. However, if you don't have a meaning for the bid, it is 'free' if you want to come up with an agreement. If you do decide to use the bid for something, you should follow these suggestions.

Use these jumps only when the opening bid is a major suit. If the opening bid is a minor suit, jumps to the four level should be preemptive and natural. These funny jumps apply only when you are jumping in a suit lower ranking than the opening bid.

Chapter Three

THEY OVERCALL
AT THE TWO LEVEL

BECAUSE THE AUCTION is at the two level, responder has fewer tools to use and less room to use them. Some of his tools may actually change to cater to the circumstances.

RESPONDER BIDS A SUIT
AT THE TWO LEVEL

WEST	NORTH	EAST	SOUTH
—	1♠	2♣	2♡

How forcing is 2♡? There are two common views and one uncommon view. The uncommon view is to play something called 'Negative Free Bids'. In this structure, 2♡ is nonforcing showing 4–10 points. I don't recommend this treatment. The only reason I mention it is that some day you will run into a pair who plays this way. If it comes up against you, it will be alerted.

The more traditional ways to play South's 2♡ bid are:

1. Game forcing.
2. Forcing for one round only.

My choice is to play that 2♡ is forcing for one round only. This is consistent with my discussion in Chapter Two where someone overcalled at the one level and opener's partner bid a new suit at the two level. I suggested in Chapter Two that a new suit by responder at the two level was forcing but did not promise another bid.

The two main reasons for playing a new suit at the two level as a one round force only are as follows. These reasons are virtually a quote from Chapter Two with a few additional comments.

1. The strengths of Two Over One bidding lie in game and slam bidding. When there is an overcall there is a modest presumption of strength in the overcaller's hand. The chance of slam has been decreased dramatically by the overcall. Even the chance of game is lessened. If games and slams aren't as likely as they would be in a noncompetitive auction it means that partscores are relatively more important than normal. I believe that you have to cater more to partscores once there has been an overcall. However true this statement is when there has been a one level overcall, it is more true when there is a two level overcall. This is because a two level overcall requires a better hand than a one level overcall. The more the overcaller has, the less chance that the opening side has a slam or a game.

2. When there is no intervention over the opening bid, opener's partner has lots of tools available. He has one over one responses and the forcing notrump. After a two level overcall, responder loses all of the one over one responses and he loses the forcing notrump response as well. It is true that you gain the Negative Double but it is a partial replacement at best. My thinking is that you still need a way to show some of your ten or eleven point hands. If you can't make a Negative Double, all you have is often a two over one response. You must cater your system to the hands that come up frequently. If slams and games are much less likely and partscores correspondingly more likely, you have to adjust your system.

When Can The Responder Stop Short Of Game?

Here are four auctions that allow RESPONDER to stop short of game after making a two over one response in competition. For a detailed explanation, go back and review Chapter Two.

1. When opener rebids his suit.

As South, you hold ♠ AJ2 ♡ 72 ◇ AJ1063 ♣ 842

WEST	NORTH	EAST	SOUTH
—	1♡	2♣	2◇
Pass	2♡	Pass	Pass
Pass			

As South, you hold ♠ 94 ♡ AJ7652 ◇ A2 ♣ J106

WEST	NORTH	EAST	SOUTH
—	1◇	2♣	2♡
Pass	3◇	Pass	Pass
Pass			

2. When opener rebids 2NT.

As South, you hold ♠ QJ953 ♡ K2 ◇ 872 ♣ AJ8

WEST	NORTH	EAST	SOUTH
—	1♡	2◇	2♠
Pass	2NT	Pass	Pass
Pass			

3. When opener raises responder's suit.

As South, you hold ♠ Q3 ♡ AJ472 ◇ K109 ♣ 985

WEST	NORTH	EAST	SOUTH
—	1◇	2♣	2♡
Pass	3♡	Pass	Pass
Pass			

4. When opener passes and the opponents compete.

As South, you hold ♠ AKJ72   ♡ J3   ◇ 743   ♣ J72

WEST	NORTH	EAST	SOUTH
—	1♡	2◇	2♠
3◇	Pass	Pass	Pass

SPECIAL NOTE. Some partnerships may wish to have a more rigid definition. You might like to say that South has to bid again if there is room to bid three of opener's or responder's suit. This is a detail for serious discussion.

When Can The Opener
Stop Short Of Game?

Here are four auctions that allow OPENER to stop short of game after responder makes a two over one response in competition. For a detailed explanation, go back and review Chapter Two.

1. When responder gives preference.

As South, you hold ♠ Q9832   ♡ KJ97   ◇ 3   ♣ AQ4

WEST	NORTH	EAST	SOUTH
—	—	—	1♠
2♣	2◇	Pass	2♡
Pass	2♠	Pass	Pass
Pass			

North has nothing extra and there is a misfit.

2. When responder bids 2NT.

As South, you hold ♠ AQ6 ♡ K10763 ◊ K3 ♣ 643

WEST	NORTH	EAST	SOUTH
—	—	—	1♡
2♣	2◊	Pass	2♡
Pass	2NT	Pass	Pass
Pass			

South has a minimum. There is no misfit, but there is no reason to expect miracles either.

3. When responder rebids his own suit.

As South, you hold ♠ A43 ♡ KQ10863 ◊ 7 ♣ Q96

WEST	NORTH	EAST	SOUTH
—	—	—	1♡
2♣	2◊	Pass	2♡
Pass	3◊	Pass	Pass
Pass			

This auction goes the same way with or without the overcall. North bids and rebids his suit which opener is entitled to pass. South, with a minimum hand and no fit, gives up at 3◊. The overcall doesn't change the method here.

As South, you hold ♠ K983 ♡ 8 ◊ AQJ63 ♣ Q106

WEST	NORTH	EAST	SOUTH
—	—	—	1◊
1♠	2♡	Pass	2NT
Pass	3♡	Pass	Pass
Pass			

4. When opener rebids his suit and responder raises.

As South, you hold ♠ Q742   ♡ KJ1084   ◇ 83   ♣ AQ

WEST	NORTH	EAST	SOUTH
—	—	—	1♡
1♠	2◇	Pass	2♡
Pass	3♡	Pass	Pass
Pass			

A minimum hand that got worse as the bidding progressed. Pass is legal. South does so.

REMINDER. When the opponents overcall at the two level and your partner bids a new suit at the two level, he may have stretched. Some of your rebids which are normally forcing may be passed by partner. The sequences above show when partner may pass an otherwise forcing bid. When opener is considering his rebid, he must be careful not to make a nonforcing bid when he has a good hand. In Chapter Two I showed some examples of the things opener can do. You should review Chapter Two carefully. There is one point I will specifically review now.

When you open, the opponents overcall at the two level, and your partner bids a suit at the two level, a raise by you does not show a big hand. Your raise can be passed. If you wish to make a forcing raise you have to cue–bid the opponents' suit. This is one of the few times you are happy to have the opponents in your bidding. It is nice to be able to raise (one way or the other) and to have clear definition.

WEST	NORTH	EAST	SOUTH
—	—	—	1◇
2♣	2♠	Pass	?

You hold ♠ Q107   ♡ AK73   ◇ QJ82   ♣ 104
Raise to 3♠ with this minimum.

You hold ♠ KJ7   ♡ A1073   ◇ AQ107   ♣ 72

Raise to 4♠. In competition this raise simply says that opener has a decent hand that doesn't want to be passed out at 3♠.

You hold ♠ AJ82   ♡ AK92   ◇ KQJ   ♣ 64

Cue–bid 3♣ to say you have a very good raise. There is no promise of a club control. Just an expression of strength.

You hold ♠ KQ73   ♡ 7632   ◇ AKJ9   ♣ 4

Jump to 4♣ showing a game forcing raise with a singleton club. Splinter raises are worth their weight in gold if used properly.

WEST	NORTH	EAST	SOUTH
—	—	—	1♡
2♣	2◇	Pass	?

You hold ♠ 843   ♡ AKJ83   ◇ KQ6   ♣ 53
Raise to 3◇. Partner can pass this.

You hold ♠ 843   ♡ AKJ83   ◇ AKJ   ♣ 53

South doesn't want the bidding to stop in 3◇ so he cue–bids 3♣ to show a good raise. When responder bids a minor suit, opener can't jump to the four level because that bid gets the partnership past 3NT, which is a likely spot. This means there are only two gradations of strength. In the previous sequence, responder bid spades, giving opener three possible ways to raise.

RESPONDER BIDS A NEW SUIT
AT THE THREE LEVEL

In the previous chapter, responder's new suit at the two
level was forcing for one round only. Had responder bid
his new suit at the three level, the partnership would be
in a forcing auction. For example:

WEST	NORTH	EAST	SOUTH
—	1♠	2♦	3♣
3♦	Pass	Pass	?

WEST	NORTH	EAST	SOUTH
—	1♠	2♦	3♣
4♦*	Pass	Pass	?

* Preemptive jump raise.

In both of these sequences, South has responded at the
three level. He has to have a good hand for this. You can
bid a new suit at the two level on light hands in
competition because the partnership has bidding room
to sort out its values. At the three level, you have to have
a good hand since you won't have room to apply the
brakes. On both of the above sequences, responder is
obliged to bid again.

Here are a selection of hands and auctions showing
how this situation might be handled. You will note that
South is always bidding a minor suit. There is no auction
where an opponent can make an overcall (as opposed to
a weak jump overcall) which forces you to bid a major
suit at the three level.

None Vulnerable

WEST	NORTH	EAST	SOUTH
—	1♠	2♦	?

What should you as South do with the following hands?

You hold ♠ 83 ♡ A7 ◇ 1083 ♣ KJ10763

South has to pass. 3♣ would be forcing to game (or to 4♣ if your partnership permitted this exception). You can't bid 3♣ and then pass partner in, say, 3♠.

You hold ♠ 62 ♡ AJ8 ◇ 764 ♣ KQ743

South still doesn't have enough to bid. A Negative Double should be acceptable, although it theoretically promises four hearts. I would double and hope that extra points made up for my three only hearts.

You hold ♠ A7 ♡ J2 ◇ 732 ♣ AQ10752

Bid 3♣. But be aware that it is an overbid. If partner has opened a light hand with only twelve points and no club help, you will be hurting. This is a calculated overbid. If North rebids 3♡, you will preference to 3♠. If North rebids 3♠, you will raise to 4♠. North must be aware of the stress you are under and not overdo things. Delicate all around!

WEST	NORTH	EAST	SOUTH
—	1♠	2♡	?

You hold ♠ 63 ♡ 92 ◇ AQ1083 ♣ KJ73

This time South can make a Negative Double. No need to bid 3◇.

You hold ♠ 9 ♡ A73 ◇ KJ10765 ♣ 762

South doesn't have the normal ingredients for a Negative Double and he doesn't have the strength for 3◇ but he does have something useful to show. Can South bid with this hand? Yes. There is a Negative Double trick South can use. By doubling and then bidding diamonds, South can show a biddable suit with limited strength. A good solution to have available.

You hold ♠ 8   ♡ A74   ◇ 862   ♣ KJ10763

This is the same hand as the above but it has the clubs and diamonds reversed. This time it is too dangerous for South to make a Negative Double. South won't have an escape route if North bids 3 ◇. South has to pass this hand. You can bid with hands like these if you can cater to all of partner's likely rebids. If you can't cater to them, you have to pass.

You hold ♠ KJ2   ♡ 73   ◇ 863   ♣ AKQ83

WEST	NORTH	EAST	SOUTH
—	1♡	2◇	3♣
3◇	Pass	Pass	?

Double. South shouldn't be expected to have much more than this in diamonds. The opponents overcalled at the two level and raised. They will have a decent trump suit. What they won't have are many tricks in the side suits. This double is one of those 'we have the points' doubles. You showed your clubs, you didn't raise hearts, and you didn't make a Negative Double for spades. Partner has a lot of negative inferences to work with. You will find with hands like this one that the opponents are going down two or three tricks (with a trump lead) and your side has nothing going at all. Remember that your partner passed 3 ◇. He has nothing special to say. If he passes your double, you will do well.

RESPONDER MAKES A JUMP SHIFT TO THE THREE LEVEL

Another situation where we can look to an earlier chapter for a comparison. In Chapter Two I showed the jump shift to the three level after a one level overcall. I suggested your jump shift show a good six or seven card suit with 7–10 points not vulnerable and 8–11 vulnerable. When the opponents overcall at the two level you can adapt the same definition, which is easy on the memory.

A few examples. You are South with None Vulnerable.

You hold ♠ J1076542　♡ 3　◇ Q106　♣ K8

WEST	NORTH	EAST	SOUTH
—	1♡	2♣	?

Bid 3♠. You ought to have seven high card points but your seventh spade will make up for it. NOTE that you have a seven card suit. That is acceptable. You shouldn't open a weak two bid with a seven card suit but that analogy doesn't apply here. If you don't jump to 3♠, you won't be able to make a descriptive catch–up bid later.

You hold ♠ Q82　♡ KJ10763　◇ Q4　♣ 103

WEST	NORTH	EAST	SOUTH
—	1♠	2♣	?

Just raise to 2♠. No need to jump to 3♡. It is possible, even likely, that you will be able to bid 3♡ later if the bidding becomes competitive, which describes your hand perfectly.

You hold ♠ AJ10963　♡ Q42　◇ Q7　♣ J3

WEST	NORTH	EAST	SOUTH
—	1◇	2♣	?

This hand qualifies for a 3♠ bid. It is the best hand you rate to have when not vulnerable. This answer raises an important question. What is the difference between jumping to 3♠ immediately as opposed to bidding 2♠ and then rebidding 3♠ on the next round?

That is hard to answer. I think the jump shift shows a marginally worse hand than bidding the suit and rebidding it.

You hold ♠ J1073   ♡ KJ7642   ◇ 3   ♣ K5

WEST	NORTH	EAST	SOUTH
—	1◇	2♣	?

Make a Negative Double. Don't give up on the spades. If partner rebids diamonds, you will show your hearts .

You hold ♠ Q86532   ♡ K   ◇ J72   ♣ Q85

WEST	NORTH	EAST	SOUTH
—	1◇	2♣	?

Do not bid 3♠. That violates every concept of what a jump shift to the three level should show. The suit is awful and you have the worst kind of points. You don't have a single high card that you can claim will take a trick. Probably best to pass.

You hold ♠ Q87642   ♡ K6   ◇ K82   ♣ 73

WEST	NORTH	EAST	SOUTH
—	1◇	2♣	?

You can't jump to 3♠ but you can reasonably try a Negative Double. You intend to bid 2♠ if partner bids 2♡. Sometimes you get away with bids like this. Sometimes you don't. If West raises clubs, North may bid hearts at the three level or the four level. You will have to bid 4♠ and the correctness of your bidding will now depend on what kind of spade support your partner has.

You hold ♠ 8   ♡ KQJ1062   ◇ 52   ♣ K1096

WEST	NORTH	EAST	SOUTH
—	1♠	2◇	?

This looks good enough to bid 2♡ and then 3♡. This is a slightly stronger sequence than an immediate jump to 3♡. Even if we were vulnerable, I would rate this hand as too good for a jump to 3♡. The solid interior cards in the heart suit and the good side club suit add up to a pretty good hand.

Both Vulnerable
You hold ♠ KQJ962 ♡ Q4 ◇ Q4 ♣ J82

WEST	NORTH	EAST	SOUTH
—	1◇	2♣	?

With a pile of garbage points, I would just jump to 3♠. The spade suit is quality but the points stink. This is a maximum hand for a jump shift in competition when vulnerable and too good for it if not vulnerable.

Both Vulnerable
You hold ♠ 862 ♡ 7 ◇ KQJ632 ♣ J32

WEST	NORTH	EAST	SOUTH
—	1♡	2♣	?

Pass. Not up to vulnerable standards. Your singleton heart is a distinct minus, your three little spades are poor, and your ♣ J32 are awful. The only good feature of your hand is your diamond suit. Given the rest of your bad features, even this suit doesn't take up the slack.

Both Vulnerable
You hold ♠ 73 ♡ AK10964 ◇ 73 ♣ J92

WEST	NORTH	EAST	SOUTH
—	1♠	2◇	?

Bid 3♡. This is a vulnerable minimum. A good suit with good spots. Your ♣ J92 may be helpful because North is likely to have a filling card for you.

When Responder Bids 2NT
Is It Forcing Or Invitational?

For most partnerships, this is a silly question. I play 2NT after a two level overcall is natural and invitational, which is the majority treatment. The more important question is what opener's rebids mean. For instance:

WEST	NORTH	EAST	SOUTH
—	1♠	2♣	2NT
Pass	?		

Is a 3♠ bid forcing? How about 3♡? What would it mean if North cue–bid 3♣? You can make a case for almost anything. One treatment is to say that 3♠ (rebidding your suit) is not forcing but that a new suit is forcing. Another scientific treatment is to play that any rebid is forcing except 3♣, which starts sign–off sequences.

I am purposely not developing this area. If you wish to play something esoteric, do so. I don't have any strong suggestions and since there are many possibilities, I will leave it to you to choose.

RESPONDER MAKES
A SIMPLE CUE BID OR A JUMP CUE BID

Partner opens, your RHO overcalls at the two level, and you make a cue bid or a jump cue bid. What does it mean?

These two cue bids can be used much like the ones I described in Chapter Two where I showed cue–bidding after a one level overcall from the opponents. For the most part, what was said in that chapter will apply here. There are some differences which I will point out in the example hands.

First, let me review the definitions.

WEST	NORTH	EAST	SOUTH
—	1♡	2♢	?

If South cue–bids 3♢, he is showing a balanced hand with game forcing values and four card heart support. It is possible that South intends to make a slam try after setting the trump suit. It is possible that South will bid this way with only three hearts, but that is unusual. It is also possible that partner has a singleton OTHER than in the opponent's suit. But unlikely. (NOTE. At the end of this section, I will discuss some optional conventions that you may wish to play.)

If South jump cue–bids 4♢, he is showing a singleton diamond, four or more trumps, and game forcing values. South may be about to make a slam try but for now North expects South to have 13–15 support points. Again, on occasion, South can jump cue–bid with just three trumps. If this happens, South will have GOOD trump and a maximum hand.

These cue bids apply whether partner opens with a major suit or a minor suit. One difference is that when your side opens with a minor suit, your subsequent bidding will tend to focus on 3NT as a contract. If your side opens a major suit, the subsequent bidding will tend to be slam oriented.

No one is vulnerable in the following hands. Since this topic was covered in depth in Chapter Two, I will show only difficult hands here.

You hold ♠ KQ8 ♡ 2 ♢ A8752 ♣ A983

WEST	NORTH	EAST	SOUTH
—	1♠	2♡	?

I would try 4♡ with this. You have the good trumps you need and you have good high card values too. You might

95

miss a club or diamond contract. That's true. The problem is that if you start with a Negative Double, you won't be able to accent your spade support AND your singleton heart. No solution is perfect here.

You hold ♠ AKQ2 ♡ KJ832 ◇ KJ ♣ 83

WEST	NORTH	EAST	SOUTH
—	1♡	2♣	?

Bid 3♣. You are showing a balanced game forcing heart raise with 13–15 support points. You happen to have a lot more than that so you will bid again if partner shows no interest in slam. Say partner bids 3♡. You will cue–bid 3♠, suggesting partner give slam another thought.

Important Question For Your Partnership

WEST	NORTH	EAST	SOUTH
—	1♡	2♣	3♣
Pass	?		

When you make your cue bid, what is the difference between a 3♡ bid by opener and a 4♡ bid by opener?

My suggestion is that you play 3♡ is a decent hand that can't do anything specific but which is willing to cooperate if partner has a big one. Play 4♡ as a hand that has no interest in slam. For example, given the above sequence, opener would rebid thusly:

You hold ♠ KJ53 ♡ AQJ83 ◇ K3 ♣ J4

North has nothing to cue–bid, but he doesn't want to discourage partner from looking for slam if he wishes. North should rebid 3♡, which says he has a good hand with no visible forward–going bid available.

You hold ♠ QJ73 ♡ KJ432 ◇ QJ ♣ K8

North wants the bidding to stop in 4♡ so he bids it. This is a warning to South that North does not like his hand for slam.

You hold ♠ 862 ♡ AQ7 ◇ AJ9765 ♣ 5

WEST	NORTH	EAST	SOUTH
—	1◇	2♣	?

This is the hand that doesn't respond well to the cue bidding structure discussed here. 3♣ theoretically shows a balanced hand. If you want to show your singleton club, you have to jump to 4♣. This is not so clear because if 3NT is your proper contract, you have lost your chance to bid it. This is a tough problem. I think you have fall back on judgment. My opinion? I would bid 3♣ and would stop in 3NT if that is what partner bids.

You hold ♠ AKJ ♡ QJ7 ◇ AQ8753 ♣ 3

WEST	NORTH	EAST	SOUTH
—	1◇	2♣	?

This hand is so good that I am going to go beyond 3NT no matter how the auction goes. Because I am willing to make that commitment, I will jump to 4♣ here, which does two things:

1. It shows a good enough hand that I am willing to go past 3NT.

2. It shows the singleton club which is a key feature.

You hold ♠ 72 ♡ AQ6 ◇ AK9863 ♣ A3

WEST	NORTH	EAST	SOUTH
—	1◇	2♣	?

Start with 3♣ showing a balanced hand with diamond

support. If partner signs off, I will cue–bid 4♣. Partner will know two or three important qualities of my hand.

1. The second cue bid will promise a club control.

2. The fact you started with 3♣ instead of 4♣ will tell North you have a balanced hand. This is a major piece of news for North. Knowing what kind of hand you have for your cue bid is a big plus.

3. He will also know you have a hand big enough to be interested in a slam.

RESPONDER MAKES
A NEGATIVE DOUBLE OR PASSES

This is a simple enough area to cover. The most relevant question is one of definition. How much does the Negative Doubler show? You need a working eight count if there is room for your partner to bid at the two level and you need an extra point somewhere if your double forces the partnership to the three level. You will find that a tiny bit of overbidding is a good idea here because it takes a lot of pressure off your partner.

None Vulnerable
You hold ♠ QJ86   ♡ J2   ◇ K1072   ♣ 832

WEST	NORTH	EAST	SOUTH
—	1♡	2♣	?

South can make a Negative Double with this because the partnership can stay at the two level. All of partner's expected rebids will be acceptable from South's point of view.

Both Vulnerable
You hold ♠ 8   ♡ 1032   ◇ KJ74   ♣ KJ832

WEST	NORTH	EAST	SOUTH
—	1♠	2♡	?

You can double with this but be aware that partner may rebid 2♠ if he has nothing else to do. Normally, partner will bid a minor suit and you will be at the three level. Sometimes you will be in a 4–3 fit when partner chooses to rebid a three card diamond suit in lieu of anything else. Be careful about getting into the bidding without some degree of safety.

Vulnerable vs. Not Vulnerable
You hold ♠ KQ   ♡ AQJ7   ◇ 763   ♣ AK106

WEST	NORTH	EAST	SOUTH
—	1♠	2◇	?

Double. Negative Doubles DO NOT HAVE an upper limit. You can double with a twenty point hand if there is no appropriate natural bid to make. Cue–bidding 3◇ here would be a terrible action. In an earlier section, I showed how the cue bid can be used as a raise of partner's suit. That treatment is much better than using the cue bid to show some random good hand.

None Vulnerable
You hold ♠ AK652   ♡ K10863   ◇ K4   ♣ 4

WEST	NORTH	EAST	SOUTH
—	1◇	2♣	?

Bid 2♠ and follow it up with some number of hearts. If you make a Negative Double, you will be in trouble if partner bids 2NT or 2◇. You won't be able to tell partner you have 5–5 in the majors with game points. If you have sufficient strength to make a natural bid, it is likely that bidding rather than doubling will be correct.

Both Vulnerable
You hold ♠ K7432   ♡ QJ542   ◊ 3   ♣ Q5

WEST	NORTH	EAST	SOUTH
—	1◊	2♣	?

Make a Negative Double. You don't have the strength to bid 2♠. By the time you get around to showing your hearts too, you will be in one game or another. Better to double and then rebid 2♡ if partner rebids 2◊.

Some Difficult Hands

At the two level, you will have an assortment of awkward hands that you know you should bid with but which don't offer an easy bid.

Not Vulnerable vs. Vulnerable
You hold ♠ A873   ♡ 73   ◊ QJ74   ♣ 743

WEST	NORTH	EAST	SOUTH
—	1◊	2♣	?

This is a dangerous hand. If you double all is well if partner bids spades. You can even survive if partner bids 2♡. You will return to 3◊ and partner will know you have this approximate hand. If you pass 2♣, you never get to show the value of your hand and if you bid 2◊, you don't get to show the spade suit. Whatever you do is tainted. My choice is double. With good diamond support, you can usually find a home. Only if the bidding forces your partner into bidding three or four hearts will you be embarrassed.

100

Both Vulnerable
You hold ♠ KJ984   ♡ 104   ◇ A108   ♣ 943

WEST	NORTH	EAST	SOUTH
—	1♡	2♣	?

Icky. You don't have enough to bid 2♠ and you need three hearts to raise to 2♡. The compromise bid is double. Most of the time partner will bid 2◇, which you will preference to 2♡, or he will bid 2♡ which you will pass. The Negative Double does two or three modestly plus things for you.

1. If you get lucky and get a spade bid out of partner, you can raise.

2. You get to make a positive noise.

3. On some sequences, you get to show a heart preference, which may allow partner to continue.

None Vulnerable
You hold ♠ 83   ♡ Q62   ◇ AJ863   ♣ 852

WEST	NORTH	EAST	SOUTH
—	1♠	2♣	?

My opinion is that South should pass. If South doubles, he has to contend with possible heart rebids from North. I think South should pass and should later jump to 3◇ if North can reopen with a double.

Vulnerable vs. Not Vulnerable
You hold ♠ 742   ♡ AQ2   ◇ K104   ♣ 10542

WEST	NORTH	EAST	SOUTH
—	1◇	2♣	?

The hand is too good to pass. I would raise to 2◇. I owe partner a diamond, but if I double, I will owe him a heart or a spade too. 2◇ strikes me as the least dangerous way to show a few points.

Both Vulnerable
You hold ♠ AQ763   ♡ 1073   ◇ 943   ♣ Q2

WEST	NORTH	EAST	SOUTH
—	1♡	2◇	?

Just raise to 2♡. Do not get involved in a Negative Double sequence when you have perfectly good support for partner's major.

None Vulnerable
You hold ♠ 63   ♡ 83   ◇ 953   ♣ AKJ742

WEST	NORTH	EAST	SOUTH
—	1♡	2◇	?

Pass. Double gets you in too much trouble to contemplate. If you have a higher ranking escape suit to bid, you can make Negative Doubles on offshape hands, but if your suit is lower ranking, you must be cautious to the point of being cowardly.

Not Vulnerable vs. Vulnerable
You hold ♠ KJ10764   ♡ Q2   ◇ 85   ♣ 865

WEST	NORTH	EAST	SOUTH
—	1♡	2♣	?

You can double and follow it up by bidding spades. Partner will know you couldn't bid spades the first time so you must have a weakish hand.

How Does Opener Continue?

I'm going to make the assumption that if you are reading this book, you have a sound working knowledge of Negative Doubles. Rather than show a number of standard example hands, I will offer some of the more obnoxious problems that opener will have to contend with. You are South.

None Vulnerable
You hold ♠ AJ763   ♡ 83   ◇ K53   ♣ KQ7

WEST	NORTH	EAST	SOUTH
—	—	—	1♠
2◇	Double*	Pass	?

* Negative Double

Nothing is a bargain here. Since North may have doubled with only seven high card points, it isn't safe to bid 2NT. It may, however, be the best bid. The other two possible calls, 2♠ and 3♣, are pretty bad. 2♠ should show a better or longer suit. 2♠ isn't forcing and partner will pass it with a singleton spade. 3♣ is bad because you have only three clubs and because partner's double didn't promise clubs. It promised hearts. I don't mind, in a pinch, bidding a three card suit, but it has to be one of the suits partner has specifically asked for. Looking the the options, I will reluctantly vote for 2NT. Obviously, if 2NT is allowable on this hand, partner has to be cautious about raising to 3NT. NOTE also that if 2NT is allowable, it is necessary for opener to bid more strongly with better hands.

REMEMBER THIS POINT. When your side makes a Negative Double, it is good for helping you find your best fit. But it is LOUSY when you don't have a fit and have to grope. After the Negative Double, there are none of the niceties that you normally enjoy. Even a jump shift by opener is not forcing. If opener has a really good hand, he has to start with a cue bid.

Vulnerable vs. Not Vulnerable
You hold ♠ AQ873   ♡ AKJ74   ◇ 73   ♣ A

WEST	NORTH	EAST	SOUTH
—	—	—	1♠
2♣	Double*	Pass	?

* Negative Double

103

You surely have a game and you are likely to have a slam. It won't be easy to bid it though. 3♡ by opener is invitational only. A jump to 4♡ will get you to game but it won't even hint at your slam interest. Constructive bidding after a Negative Double is not easy. If you want to make a forcing bid, you have no choice but to make a cue bid. Bid 3♣. Your later bidding will show that you were interested in a heart slam.

None Vulnerable
You hold ♠ AQ7   ♡ J73   ◇ AQ94   ♣ 852

WEST	NORTH	EAST	SOUTH
—	—	—	1◇
2♣	Double*	Pass	?

* Negative Double

I lifted this problem from the February, 1991 *Bridge World*. It is typical of what happens when opener doesn't have the hand that the Negative Doubler is hoping for. What should opener bid? The Bridge World panel of thirty experts was divided in its opinion. They voted:

2♡	13 votes
2♠	9 votes
2◇	8 votes

I think it is fair to say that this is not an easy problem. The voters for 2♡ chose it because they thought it was the most flexible bid plus it kept the bidding low. The 2♠ bidders said they wanted to bid where their strength was. The 2◇ bidders hoped partner would bid a major suit. They also expressed fear that if they bid a major suit, North would raise to game. My vote? I lean toward 2♡ and would accept 2♠. I don't like 2◇ because it gets you to some 4–2 fits. Even a 4–3 diamond fit won't be a bargain because it will pay less than the available 4–3 major suit fits.

Both Vulnerable
You hold ♠ A54   ♡ 953   ◇ AKJ8   ♣ J52

WEST	NORTH	EAST	SOUTH
—	—	—	1◇
2♣	Double*	Pass	?

* Negative Double

With very good diamonds and relatively poor major suits, I would rebid 2◇, following the instincts of the eight players who voted for 2◇ on the previous hand.

Vulnerable vs. Not Vulnerable
You hold ♠ Q10652   ♡ 3   ◇ AJ107   ♣ AQ3

WEST	NORTH	EAST	SOUTH
—	—	—	1♠
2◇	Double*	Pass	?

* Negative Double

Once in a while you may choose to pass a Negative Double for penalties. In this case, you have a fairly happy pass. You have good diamonds and you have good strength. Another consideration is that you have nothing decent to bid. I hate to rebid a five card suit since partner will often pass with a singleton. I hate to bid 3♣ because partner doesn't have to have club support. The only thing I can count on partner for is four hearts and sevenish high card points. 2NT is a possible bid but it doesn't feel right either. The spade suit is too poor to set up and the singleton heart means there won't be heart tricks either. GIVEN that 2◇ is likely to go down and that 2NT is a poor choice, I go for the penalty pass.

What Are Opener's
Obligations To Reopen?

As with a one level overcall passed back to the opening bidder, the opening bidder is expected to use his judgment. A no rule that says opener HAS to reopen is one of the worst rules I have ever run into. At the table against pretty good players, I have seen disasters like these. Do not bid like South does in the following hands.

None Vulnerable
You hold ♠ KQ863 ♡ A5 ◇ 1073 ♣ AQ3

WEST	NORTH	EAST	SOUTH
—	—	—	1♠
2◇	Pass	Pass	?

In spite of this pretty good hand, it would be a big error to reopen with 2♠ or with a double. South should pass. His ◇ 1073 are a warning sign that North does not have a penalty pass. If North couldn't look for a penalty, he would have bid or made a Negative Double if he had the values for it. He did neither. North has a poor hand. South should pass. Here is a possible set up for North–South.

NORTH	SOUTH
♠ 94	♠ KQ863
♡ Q9742	♡ A5
◇ Q84	◇ 1073
♣ J94	♣ AQ3

North–South have six or seven potential tricks against a diamond contract and about the same number of tricks in a heart or spade contract. Reopening the South hand is the equivalent of trading in a plus score for a minus score.

Both Vulnerable

You hold ♠ AQJ53 ♡ AJ73 ◇ AKJ7 ♣ None

WEST	**NORTH**	**EAST**	**SOUTH**
—	—	—	1♠
2♣	Pass	Pass	?

When you have a hand this good, you want to get the most out of it. That's natural. Here, you started with 1♠ on a hand that is a smidgeon away from a strong two bid. When West overcalls 2♣, passed around to opener, the hand still has a lot of potential. South has to find a way to continue. In practice, I see this hand cue–bid 3♣. The explanation is that North might pass a double and South doesn't want that to happen.

Is it correct for South to bid 3♣ with this mountain? The answer is a very strong no. A solid rule for you is this: If you have the shape for a takeout double, you should do so no matter how strong you are. This hand is a fine example. If South bids 3♣ and North bids 3♡, how does South continue? 4♣ is a possible bid but North won't be sure what kind of hand that South has.

If South doubles, as he should, two things may happen.

1. North may pass 2♣ doubled. If this happens, 2♣ will go down a lot. Here is a possible setup of the North–South hands where North chooses to pass 2♣ doubled.

NORTH	**SOUTH**
♠ 8	♠ AQJ53
♡ 1082	♡ AJ73
◇ Q864	◇ AKJ7
♣ KJ874	♣ None

In clubs, North–South should get two or three spade tricks, one or two heart tricks, one or two diamond tricks, and two or three club tricks. This adds up to anywhere from +500 to +1100.

Considerhow North–South will do if they bid to a diamond contract or a notrump contract. In diamonds, North will do well to make five diamonds and in notrump, nine tricks will be a struggle.

2. The other thing is that North will bid a suit. Say North responds 2♢. South can make a precise bid now by jumping to 4♣ showing a huge hand in support of diamonds with a singleton or void in clubs. North will remember that he hasn't shown any values yet so South must have a rock to invite a slam.

Compare these two sequences. How informed do you feel as North in Sequence One versus Sequence Two?

Sequence One

WEST	NORTH	EAST	SOUTH
—	—	—	1♠
2♣	Pass	Pass	3♣
Pass	3♢	Pass	4♣
Pass	?		

Sequence Two

WEST	NORTH	EAST	SOUTH
—	—	—	1♠
2♣	Pass	Pass	Double
Pass	2♢	Pass	4♣
Pass	?		

Here are four North–South hands. How would you want them to be bid after the 2♣ overcall?

South holds ♠ AQJ53 ♡ AJ73 ◇ AKJ7 ♣ None

North holds:

1. ♠ 82   ♡ K5   ◇ Q9862   ♣ 10752
2. ♠ 8   ♡ K5   ◇ 1098642 ♣ 10752
3. ♠ K   ♡ 1064   ◇ 1098542 ♣ 1075
4. ♠ 82   ♡ 864   ◇ 86542   ♣ 1073

The South hand makes 6 ◇ or 7 ◇ opposite Hands One and Two. The South hand probably makes 7 ◇ opposite Hand Three. The South hand might even make 6 ◇ opposite Hand Four although that would be quite lucky. I would hope to reach 6 ◇ opposite the first three hands and would expect to struggle in 5 ◇ on the last hand.

The important part of these examples is this. When South reopens with a double he has room to tell North about his huge hand and the good fit. There is enough time in the auction to get North to appreciate any useful card he may have. When South reopens with a cue bid, the auction becomes heavy and lethargic. North knows that South has a good hand, but doesn't know what kind of hand South has until the auction is well along.

This discussion has come a long way from the original issue. I repeat the initial thought. When you open the bidding and there is an overcall passed around to you, DO NOT CUE–BID JUST TO SHOW A BIG TAKEOUT DOUBLE HAND. If your hand is suited to a takeout double, then double regardless of your hand strength. If you have a hand which wants a bid from partner but is too distributional to double, THEN you can make a cue bid. It is almost too rare to contemplate, but I give these two examples 'just in case'.

1. You open 1♡ and LHO overcalls 2◇, which is passed around to you. This is your hand:

♠ AKQ7 ♡ AQJ98753 ◇ None ♣ 7

No natural bid comes close to showing this hand. In fact, some of your nominally strong natural bids aren't even forcing. 2♠ and 3♡ are both passable. Double could produce some frightening results. With this hand, you have to reopen with 3◇ and then hope to catch up.

2. You open 1◇ and LHO overcalls 2♣ which is passed around to you. This is your hand:

♠ Q   ♡ AKJ   ◇ AKQJ875   ♣ 73

3NT is your most likely game, but no natural bid suggests this hand. If you bid 3◇, partner won't imagine the strength of your hand. Cue–bidding 3♣ will imply something like this hand and will get you to 3NT if it is playable.

RESPONDER JUMPS TO THE FOUR LEVEL

There isn't much to offer in this section except a couple of ideas for you to look at and consider. I'll keep this one short. Here are two situations.

WEST	NORTH	EAST	SOUTH
—	1♠	2◇	?

Using this auction, what does it mean if South bids 4♣, 4◇, 4♡, or 4♠? Here are the possibilities.

1. 4♣. A jump in an unbid minor.

   You can play this as a splinter bid showing four or more spades, an opening bid, and a singleton club. You can also play 4♣ as a fit showing jump meaning you have a club suit, an opening bid, and four card spade support. And finally, you can play it as a weak preempt in clubs.

In this case, I feel pretty strongly about using the jump as a splinter bid. If, for no other reason, it is at least consistent with the jump to 4 ◇ (see next line).

2. 4 ◇. A jump cue bid. This was discussed earlier. The jump cue bid shows a singleton in their suit with game values and trump support. There is no alternative to this interpretation.

3. 4 ♡. A jump to game in an unbid major. You can play this as a splinter raise but most partnerships like to play this as a natural, albeit preemptive, bid. This strikes me as the best treatment. Using this jump as natural is less likely to lead to an embarrassing system forget.

4. 4 ♠. The jump raise is, as always, a preemptive natural bid.

Chapter Four

THEY MAKE A TAKEOUT DOUBLE

THIS IS ONE OF THE MOST MISUNDERSTOOD bidding areas for unseasoned players. It is obviously an important bidding area because of its frequency. In one of my earlier books, *Judgment at Bridge*, I devoted many pages to this topic. I am going to make the assumption that anyone who is reading a book focusing on the Two Over One system will have experience dealing with takeout doubles. In this book, I will present a shortened version of bidding after a takeout double. In addition, I will introduce a recent product of science which is rapidly gaining popularity.

Long ago, it was thought that the only way to show a decent hand was to redouble when you had ten points and to bid something when you had less than ten points. A corollary to this was that a new suit at the one level was not a forcing bid. I promise you that this is a terrible method to play. This style of bidding might have worked in the past, but players today are wiser and they know how to make mincemeat out if you when you redouble to show your ten point hands. You are South.

None Vulnerable
You hold ♠ 83 ♡ KQ83 ◇ KJ3 ♣ Q1095

WEST	NORTH	EAST	SOUTH
—	1◇	Double	?

If you play that you must redouble with all ten point hands, you will have to do so with this hand. If the opponents behave and pass as you would like them to, you may survive, but if they bid even one or two spades, you won't be able to describe all the things you want to show. Imagine the bidding continues this way:

WEST	NORTH	EAST	SOUTH
—	1♢	Double	Redouble
1♠	Pass	2♠	?

You would like to show your diamond support and you would like to show your heart suit. Not possible. NOTE that if you bid 3♡, it will be forcing and it will virtually commit your side to a game. You don't have enough points for that. Not only that, if you bid 3♡, North will expect you to have five of them. I ask you. If you have to fight with your system to make it work, if it gets you into more trouble than it saves you from, if it reduces your decisions to guesswork, then why use it? The following structure will give you much better definition.

RESPONDER BIDS A SUIT AT THE ONE LEVEL

When your partner opens the bidding and your opponent makes a takeout double, there are three things you may wish to do.

1. You may wish to pass and stay out of the auction.

2. You may wish to double the opponents.

3. You may wish to bid to your side's best contract. It used to be that if responder had a weak hand with shortness in opener's suit, he would bid something. 1♣–Double–1♠ would be nonforcing, implying a poor hand that didn't

114

want to play in 1♣ doubled. Then some bright player noticed that the person who should decide whether to play in 1♣ doubled was not opener's partner, but opener himself. Why should responder be the judge? Then someone noticed that when they redoubled with all their ten point hands, there were too many bad results along the lines of the example in the introduction. After trial and error, it was discovered that it was better to play one level bids were forcing. This made it easy for the partnership to show what it had. Showing partner what suits you have is more important than telling partner that you have ten or more points.

Here are some examples. For a larger discussion, refer to my book *Judgment at Bridge*. This auction will apply in all of the following example hands.

None Vulnerable

WEST	NORTH	EAST	SOUTH
—	1♦	Double	?

You hold ♠ A973   ♡ Q1075   ♦ 763   ♣ J2

Bid 1♡. It is okay to bid a four card suit over the double. If your side has a major suit fit, 1♡ will help you find it. If you don't bid 1♡, you will lose the heart suit and probably the spade suit as well. Basically, your intention is to bid as if there had been no takeout double. Some of my students have asked me why I would look for a major suit fit with this hand when East has shown the major suits with his takeout double. My answer is that East's double promises only three cards in each major. If East has:

♠ KQ82   ♡ K93   ♦ A3   ♣ Q1083

he would correctly double 1◇. Our side may have a 4—4 heart fit in spite of East's double.

None Vulnerable

WEST	**NORTH**	**EAST**	**SOUTH**
—	1◇	Double	?

You hold ♠ A104   ♡ 9743   ◇ J74   ♣ KJ3

I would just bid 1NT. You should try to show your major suits if you have them, but you don't have to show this one. 1NT shows a good seven points up to a poor ten points. This hand qualifies perfectly. (See later section on bidding 1NT over a takeout double.)

You hold ♠ KJ872   ♡ 3   ◇ K73   ♣ QJ82

Bid 1♠. You have redouble points but you should still bid naturally. It is almost always better to look for your own contract than to try to double the opponents. You will find that it is MUCH easier to find your best spot if you can start with a natural bid rather than a redouble showing ten points but which says nothing about your distribution. If you start with a natural bid, it will be relatively easy to show partner how many points you have. If you start with redouble, you will often have trouble showing your distribution.

If you redouble, the opponents are sure to bid hearts. Say West bids 1♡ and East raises to 2♡. You will have to bid 2♠ in order to show your suit. If partner doesn't have a spade fit and also has a minimum hand, it may be hard to stop in a safe partscore.

You hold ♠ QJ82   ♡ AQ83   ◇ 93   ♣ Q105

Bid 1♡ or redouble. Redouble is okay on this hand because there is nothing the opponents can bid to bother you as they could on the previous hand. NOTE that if West bids 2♣, you will double it.

None Vulnerable

WEST	NORTH	EAST	SOUTH
—	1♦	Double	?

You hold ♠ A108   ♡ J9762   ♦ 63   ♣ J42

Bid 1♡. Not beautiful, but it is the bid you would have made had East passed. In general, if you aren't ashamed of your bid, you should go ahead and make it when East doubles. If North rebids 1♠, you will pass it.

You hold ♠ A2   ♡ AQ82   ♦ J10763   ♣ Q6

Definitely bid 1♡. If you redouble, you won't be able to show partner that you have hearts, diamond support, and a game forcing hand. Bid 1♡ and follow up with whatever methods your system uses. For instance, if partner rebids 1NT, just raise to 3NT. If partner rebids 1♠, you should jump to 3♦ if it is forcing. Otherwise you should bid the fourth suit, 2♣, and continue appropriately. Compare this with what happens if you redouble. West will bid, say, 1♠. Let's take the charitable view that 1♠ is passed back to you. What do you do? You can't bid 2♡ because it shows five hearts and is more or less game forcing. If you raise diamonds, you may lose a 4–4 heart fit.

   And it can be worse for you. If East raises to 2♠ or 3♠, you will be more constricted yet in terms of what you can do. Forget about redoubling unless you know you are ready for the worst.

You hold ♠ A73   ♡ KJ82   ♦ 4   ♣ Q8752

Again, start with a natural 1♡ bid and develop the bidding as if there hadn't been a double.

You hold ♠ Q7642   ♡ J9652   ♦ 4   ♣ 82

Pass. If you bid something, you rate to hear partner jump to 2NT or 3♦, or something equally unpleasant.

RESPONDER BIDS A SUIT
AT THE TWO LEVEL

This is the trickiest bid . It is easy to define. It is less easy to explain. The definition is simple. An auction like:

WEST	NORTH	EAST	SOUTH
—	1♠	Double	2♦

IS NOT A NORMAL FORCING TWO OVER ONE RESPONSE. It shows a decent five or six card suit and about 6–9 points and is NOT FORCING. Opener can pass. Why is it right to play a two over one is not forcing? I think the reason is one of practicality. Responder will almost never have a good enough hand to qualify for a true two over one response when RHO has the strength for a takeout double. There will be many hands where responder has a fair suit and a few points and wants to take this opportunity to be heard.

None Vulnerable

WEST	NORTH	EAST	SOUTH
—	1♡	Double	?

You hold ♠ 83　♡ 105　♦ AQ10764　♣ 1094

Bid 2♦. This is the classic 2♦ bid as defined in this discussion.

You hold ♠ 943　♡ 3　♦ KJ1095　♣ J753

I would bid 2♦ with this. The opponents will probably buy the hand in spades. 2♦ will help partner defend. Also, if partner wants to compete, my 2♦ bid may be the thing to help him decide whether to do so.

You hold ♠ QJ96　♡ 73　♦ 82　♣ A10763

Bid 1♠. You don't want to give up this good of a spade holding.

None Vulnerable

WEST	NORTH	EAST	SOUTH
—	1♡	Double	?

You hold ♠ J53 ♡ J3 ◇ A93 ♣ Q8753

Bid 1NT. 2♣ should show a better suit. Remember. If partner has a singleton club, you are in trouble. You want to have a good enough suit that you won't be hurting if there is a misfit.

You hold ♠ 7 ♡ Q4 ◇ 8652 ♣ A109763

Bid 2♣. I recommend against making a weak jump bid of 3♣. If your partner is short in clubs, you will be exposed to a penalty double. East showed something in clubs with his takeout double so West will be able to double 3♣ without too much in the suit.

You hold ♠ AQ73 ♡ 4 ◇ 64 ♣ AQ8752

Redouble. 2♣ would not be forcing and 1♠, while forcing, would never allow you to show your shape. You have to redouble and then bid clubs and possibly spades if the auction allows. This is not an easy hand if you play new suits at the two level as nonforcing. Fortunately, this is a rare problem. I can't remember more than one such hand in the last ten years.

RESPONDER JUMP SHIFTS TO THE TWO LEVEL

This is an easy section to address. There are three or four things you can use but unless you want to go in for the esoteric, only one of them is worth considering. The four things you can use a jump shift for are the following. Say the bidding starts 1♣–Double–2♠. These are the things you can use it to show.

1. You can use the 2♠ bid as some kind of strong bid showing an opening bid with a spade suit. In my opinion, this is the worst of the four treatments shown here. If you play 1♠ as a forcing response over the takeout double, the jump shift to 2♠ to show a good hand is totally unnecessary.

2. You can use the 2♠ bid to show some kind of good hand with a spade suit AND with a club fit. (The name of this treatment is the Fit Showing Jump.) This is a sensible treatment but it needs lots of discussion. The fact is that it isn't used by very many partnerships.

3. You could conceivably use the jump to 2♠ to show a singleton spade and a good club fit. This treatment will work well when it occurs, but it suffers greatly from lack of frequency.

4. The treatment used by over 90% of today's players is to play that 2♠ shows a weak hand with a fair suit. It is a preemptive bid tending to deny the strength to bid just 1♠, which would be forcing. Here are some examples. You will find the concepts here are very similar to the ones shown in Chapter Two where responder jump shifts after a one level overcall.

None Vulnerable

WEST	NORTH	EAST	SOUTH
—	1◇	Double	?

You hold ♠ J97653   ♡ 43   ◇ J83   ♣ Q6

It isn't my idea of good bridge to bid with this hand, but it is an example of how far successful players may go to pressure the opponents. I think pass is the right bid with this poor a suit. If the spades were J109763, I could see bidding 2♠. If you are too aggressive, you will be doubled. West knows that East has three spades or more and twelve points or more. West can and will double you so you need some spots to see you through. NOTE the difference between these two jumps to 2♠.

WEST	NORTH	EAST	SOUTH
—	—	1◇	2♠

WEST	NORTH	EAST	SOUTH
—	1♣	Double	2♠

On the first sequence, West knows East has an opening bid but that is about it. West is so uninformed that modern bidding has rejected the penalty double in favor of the Negative Double. If your 2♠ jump is in trouble, you may escape if the opponents aren't able to double you.

On the second sequence, West knows East has an opening bid and he also knows that East has three or more spades. In this circumstance, West has no need for Negative Doubles. West knows if a fit exists and he can show that fit if he wishes. If West thinks you are in trouble in 2♠, he can double and it will stick.

None Vulnerable

WEST	NORTH	EAST	SOUTH
—	1◇	Double	?

You hold ♠ 43   ♡ KJ10652   ◇ 64   ♣ 763

This is an acceptable jump to 2♡. You have a good suit and that is all that is required. There isn't much room for side cards. If you have a decent suit and a high card on the side, you probably have enough to bid one of your suit, which is forcing.

None Vulnerable

WEST	NORTH	EAST	SOUTH
—	1◇	Double	?

You hold ♠ QJ1076 ♡ 54 ◇ 53 ♣ 10763

Some partnerships are willing to mix things up and bid 2♠ on hands like this. Five card suits are not safe if partner has a singleton. Still, 2♠ does take away bidding room. You have to decide what your agreements are. It may work. If you need a good board, this is a reasonable way to try for one. It won't work in the long run, though, so I don't think this trick should be in your arsenal.

You hold ♠ 74 ♡ J84 ◇ 5 ♣ Q1087542

If you want to preempt with this hand, you have to bid 3♣. I define three level jumps differently from two level jumps. I would pass or bid 2♣ with this hand. I will elaborate on this later.

None Vulnerable

WEST	NORTH	EAST	SOUTH
—	1◇	Double	?

You hold ♠ AQ10764 ♡ 743 ◇ J4 ♣ 97

Bid 1♠. This hand is too good for a jump response.

You hold ♠ K653 ♡ J109743 ◇ 6 ♣ J7

Bid 1♡. The hand is okay strengthwise for a 2♡ bid but you have four pretty good spades and you don't want to lose them. East's double doesn't promise four spades. It promises only three spades. It is possible North has four spades. Bid 1♡. If North rebids 1♠, you will raise to 2♠. If North rebids 1NT, you will rebid 2♡. If North rebids 2♣, you will again rebid 2♡. And if North rebids his suit, 2◇, you should just pass.

RESPONDER MAKES A SINGLE JUMP SHIFT TO THE THREE LEVEL

There are many things you can do with the jump shift to the three level over a takeout double and this time, some of them are quite useful. Here is a list of possibilities. You will have to choose one. NOTE that I am including the Jordan 2NT response in this section. It doesn't belong here in theory, but since it can affect your jump shift structure, I have included its discussion in this chapter.

WEST	NORTH	EAST	SOUTH
—	1♡	Double	3♢

You can use the 3♢ bid as natural showing a six or seven card suit with invitational strength. This is a good treatment and I recommend it. One of the good things about it is that you no longer have to redouble first and then bid your suit. Redoubling doesn't ensure you will have room to do all the things you wish. Sometimes redoubling can lead to embarrassing auctions. On the other hand, using the three level jump as a good hand has the disadvantage of being a rare animal. Because it won't come up very often, you may decide to use a different treatment. This is a typical hand for 3♢ after RHO doubles 1♡.

None Vulnerable
You hold ♠ 73   ♡ K3   ♢ AJ10953   ♣ Q108

WEST	NORTH	EAST	SOUTH
—	1♡	Double	?

If you redouble, the bidding may be up to 2♠ when it gets back to you. You will have to bid 3♢ to show your suit. New suits after a redouble are forcing so the bidding has to continue. This hand is good enough to redouble but it isn't good enough to push beyond 3◇. NOTE that 3◇, as used here, is invitational showing 9–11 high card points and a good six card or longer suit.

You can use the 3◇ bid to show diamonds plus a heart fit (the fit showing jump). This is a fair treatment. It makes more sense to play that jumps to the three level are fit showing than jumps to the two level. It isn't likely you will have a suit good enough to want to play at the three level, but it is likely you will have a hand that wants to raise partner to the three level. NOTE that you have to decide what values this bid shows and you have to decide whether it promises three or four card trump support. Keep in mind that if you use the Jordan 2NT response (discussed later in this chapter), it will affect what you do with the fit showing jump. Here are some possible hands for the fit showing jump after partner opens 1♡ and RHO doubles.

None Vulnerable

WEST	NORTH	EAST	SOUTH
—	1♡	Double	?

You hold ♠ 843   ♡ QJ82   ◇ 52   ♣ AQ107

If used to show limit raise strength, you could jump to 3♣ with this hand. NOTE that you have four trump (I think the bid is best used with four card trump support) and a concentration of strength in clubs and hearts.

You hold ♠ 72   ♡ J73   ◇ K63   ♣ AKJ83

I think it is okay to play that fit showing jumps promise limit raise strength OR BETTER, but I wouldn't do so with this hand because it has only three hearts. I would redouble and then force to 4♡. Partner will know I have only three hearts because I didn't start with the Jordan 2NT (discussed in the next section).

You hold ♠ Q7 ♡ J932 ◇ KJ4 ♣ A852

Use the Jordan 2NT response, which I will discuss shortly. The fit showing jump, if you choose to use it, should show a GOOD four or five card suit and four pretty good trumps. This hand has poor clubs plus it has most of its strength in the other two suits.

The jump to 3◇ can also be used as a splinter bid showing heart support plus a singleton diamond. Another decent treatment. Be sure you have your definitions down. What points does it show? How many trumps does it guarantee? Here are some hands to consider.

None Vulnerable

WEST	NORTH	EAST	SOUTH
—	1♡	Double	?

You hold ♠ 873 ♡ AK52 ◇ 5 ♣ J10653

If 3◇ shows a singleton diamond plus limit raise strength, this hand is acceptable. If 3◇ promises game forcing values, you can't bid it with this hand. Change the hand to:

♠ 873 ♡ AK52 ◇ 5 ♣ K10964

and 3◇ would be okay. Using these splinter bids over a takeout double will help your partner decide what to do in the bidding and they may help your partner's defense if the opponents buy the hand. The splinter bids have a down side too. They let the opponents double and perhaps find a sacrifice, and they may give the defenders some inferences they can use on opening lead.

You hold ♠ 2 ♡ KJ872 ◇ AQ104 ♣ 1084

No matter what conventions you play and no matter how much you discuss them, questions will arise about their use that you didn't anticipate. If you decide to play three level splinters over takeout doubles (whatever range of

points you decide on), it will eventually occur to you that
3♠ on this hand and this specific auction should also be
a splinter. I offer this hand only to help you clear up your
partnership agreements in the event you decide to use
splinter responses.

The last possibility for a three level jump shift after a
takeout double is to play the jump is preemptive. It
makes sense to use this treatment for two level jump
shifts where you are a trick lower. At the three level,
though, you are more vulnerable to a penalty double if
you have done the wrong thing. I am reluctant to choose
this treatment even though it is fairly popular. Another
reason I recommend against this treatment is that it will
come up rather infrequently. You need a seven card suit
for this bid and that won't happen too often. Remember,
your RHO has promised length in the unbid suits too.

RESPONDER MAKES
A DOUBLE JUMP SHIFT
TO THE THREE LEVEL

This response isn't going to come up very much no matter
how you play the bid. If the bid is natural, you need a
good enough suit to overcome the bad split promised by
the takeout double. Since there is nothing wonderful to
use this jump for, even in the world of science, it should
probably be natural and weak with the understanding
that it won't happen more than once a year.

None Vulnerable

WEST	NORTH	EAST	SOUTH
—	1♣	Double	?

You hold ♠ KJ108643   ♡ 74   ◇ 93   ♣ 106

3♠ is okay. The key factors are that you have a suit that can stand a bad split and you don't have any surprise high card points. Vulnerable vs. Not Vulnerable, 2♠ would be enough.

You hold ♠ 8   ♡ Q1065432   ◇ J74   ♣ 93

It's tempting to bid 3♡ but it invites disaster. The bad suit is a serious warning sign, especially given the warnings of East's takeout double. If we were Not Vulnerable vs. Vulnerable, I would think about bidding 3♡ but would really like to have the nine of hearts to fill in the suit.

THE JORDAN 2NT RAISE
AFTER A MAJOR SUIT OPENING

Many of the meanings for jump shifts to the three level over a takeout double were natural, but some of them were artificial raises of opener's suit. Another convention which is used by almost all tournament players is the Jordan 2NT Raise. It works this way. When partner opens a suit and RHO doubles, a jump to 2NT by responder shows a strong raise of partner's suit. It is usually defined as showing limit raise strength or better and shows four or more trumps. Some partnerships do it with three trump, which in my opinion is a terrible way to play. Here are some examples of the Jordan Raise with comments. NOTE that in these examples, partner opens in a MAJOR suit.

None Vulnerable

WEST	NORTH	EAST	SOUTH
—	1♠	Double	?

You hold ♠ Q873   ♡ A9   ◇ K854   ♣ J82

Bid 2NT. This is the average hand for a Jordan Raise. It has ten so–so high card points plus a doubleton. As noted above, it contains four trumps.

None Vulnerable

WEST	NORTH	EAST	SOUTH
—	1♠	Double	?

You hold ♠ K106   ♡ KJ652   ◇ K42   ♣ 82

This hand shows one of the strengths of the Jordan Raise as I would play it. If you use this convention only with four trumps, you can redouble with this hand and later raise spades. Because you redoubled first and then raised spades, North will know you have only three trumps.

Do you think it is all that important to tell partner how many trumps you have? Absolutely! If partner knows you have four trumps, he will be able to judge competitive auctions more accurately than he can if he is unsure about your trump length. If he knows you have four trumps, it might give him reason to bid on. If he knows you have three trumps, it might give him reason to double. For example, you have K9653 opposite A82. How many trump losers do you have with this combination? The answer depends on how lucky you are.

If trumps are 3–2, you have one loser. That will happen about 68% of the time. If trumps are 4–1, you will have two losers. This will happen about 28% of the time. And if you are really unlucky and find trumps 5–0, you will have three losers and you will be doubled for your troubles. This will happen about 4% of the time.

Now, let's add the four of trump to dummy so that declarer has a nine card fit instead of an eight card fit. You have K9653 opposite A842. Now how many losers do you have? If trumps are 2–2, you have no losers. This happens about 41% of the time. If trumps are 3–1, you have one loser. This happens about 50% of the time. If you are unlucky in your nine card fit and they divide 4–0, you will lose two trump tricks. This will happen almost 10% of the time.

If you work this out, it will turn out that the eight card fit averages almost one and a half losers per hand and the nine card fit averages about half of that. That is a large discrepancy and one which will give your partner headaches if he has to guess how many trump you have.

None Vulnerable

WEST	NORTH	EAST	SOUTH
—	1♠	Double	?

You hold ♠ KJ64   ♡ 73   ◇ AQ104   ♣ K73

Start with 2NT and then continue to game. This gets across to partner that you have game values plus four trumps.

You hold ♠ AQJ4   ♡ 83   ◇ KJ3   ♣ AK62

Bid 2NT and then make a cue bid. It is always a good idea to set trumps so partner will know what your later auction is all about. Your auction won't be perfect but it will be in the ball park of what partner thinks you have.

You hold ♠ Q1086   ♡ 7   ◇ A74   ♣ KJ1084

If you have decided to play fit showing jumps, you won't bid 2NT with this hand. It has a good club suit, which qualifies the hand for a 3♣ response. If you have decided to play splinter raises over the double, you won't bid 2NT with this hand because it has a singleton heart. If you use Jordan Raises, which, if any, of the jump shifts to the three level should you use as well or should you use the jump shift as some sort of natural bid? This is a fair question. Of the four treatments shown above, three are acceptable.

Using the jump as natural showing a ten point hand with a good six or seven card suit is excellent when it comes up. It is just too rare an event though for me to insist on this treatment.

Using the jump as fit showing or as a splinter both make sense too. But they suffer from something else. They give away information to the opponents. When you are bidding games, the blunderbuss approach works well because of the vagaries of the opening lead. Having an uninformed defender on lead is an asset to your close games. It is when you are bidding slams that you need precise information. This won't happen often because the takeout doubler usually has enough points to make slams unlikely. Because neither of these two scientific treatments gain you that much over what you get by using Jordan Raises, I would tend to stick with natural and invitational jumps to the three level.

REVERSE JORDAN RAISE
AFTER A MINOR SUIT OPENING

WEST	NORTH	EAST	SOUTH
—	1 ◇	Double	2NT

What does 2NT mean? If you are using the Jordan Raise in the major suits, you may be tempted to use the convention in the minors too. If you make this agreement, you will sooner or later run into this hand. Partner bids 1♣ and RHO doubles finding you with:

♠ 43   ♡ KJ5   ◇ 1074   ♣ AQ1093

Ah. The perfect hand for Jordan. You bid 2NT, showing a limit raise with club support. Partner raises you to 3NT and West leads the queen of spades. This is what you see.

	PARTNER	YOU
	♠ K9	♠ 43
	♡ A982	♡ KJ5
	♢ K3	♢ 1074
	♣ KJ874	♣ AQ1093

WEST	NORTH	EAST	SOUTH
—	1♢	Double	2NT
Pass	3NT	(All Pass)	

Sure enough, the defense takes five spade tricks. LHO ends up on lead and switches to the two of diamonds. The defense takes only four diamond tricks and you have to score up 3NT down five. "Looks like they are cold for 3NT," says partner. "Good thing we got there first."

What went wrong? Responder has a limit raise and opener has a good enough hand to bid game. In fact, when you look at the scores, you discover that everyone in the room was in 3NT with your cards. And they all made it. Some declarers made ten tricks and one made eleven! Looking back at how you played the hand, it was clear that the defenders were entitled to the first nine tricks. You couldn't do anything about it.

The discrepancy is not in how you played the hand but how you bid it. The Jordan Raise was great. It told partner exactly what you had. Unfortunately, the bid you used to tell partner your message was 2NT. This put you on play instead of partner which in turn put West on lead instead of East.

This is a relatively common problem with Jordan if you use the bid in the minor suits the same way you use it in the major suits. When your side is bidding majors, you can bid all the notrump you want along the way. The final contract will be a major suit. When your side is bidding minors, you want a method that plays notrump from the right side since notrump will be the final contract on many of your good hands.

Since Jordan Raises automatically and arbitrarily make responder bid the notrump and since that is often bad, it makes sense to look for a solution.

A solution which offers modest improvements is to play Reverse Jordan Raises. These work exactly as their name suggests. 1◇–Double–3◇ shows the limit raise and leaves the partnership to sort out the notrump issue if necessary. 1◇–Double–2NT shows the preemptive raise. This combination solves some of the problems but it also has its drawbacks.

The good part of this combination is that it fixes the objection noted above. You will always play 3NT from the right side when the auction starts 1◇–Double–3◇. A nice extra is that there is nothing WRONG with playing the jump raise as a limit raise. There is usually a dark side to conventions and there is none here.

There are a couple of bad side effects, however, from using 1◇–Double–2NT as a preemptive raise. Neither of them feel awful and in fact won't be felt that often. But they can happen and they will happen and you won't like it when they do happen. These are the bad things that occur when you use 2NT as a preemptive raise.

1. On those hands where you want to be in 3NT, you will still play it from the wrong side. It will be a rare occurrence but when it happens, it will surely be bad. When the bidding goes:

WEST	NORTH	EAST	SOUTH
—	1◇	Double	2NT
Pass	3NT		

there is almost no chance that declarer will like the opening lead. Declarer, remember, has a weak hand and his partner has a monster.

2. Using 2NT to show the weak raise leaves LHO with more room to bid. Look at these two sequences.

WEST	NORTH	EAST	SOUTH
—	1♣	Double	3♣

WEST	NORTH	EAST	SOUTH
—	1♣	Double	2NT

On the first sequence, West can bid a suit or he can use the Responsive Double or he can cue–bid at the four level. On the second sequence, West can bid a suit or he can double or he can cue–bid at the three level OR the four level.

It may not look like you are giving the opponents that much extra room, but in practice, West will be happy he has the three level cue bid available. NOTE also that if the bidding goes 1◇–Double–3◇, West can't bid 3♣, which he would be able to do over 1◇–Double–2NT. These are small deficiencies in the Reverse Jordan structure, but they are deficiencies and they can annoy.

There are other things you can do. Here is a list of them which you can mull over and adopt or reject.

Option One

WEST	NORTH	EAST	SOUTH
—	1♣	Double	?

3♣   Preemptive.

2NT   Shows a balanced limit raise that doesn't mind declaring notrump. Opener can pass 2NT, he can sign off in 3♣, or he can raise to 3NT.

REDOUBLE   If responder redoubles first and then raises opener's minor, it shows a distributional limit raise or one with concentrated values.

This structure works fairly well. I think it is important to keep the double raise as the weak bid, which this structure does for us. It also allows responder to differentiate between balanced limit raises and distributional limit raises.

None Vulnerable

WEST	NORTH	EAST	SOUTH
—	1◊	Double	?

You hold ♠ 73 ♡ Q83 ◊ K10875 ♣ 1093

Bid 3◊. The double raise is preemptive in this structure. This hand is average. Responder could have another point or two and might make the bid without the queen of hearts. Three to seven high card points with five trumpS is par.

You hold ♠ 83 ♡ 92 ◊ AJ98 ♣ 107642

I would recommend bidding 3◊. You would like a fifth trump but you don't promise it. As long as you have good shape and as long as your trumps are good ones, the double raise is a good choice.

You hold ♠ J82 ♡ KQ ◊ K9732 ♣ Q43

Using OPTION ONE, you can respond 2NT, which is seminatural and not forcing but which does promise trump support. It is likely you have five trump. If you were 4–3–3–3 with only four card support, you could just redouble and then follow with 1NT.

You hold ♠ Q9 ♡ AJ8 ◊ Q763 ♣ J1096

Point count says you can redouble or make a limit raise. I would not want to end up giving a diamond raise on this hand. My choices are to bid 1NT now or to redouble and hope that I can bid 1NT later. If I redouble and the bidding is at the 2♡ or 2♠ level, I won't like my choices at all. I lean toward 1NT now. We won't miss a game unless partner has fifteen points and since he didn't open 1NT, I will take that chance.

None Vulnerable

WEST	NORTH	EAST	SOUTH
—	1♢	Double	?

You hold ♠ K82   ♡ 82   ♢ AJ762   ♣ QJ5

Redouble and then raise.

Option Two

Credit science with this one. If you are unhappy with all of the above ideas, you can try something really strange. OPTION TWO works this way.

WEST	NORTH	EAST	SOUTH
—	1♣	Double	?

3♣   Preemptive, as it should be.

2NT   Shows the balanced eleven point hand with stoppers and support for partner. This treatment was discussed above as part of OPTION ONE.

2♢   or 1♢–Double–3♣ (responder jumps in the other minor suit) shows a shape limit raise.

RESPONDER JUMPS
TO THE FOUR LEVEL
IN A LOWER RANKING SUIT

There is virtually no way this bid can have a natural meaning so it makes good sense to adopt a conventional treatment or to ignore the bid. In this case, the Fit Showing Jump and the Splinter Response both have merit. NOTE that these two conventions won't come up very often so don't use either without discussion. An unsuspecting partner won't be happy if he learns about your new conventions in the middle of a competitive auction.

The Fit Showing Jump is usually reserved for semipreemptive hands. You can't use a wide range of strength for this bid because there is no bidding room for opener to find out what you have. Here are some example hands.

None Vulnerable

WEST	NORTH	EAST	SOUTH
—	1♡	Double	?

You hold ♠ 72 ♡ J10763 ◇ 4 ♣ AQ1083

4♣ would be acceptable. You have a hand that wants to bid 4♡ and by raising via a 4♣ bid, North will have more knowledge of how to continue when the opponents bid. Since they are likely to get into the bidding, this treatment can be a lifesaver. The convention does have the usual down side in that it leaves your opponents with extra bidding room. It is possible that your 4♣ bid will allow West to come in with 4◇.

You hold ♠ KQJ8 ♡ K9863 ◇ 3 ♣ 964

You may wish to extend the Fit Showing principle to this specific sequence as well. If so, your response is 3♠. NOTE that is is okay to jump in a four card suit. The idea is that you are showing partner where your values are.

None Vulnerable

WEST	NORTH	EAST	SOUTH
—	1♡	Double	?

You hold ♠ 84   ♡ AJ86   ◇ 74   ♣ AQJ53

This is a tough hand. A Fit Showing 4♣ bid shows a weaker hand. If you bid 4♣ with this North won't envision this good a hand. When he signs off in 4♡, you will have undisclosed values and no way to show them. I don't know how to handle this hand perfectly. I think the right approach is to bid 2NT, the Jordan Raise, and then cue–bid clubs if possible.

The Splinter Response has much the same requirements of the Fit Showing Jump. The only difference is that responder jumps in his singleton instead of in his strong side suit. The Splinter Response shows the same specific point range since it is too space consuming for later elucidation. A couple of examples should be enough.

None Vulnerable
You hold ♠ 872   ♡ Q873   ◇ AJ762   ♣ 2

WEST	NORTH	EAST	SOUTH
—	1♡	Double	?

Bid 4♣ if you are using the splinters. One nice thing about this convention is that if they bid 4♠ and North leads clubs, your deuce won't discourage him from giving you a ruff or two. Conventions can help or haunt you in curious ways.

In my opinion, there isn't much reason to get involved with the conventions of the last three sections with the exception of the Jordan Raise. If you have to wait months for a bid to come up it is a waste of time. If you wait months for a bid to come up and you alert that partner is splintering and he is in fact fit showing, it is more than just a waste of time. It is a disaster.

If I am asked to give a final opinion, I vote for the following, most of which has already been noted.

1. Play the Jordan Raise.

2. Play the jump shift to the three level as invitational and natural.

3. Play the jump shift to the four level as showing a singleton. This is the closest decision in the group. There is little to choose between the Splinter Raise and the Fit Showing Raise. I asked some of my scientific friends which treatment they preferred and they all shrugged and mumbled that they used one or the other of the conventions (some used neither), and no one thought enough of their treatment to make me think I should tout it.

NOTE that you must decide how many points the four level jump shows, regardless of which treatment you choose. If you use a convention without discussion or if you use a convention just because you have it in front of you it will be worse than having no convention at all. Unless of course, you decide not to play either one.

RESPONDER BIDS 1NT

Not much to offer here. One player I know refuses to bid 1NT at all. He feels that if he has a 1NT response, he can do just as well to pass and bid later. I don't entirely agree with this opinion. But I can see the merit of it. There is a new convention (Cappelletti over Doubles of 1♡ or 1♠) which is gaining a following. In this method, a 1NT response over a takeout double is a transfer to clubs. The users of this convention feel that the normal meaning for 1NT is worth giving up in order to show a club suit. In other words, they don't think so much of the 1NT response that they insist on keeping it. In a couple of chapters I will discuss Cappelletti in detail.

If 1NT Over A Takeout Double Shows A Balanced Hand, How Many Points Does It Show?

Assuming you wish to keep the traditional meaning of 1NT over takeout doubles, you have to have enough points that you won't get massacred.

WEST	NORTH	EAST	SOUTH
—	1♡	Double	?

If East hadn't doubled, you would have bid a notrump on hands with as few as six points and as many as ten. Some players fudge and do it with five. In fact, if you play 1NT is forcing in response to one of a major, you might bid 1NT with a two count hoping to steal the hand from the opponents.

When East doubles, your obligations change. It is not necessary to keep the bidding open with a five or six point hand and some poor sevens are worth leaving alone. The range used by most players is a good seven to a poor ten that isn't suited for a redouble.

Note To Forcing Notrump Players

If you play a forcing notrump structure, IT DOES NOT APPLY after a takeout double. You have enough weapons, including a redouble, that you don't need the forcing notrump.

Here are some examples of what to do when RHO doubles your partner's opening bid. Since your considerations vary a little according to what suit partner opened, I'll look at more than one possibility.

None Vulnerable

WEST	NORTH	EAST	SOUTH
—	1♣	Double	?

You hold ♠ 1073   ♡ KJ3   ◇ Q1074   ♣ Q83

This is the average 1NT bid over a takeout double. You could bid 1◇ but 1NT is more descriptive. If the opponents bid, your partner will have a better idea what to do if your response was 1NT as opposed to 1◇.

You hold ♠ 643   ♡ K1094   ◇ AJ4   ♣ 1073

Even though you have the points and the shape to bid 1NT, I much prefer 1♡. RHO's double does not preclude your side having a 4–4 heart fit. Your heart suit is good so you won't mind being raised with only three card support.

None Vulnerable

WEST	NORTH	EAST	SOUTH
—	1♣	Double	?

You hold ♠ KQ8   ♡ 9532   ◇ J74   ♣ QJ4

This approximate hand was discussed in an earlier section. I thought responder should skip the heart suit and just respond 1NT. I accept you may miss a 4–4 heart fit.

You hold ♠ Q84   ♡ Q86   ◇ J954   ♣ J43

It is all right to pass when you have nothing to say. This hand looks speechless to me. If you pass and partner doesn't bid again, you won't miss anything.

Not Vulnerable vs. Vulnerable

WEST	NORTH	EAST	SOUTH
—	1♡	Double	?

You hold ♠ J73　♡ Q　♢ Q873　♣ J10763

Pass. 1NT shows a decent seven to a poor ten count. This hand is a very poor six. NOTE that you can't bid 2♣. 2♣ shows a weak hand but it also shows a good suit. If all your strength was in clubs, it would be okay.

You hold ♠ 754　♡ 2　♢ 7642　♣ AQ1097

With this, bidding 2♣ would be all right systemically and it would be all right in practice. Among other things, it will help partner if they play the hand and he is on lead.

Not Vulnerable vs. Vulnerable

WEST	NORTH	EAST	SOUTH
—	1♡	Double	?

You hold ♠ Q84　♡ K82　♢ Q72　♣ 10763

Raise to 2♡. A major suit raise takes priority over takeout doubles. If you bid 1NT or if you pass, you may not get to show your heart support. More on this later.

You hold ♠ Q6　♡ Q8　♢ KQ53　♣ J5432

This is the ten count that bids 1NT instead of redoubling. If you redouble, you will have to bid when the opponents bid one or two spades and nothing looks good. Better to bid 1NT and have a point in reserve than to brag about your ten points and then have no way to discuss them on the next round.

RESPONDER REDOUBLES

It used to be that all ten point hands redoubled. This worked fine if the opponents behaved and stayed out of the auction. Bridge has changed a lot since in the last fifteen years. Good opponents no longer regard your redouble as a warning. They regard it as a challenge. You might think that an opponent with only two or three points couldn't do much to hurt you but don't you believe that for a second. An underarmed opponent can give you problems you don't want to know about. Here are a couple of hands showing the automatic redouble at its worst.

Vulnerable vs. Not Vulnerable
You hold ♠ 73   ♡ AQ84   ◇ KJ653   ♣ 93

WEST	NORTH	EAST	SOUTH
—	1◇	Double	?

If you redouble, what is your next bid when West bids 1♠, passed around to you? Do you raise diamonds and never find your heart fit? Do you bid 2♡? If you do, it will properly be construed as forcing and will probably get your side to game on inertia. Or do you cue–bid 2♠ and try to get partner to bid notrump? Even if he does bid notrump, do you know what to do now?

Next question. Let's assume you didn't feel bothered by the 1♠ bid and that you were happy with your solution, whatever it was. (I don't believe you, by the way.) How will you proceed if East raises to 2♠ instead of passing? Do you raise to 3◇, which loses the heart suit, or do you bid 3♡, which promises five hearts and forces the bidding to game? Annoying, isn't it? Your side has 24 or more high card points and you have no correct way to bid your hand.

Much better for South to respond 1♡, forcing, and then to continue as if the double didn't exist. So far I have been charitable. I have kept the opponents' bidding at a manageable level. Here is an even better hand for you to contend with. Don't forget that you are vulnerable and they are not.

Vulnerable vs. Not Vulnerable
You hold ♠ A10764   ♡ 4   ◇ QJ7   ♣ KQ83

WEST	NORTH	EAST	SOUTH
—	1♣	Double	?

Here's what will happen to you if you redouble. West will jump to 3♡ and the auction will continue thusly.

WEST	NORTH	EAST	SOUTH
—	1♣	Double	Redouble
3♡*	Pass	4♡	?

* Preemptive

If you ask what 3♡ means, it is preemptive. It shows five or six hearts and promises no high card strength at all. East's raise to 4♡ represents East's judgment that 4♡ is the right bid. We don't know if he expects to make 4♡ or whether he is bidding 4♡ as a sacrifice. What do you do now with your opening bid? Here are your choices.

1. You can bid 4♠.
2. You can bid 5♣.
3. You can double.
4. You can pass.

Are you comfortable, let alone happy, with any of these bids? I personally would feel revolted if someone came to me with this bidding problem. Here's why.

1.   If I bid 4♠, the auction will end there. Why should 4♠ be the right contract? We might belong in 5♣, 6♣, 6♠, or 4♡ doubled.

2. If I bid 5♣, I have the same worries as above. Why should 5♣ be better than 4♠?

3. If I double, I will have to sweat out the rest of the hand. Maybe we should be in 4♠. Should I have raised clubs? Are we going to beat 4♡ doubled enough to make up for our game? Uh oh. Declarer is crossruffing the hand. He has seven—no, make that eight tricks. We can't beat it enough for game. I don't believe this. I'm not sure we are going to beat it at all. Whew. Nice play partner. Down one. We get a hundred. How many spades did you have? Nuts. We make four spades. In fact, five is cold if I guess the spades and I can make six if I can guess East's distribution. Sorry partner. Guess I shouldn't have doubled. etc.

4. If I pass, it invites partner's opinion. Even though this is the best bid of the lot, it is still poor. Partner has to guess what to do and he doesn't know the most important features of my hand, starting with the good five card spade suit. If North has three spades and 4♠ is the right contract, there is no way North will come up with that decision.

The answer is a simple one. **Save your redoubles for hands where the opponents can't run over you**. The key here is that there is no suit the opponents can bid which will embarrass you. If you have redouble values, you should take this approach.

1. If you have a suit of your own you should tend to show it if you can. This means that if you can bid the suit at the one level, which is forcing, you should do that. If your suit is lower ranking and you can't bid it at the one level, you may have to redouble and hope for the best.

2. If you have four card support for partner and no major suit that needs bidding, you should show that support in whatever manner your system calls for.

3. If you have three card support for partner, you must start with redouble. It is not good to make a strong raise on the first round with three trump. This is a major rule in my mind. I can't remember violating it.

4. If you can handle anything the opponents do, you should probably redouble.

Here is a selection of hands which give you a choice of redoubling or doing something else.

None Vulnerable

WEST	NORTH	EAST	SOUTH
—	1◇	Double	?

You hold ♠ Q83   ♡ KJ8   ◇ KJ6   ♣ J1072

Redouble and then bid 1NT unless partner has doubled something in the meantime.

You hold ♠ 63   ♡ AQJ83   ◇ K108   ♣ 842

Bid 1♡. You have redouble strength, but you have no real interest in doubling them in spades. Your heart suit is the most important feature of your hand. Show it while you can. If you redouble, you will have to bid hearts at the two or three level and this will more or less commit you to game even if partner has a minimum. If you bid 1♡, your auction will continue as if East hadn't entered the auction.

You hold ♠ K73 ♡ 8 ◇ QJ6 ♣ AQ9863

Redouble. This is a bad hand for my method. It would be nice to play that 2♣ was a normal forcing bid. But it isn't. This is a sad hand but it is also a rare hand. You won't see many of these. What you hope to do is to redouble and then bid clubs, which will create a force. NOTE that in my methods, a 3♣ bid would show 10–11 points with six good clubs. You can't do that with this hand because it is too good. You intend to force to game so you can't start with a nonforcing bid.

You hold ♠ K4 ♡ 93 ◇ 83 ♣ AQ98753

You have the strength for a redouble but no assurance you will be able to show the clubs AND retain control of the auction. Bid 3♣ if you use this jump to show a 10–11 point hand with a good six or seven card suit. This treatment allows partner to pass if he must but he can bid on if your bid encourages him.

None Vulnerable

WEST	NORTH	EAST	SOUTH
—	1♡	Double	?

You hold ♠ AJ106 ♡ 87 ◇ J104 ♣ KJ72

A classic redouble. You intend to double the opponents in whatever they bid. Even if they bid 2◇, you have a good double.

You hold ♠ A7653 ♡ QJ8 ◇ Q10 ♣ Q32

Redouble. You hope to be able to bid 2♡ on the next round, showing redouble strength and exactly three trumps. Bidding 1♠ makes no sense. Your side isn't going to play in spades. It is going to play in hearts. If you bid 1♠, you will have to jump in hearts to get across your strength. If partner has a minimum opener, 2♡ will be high enough.

146

You hold ♠ 843   ♡ QJ653   ◇ AJ3   ♣ Q8

Bid 2NT showing a limit raise. DO NOT REDOUBLE with four card or better support for a major suit. Even if you have twenty support points, you should start by telling partner you have four trumps. You will show additional points on the next round. I promise you, the sooner partner knows you have support, the sooner he will be able to contribute sensible decisions into the auction.

RESPONDER RAISES
TO THE TWO LEVEL

When partner opens the bidding and gets doubled, the most common thing for responder to do is to offer a single raise. The only question is deciding what range the raise shows. For instance, after 1♠–Double–?, what is the best and the worst hand responder can have for a 2♠ bid?

Here are some useful considerations to help you with your decision.

1. If you have a weak hand, this may be the last time in the auction that you can show support.

2. If you have a weak hand, your side isn't going to be able to make anything unless partner has a good hand and even then, he may not be able to compete UNLESS HE KNOWS about your fit.

Remember, the goal of bidding is to find a fit and then to find the level. Finding the fit is the immediate issue. Since East's takeout double tells you there is going to be bidding, you want to let partner in on the secret of your few points and your support so that he can make later decisions. Here are some possible raise decisions.

None Vulnerable

WEST	NORTH	EAST	SOUTH
—	1♣	Double	?

You hold ♠ 743 ♡ K3 ♢ 10763 ♣ Q1076

Absolutely, raise to 2♣. True, North may have only three clubs, but he doesn't have to have three only. He may have four of them. He may have more. He may have twelve points. He may have twenty. Your raise will help his judgment immensely. For whatever it's worth, I would rather bid 3♣ than pass with this hand.

You hold ♠ 64 ♡ 973 ♢ 96542 ♣ AJ8

Pass if you must, but I wouldn't be unhappy to raise with this hand.

The more common decisions come when partner opens one of a major. Raising with three trumps is no problem so the issue is how few points you need to raise. Experience has shown that responder has to bid aggressively in this position. Failure to raise causes lots of lost partscores, a few games, and some saves, to say nothing of pushing the opponents one level higher.

None Vulnerable

WEST	NORTH	EAST	SOUTH
—	1♠	Double	?

You hold ♠ 10875 ♡ 84 ♢ 843 ♣ QJ74

Some players raise to 3♠ with this hand. I don't think this is necessary, but it does show the importance that good competitors give to getting their two cents in. I would raise to 2♠ only. Be clear that this is a normal bid over a takeout double. South isn't taking great liberties with this raise.

You hold ♠ K93   ♡ 843   ◇ 83   ♣ J8532

Another mandatory raise to 2♠. This time you have only three trumps but they include an honor. You should raise to 2♠ even if you didn't have the jack of clubs. In fact, I know a few very good players who would raise to 2♠ without the jack of clubs and without the doubleton diamond.

You hold ♠ K104   ♡ 843   ◇ 842   ♣ 9852

I wouldn't raise with this, but I have seen it done with good effect. You have to decide if this hand meets your requirements.

You hold ♠ 973   ♡ A5   ◇ 8432   ♣ 10973

You can raise with three little trumps as long as you have something that will please partner if your hand becomes dummy. The doubleton ace of hearts is a sure value so even if your trumps disappoint partner, your hand won't be an entire loss.

You hold ♠ 873   ♡ Q843   ◇ Q97   ♣ Q104

I suggest passing. You know the bidding will be competitive and that your partner will be bidding again on many hands. This hand isn't going to please him. Worse yet, if your partner competes and goes down, you will discover that your queens were enough that the opponents couldn't make anything. Pass this and if possible come back in with 2♠ later. Partner will know you have a crummy hand along these lines.

You hold ♠ K95   ♡ 862   ◇ KJ976   ♣ J3

If you have been in agreement with some of the earlier cream puff raises, you will be feeling some doubts about this one. This hand is much better than the three point minimum discussed a moment ago but it is still short of a redouble. Can it be right to raise to 2♠ with some three point hands and also with eight and nine point hands? There is a definite problem here. Four solutions are currently in effect.

1. Raise with the three point hand and with the nine point hand and hope for the best. In practice, this isn't as bad as it sounds. Still, when you do the wrong thing, you will wish for something better.

2. Eddie Kantar taught me this one. His method is to raise with the little hands. If he has eight or nine points, he passes and then raises later. This works okay as long as there is a later. If the bidding is at the three level, this method has obvious drawbacks.

3. You can play that a raise shows 3–7 points and that a 2♣ bid becomes an artificial raise promising a really good seven points up to a nine count that wasn't worth a redouble.

4. You can play Cappelletti Raises.

Both of these last two treatments are artificial. You can use the Two Club Raise easily enough but the Cappelletti Raises are more complex than anything I have talked about in this or in any other book I have written. The next section will cover both of these methods.

THE TWO CLUB CONSTRUCTIVE RAISE

In an effort to overcome the problems of the previous section, someone came up with a solution that does work although not without cost. It works like this. When your partner opens one of a major and RHO doubles, you show support in this fashion.

1. With a poor raise (three to a so–so seven points) you make your normal single raise.
2. With a good raise (seven good points to nine support points) you bid 2♣ over the double.
3. With more you either redouble or use the Jordan 2NT raise.

These hands would qualify to raise 1♡ to 2♡ over a takeout double.

1. ♠ 73   ♡ K73   ◇ 108753   ♣ 743
2. ♠ 743   ♡ J83   ◇ 83   ♣ K10754
3. ♠ AJ43   ♡ 1096   ◇ 3   ♣ 95432
4. ♠ K94   ♡ K763   ◇ 853   ♣ 953
5. ♠ J73   ♡ Q83   ◇ K832   ♣ Q73

These hands range from three high card points which have a useful feature up to eight high card points which have poor points and poor distribution. REMEMBER that you are allowed to pass with three card trump support and six points if you have no redeeming features.

The following hands would qualify to bid 2♣ after RHO doubles partner's 1♠ opening bid.

1. ♠ Q104   ♡ 85   ◇ 943   ♣ AJ1084
2. ♠ 1084   ♡ K43   ◇ KQ652   ♣ 84
3. ♠ K973   ♡ K3   ◇ 873   ♣ 10853
4. ♠ K73   ♡ J106   ◇ J763   ♣ A74

These are hands which would be happy to raise if East hadn't doubled. Responder has six excellent high card points with a little shape (Example Three), up to a nine count with poor shape (Example Four). Note the first hand. It has five good clubs. This is a coincidence. The 2♣ response promises support and a decent hand. It says nothing about clubs.

I think this convention works well enough to deserve your consideration. If you adopt this convention, though, you have to remember it. 'Forgets' are not appreciated. Also, you lose the ability to bid a natural 2♣. This is a real loss. My opinion? Use this convention if you wish and you will gain enough to make up for the loss. One reminder. If you use the Drury* Convention, you will have a conflict if partner opens in third or fourth seat and is doubled. I suggest you use the Two Club Raise after a first or second seat major suit opening and takeout double and the Drury Two Club Convention after a third or fourth seat opening and takeout double.

*Drury is a worthwhile convention. If you wish a thorough discussion of it, refer to my book *Passed Hand Bidding* published by Lawrence and Leong Publishing.

THE CAPPELLETTI CONVENTION

Mike Cappelletti has come up with an interesting bidding structure over takeout doubles. It is named appropriately enough, Cappelletti Over One of a Major Doubled. He had the courtesy to abbreviate it to C/1MX, which is easier to type. I will refer to it in the remainder of this discussion as CAP which is even easier to type.

CAP solves a large number of problems that occur when RHO doubles your partner's opening one heart or one spade bid. I will present the basic method here but I warn you that it is more than just a convention. It is almost an entire system unto itself. Also, even though CAP has been around only a few years, creative minds in the bridge world are introducing changes.

Here is the nutshell outline. Your partner opens one of a major and East doubles for takeout. Let's assume partner opened 1♡ for the sake of discussion. Here is what responder's bids mean. NOTE that 1NT, 2♣, and 2◇ (the suit below opener's major) are all transfer bids.

WEST	NORTH	EAST	SOUTH
—	1♡	Double	?

You hold ♠ QJ763 ♡ 83 ◇ K984 ♣ K3

Bid 1♠. This is a natural bid. CAP does not affect this sequence. If your current system says to bid 1♠ with this hand, you should continue to do so. The CAP system applies only to 1NT and two level bids up to two of opener's suit.

WEST	NORTH	EAST	SOUTH
—	1♡	Double	1NT

1NT shows one of two hands. Initially it is a transfer to 2♣. Responder will show on his next bid what his intentions were. The most common hand for this bid is a seven to nine point heart raise with only two trumps.

You hold ♠ A73 ♡ 105 ◇ K876 ♣ 9842

Start by bidding 1NT. Partner will bid 2♣ and you will correct to 2♡ showing 7–9 points with a doubleton heart. NOTE that this sequence says nothing about clubs.

You hold ♠ KJ3 ♡ 93 ◇ AJ985 ♣ 763

Bid 1NT. Partner will bid 2♣ and you will continue with 2◇. This is a CAP trick which shows five good diamonds AND the 7–9 point heart raise with a doubleton heart. If your clubs and diamonds were reversed, you couldn't show the club suit.

Responder may have a real club suit. In this case, responder will pass 2♣ with 5–9 points and will continue bidding if he has ten or more.

You hold ♠ 84 ♡ 92 ◇ Q983 ♣ AQ1084

Responder transfers to 2♣ and passes when opener bids 2♣ as asked.

You hold ♠ 84 ♡ 92 ◇ Q98 ♣ AQJ1083

This time responder has invitational values. When opener bids 2♣ responder will raise to 3♣ showing game interest and a six card suit.

WEST	NORTH	EAST	SOUTH
—	1♡	Double	2♣

As with most CAP bids, this one (2♣) is a transfer. Responder is asking opener to bid 2◇. Responder will continue to describe his hand after opener bids 2◇. If responder has a weak hand with diamonds, he will pass 2◇. If responder has an invitational hand with diamonds, he will raise to 3◇.

WEST	NORTH	EAST	SOUTH
—	1♡	Double	2◇

Two of the suit below opener's major is also a transfer. It shows a good raise with 7–9 support points. Similarly, if the bidding started 1♠–Double–?, a 2♡ bid by responder would show a good raise for spades.

WEST	NORTH	EAST	SOUTH
—	1♡	Double	2♡

When responder raises opener's major, it shows a crummy raise with 3–6 points. This is an important distinction for opener because he needs to know whether to compete when West bids, as he will on many hands.

WEST	NORTH	EAST	SOUTH
—	1♡	Double	?

Other bids such as 2♠, 2NT, 3♣, 3◇, and 3♡ will need defining. I suggest, as does Cappelletti, that you use something like the following structure for these bids.

2♠	A normal weak jump shift.
2NT	This continues to be the Jordan Raise.
3♣, 3♦	Since you can transfer into the minor suit with CAP, you don't need these bids as natural any more. These can be used as fit showing jumps or some kind of splinter bid. Cappelletti likes these as fit showing jumps and that seems okay to me.
3♡	This continues to be natural and weak as discussed in the next chapter.

How Does Opener Respond To A CAP Bid?

The discussion above assumed throughout that opener bid as asked by responder and that responder could continue with his plan. Opener, in fact, is not obliged to obey responder's transfers. If responder transfers, the bid is forcing and opener can not pass, but he is entitled to make a different bid if his hand calls for it. Since most of opener's digressions are logical, I will give some examples only and will leave the rest to you.

WEST	NORTH	EAST	SOUTH
—	—	—	1♡
Double	1NT *	Pass	?

* Cappelletti relay to 2♣

North has asked South to bid 2♣. South will usually follow instructions but it is not mandatory. Here are some examples.

You hold ♠ Q2   ♡ AKJ985   ♦ A1032   ♣ 5

Rebid 2♡. Opener has no interest in clubs and more importantly, he has a fine heart suit to rebid.

You hold ♠ KJ4 ♡ AKJ73 ◇ 9873 ♣ 3

Opener has to rebid something. He can't pass. North will usually have a modest hand but he may have a good one. Since opener has nothing special to show and has a minimum hand, he should rebid 2♣. This does not show club support, it just implies a boring hand with nothing good to do.

You hold ♠ A8 ♡ Q10875 ◇ AQJ84 ♣ 3

Rebid 2◇. You have something good to introduce.

You hold ♠ 98 ♡ KQJ9864 ◇ A ♣ AQ8

Rebid 3♡ or even 4♡. This is one area that needs your partnership defining. I think 3♡ is forcing so that ought to do the trick whatever partner intends to do.

You hold ♠ A84 ♡ AQ764 ◇ 3 ♣ AJ94

A tough hand for CAP. If responder has clubs, this hand can almost look for a slam. If responder has 7–9 points with a doubleton heart, a partscore may be enough. I would guess to bid 2♣. This hand is offered only to show that all conventions have their awkward moments. It is not intended as a criticism.

CAP offers a lot of benefits if you are willing to put in the time. This convention has one immediate advantage in that it will come up a lot. A convention that is both useful and has a high rate of usage gets my vote. I will note here that this convention is much more detailed than the three or four pages here suggest. A full discussion of this convention and its many nuances would take thirty pages. As of this moment there is a twelve page booklet on CAP published by Cappelletti himself, a couple of pages in Amalya Kearse's Bridge Conventions Complete and an article in the ACBL Bulletin by George Rosenkranz. One of these days someone will write up the convention in the entirety it deserves. Maybe I will do it.

RESPONDER RAISES
TO THE THREE LEVEL

An easy topic to finish the discussion on bidding over doubles. When partner opens the bidding and is doubled, a jump by responder shows a weak hand with four or more trumps and some sort of shape. (A possible exception to this rule is discussed in the Jordan section regarding jump raises in a minor suit.)

Some players like to use the jump raise over a double as still being a limit raise or even a game forcing raise. This is an ill judged philosophy. For starters, you will wait for eons until you have a game forcing hand with trump support. And secondly, you give up the benefits of the preemptive jump raise. The only sensible way to play jump raises over takeout doubles is as preemptive in the major suits. If I have my way, the jumps will be preemptive in the minor suits as well.

How strongly can you pursue this theory? Here are some example hands. NOTE the vulnerability changes from hand to hand.

None Vulnerable
You hold ♠ 63 ♡ KJ84 ◇ 107643 ♣ 82

WEST	NORTH	EAST	SOUTH
—	1♡	Double	?

A classic jump to 3♡. It meets all three of the usual criteria. You have a weak hand. You have four trump. You have distribution. Because the hearts are so good, I would bid 3♡ with this hand on any vulnerability. Good trumps are the best defense you can have against a penalty double.

Vulnerable vs. Not Vulnerable
You hold ♠ Q83   ♡ 84   ◇ AJ73   ♣ K1094

WEST	NORTH	EAST	SOUTH
—	1♠	Double	?

Do not bid 3♠. It is wrong for many reasons.

1. You have only three trumps. A double raise promises four or more. Even playing five card majors, you need four trump to jump.

2. Your hand is too strong. With limit raise strength, you should start with a redouble and then bid 2♠ if possible. That will show 10–11 support points and three trumps.

3. You have so–so shape. Frankly, hands with three trumps are almost defined as having poor shape. It is easy for the defenders to lead trump and cancel out your ruffing strength. If you have four trumps, the defenders have to work harder to keep you from ruffing. It is possible that they can't stop you simply because they don't have enough trumps of their own to keep leading them.

None Vulnerable
You hold ♠ Q73   ♡ QJ543   ◇ 872   ♣ J6

WEST	NORTH	EAST	SOUTH
—	1♡	Double	?

2♡ looks like enough. You have five trumps, but your shape is poor and you have some side high cards which may turn out to be winners on defense.

For this chapter, the most important thing I can offer is that you do play the jump raise as preemptive and that you never do it without four or more trumps.

Chapter Five

THEY OVERCALL
A STRONG NOTRUMP

IT USED TO BE THAT WHEN AN OPPONENT OVERCALLED a strong notrump showing 15–18 points with a stopper in the opened suit, everyone shut up out of respect for all those points.

Times have changed. It is true that the one notrump bidder may have the best hand at the table and it is true that the opening side probably doesn't have a game. It is not automatically true, however, that the opening side can't make a partscore. Games and slams are the big prizes of successful bidding but partscores remain the most likely result on any given hand.

Do you have a sense for what a partscore is worth? At matchpoints, for example, how many matchpoints do you get if they make two hearts and you could have made three diamonds? My guess is that you will get an average of 2–3 matchpoints for the –110 and you would have gotten 9–10 matchpoints if you made +110 yourself.

If you are playing at IMPS, the cost to you is at least as great. If you let the opponents make 110 when you could have had the same score, that costs you 220 points, which equates to six IMPS. Did you know that if you make a nonvulnerable game that wasn't bid in the other room, your gain is just six IMPS? Interesting. A partscore swing can be worth as much as a game swing!

Going back to the question of bidding over a 1NT overcall, it is clear that a partscore is worth going after.

True, you have to respect those 15–18 points, but you don't have to be in awe of them. If you have a few points but also have a good suit with some shape, the percentages are greatly in favor of bidding.

In general there are five things you can do.

1. You can double 1NT for penalty.
2. You can raise partner's suit .
3. You can bid a new suit.
4. You can pass.
5. You can bid 2NT!

THE PENALTY DOUBLE

Barring some distributional reason suggesting a different action, you should double a 1NT overcall with all nine point hands and with any eight point hand that has an obviously good lead.

Opener is not obligated to sit for the double. If opener has a weak distributional hand, he can pull the double. You should not pull the double just because you have a weak opener or just because you have a distributional opener. You need both weakness and shape to pull.

None Vulnerable

WEST	NORTH	EAST	SOUTH
—	—	—	1♠
1NT	Double	Pass	?

You hold ♠ AJ762 ♡ KQ1094 ◇ J3 ♣ 4

Assuming you opened this hand, you can bid 2♡ over North's double.

None Vulnerable

WEST	NORTH	EAST	SOUTH
—	—	—	1♠
1NT	Double	Pass	?

You hold ♠ KQ1094　♡ AJ762　◇ J3　♣ 4

This hand can pass 1NT doubled. The reason is that on this hand, you welcome a spade lead. On the previous hand, North is likely to lead spades, which is not what you really want. When the suit you opened in is good, you will be happy if partner leads it. It means the defense is doing something good.

You hold ♠ KQJ1073　♡ A1065　◇ 4　♣ 105

Let's pretend you opened this ten count with 1♠. If North doubles a 1NT overcall, you can pass. With a spade lead, you have six tricks in your own hand plus you have a sure entry.

You hold ♠ J9652　♡ K2　◇ K3　♣ KQ105

Pass. Hard to imagine pulling the double with a balanced or near balanced hand.

You hold ♠ A1086542　♡ 83　◇ AQ　♣ Q10

Pass again. You have scattered honors and you don't have any shape outside the seven card suit.

You hold ♠ A1086542　♡ AQ　◇ Q762　♣ None

I might pull the double, but it isn't 100% clear. If North has something like:

♠ 93　♡ J983　◇ K73　♣ AJ107

1NT doubled has scads of losers.

You hold ♠ Q1087543　♡ 3　◇ 4　♣ AKQ6

Bid 2♠. North won't know about your club strength until

it's too late. NOTE that when you pull to your original suit, you are doing so in the face of West's notrump bid. West says he has your suit stopped and North's double doesn't promise support. If you rebid your suit, you need a seven card suit.

None Vulnerable

WEST	NORTH	EAST	SOUTH
—	—	—	1♠
1NT	Double	Pass	?

You hold ♠ QJ10862 ♡ K72 ◊ A87 ♣ J

This is a pretty good six card suit. The reason you don't rebid it is that you are happy to defend. With a spade lead, your hand has six potential tricks. If North doesn't lead a spade, you may be in trouble. But not automatically. If North happens to lead a red suit, that is fine with you.

You hold ♠ K107652 ♡ 8 ◊ K3 ♣ AQ98

I would pass with this hand. If I decided to rebid, I would bid 2♣, not 2♠.

You hold ♠ K107652 ♡ Q8 ◊ K3 ♣ A98

Pass for sure. Your hand is balanced and you have your normal allotment of points. Bidding 2♠ on this is begging for a poor result.

RAISING PARTNER'S SUIT

This is a common choice when RHO bids 1NT. One important point to note here: When your RHO bids 1NT over your partner's opening bid, your side won't have a game. Bidding by your side should be defined as competitive and not as looking for a game.

None Vulnerable

WEST	NORTH	EAST	SOUTH
—	1◇	1NT	?

You hold ♠ 2   ♡ J1074   ◇ Q973   ♣ Q863

Raise to 2◇. You can't possibly get hearts into the picture. But you can show your diamond support. You pay off if partner is 4–4–3–2 but that is a pessimistic view. There are too many good things that can happen including the possibility that partner can compete.

You hold ♠ A5   ♡ 4   ◇ Q10653   ♣ 65432

I think you can make a good case for jumping to 3◇. Jumps are not forcing or invitational over a 1NT overcall. Jumps are weak and preemptive. On this hand it is clear that the opponents have a major fit or two. West can bid either major if he wishes but if he wants to show both majors, he has to cue–bid 4◇. It is possible they will find the wrong fit.

None Vulnerable
You hold ♠ K2   ♡ 10763   ◇ 832   ♣ 9874

WEST	NORTH	EAST	SOUTH
—	1♡	1NT	?

Raise to 2♡. This sequence is not forward going. It does not promise a good hand. It shows heart support only and enough of a wish that 2♡ will be an okay spot. There is nothing in this bid to suggest an interest in going higher.

You hold ♠ 10964   ♡ Q106   ◇ 87532   ♣ 9

Well? Raising could work. You have only three trump but you also have a singleton plus two honors in hearts. Bidding with this hand will require a partner who can remember that East bid 1NT.

You hold ♠ AQ2 ♡ 1094 ◇ 63 ♣ Q8752

I would raise to 2♡ with this hand too. The 1NT bid has warned you that any heart finesse will lose so if your side has a game to bid, it is less likely to succeed than in an uncontested auction. It is true that you have eight high card points. You might double. If the opponents were vulnerable, double would be a better choice because down one would be a satisfying +200. Against nonvulnerable opponents, bidding 2♡ rates to be better because it puts you in strong contention for +110 or +140, which is better than beating 1NT doubled just one trick.

Both Vulnerable

WEST	NORTH	EAST	SOUTH
—	1♡	1NT	?

You hold ♠ 2 ♡ 109763 ◇ Q10875 ♣ 83

3♡, preemptive, is best. North will not play you for a good hand. Good hands would double 1NT. 3♡ is a weak bid showing lots of trumps and good shape. Don't bid a conservative 2♡, which leaves West bidding room. Make him work to show his hand.

BIDDING A NEW SUIT

Bidding a new suit isn't as safe as raising partner's suit because you don't have a known fit. If you decide to introduce a suit, you can count on partner to have opening bid high cards but you can't depend on him for any trump help. For this reason, you usually need a six card suit when you bid over the 1NT overcall. If you bid a new suit, it is not forcing. It is not even encouraging. Partner is expected to pass. If he has something special to show, he can do so. But he shouldn't bid on the assumption that your new suit is forcing. It isn't.

Both Vulnerable
You hold ♠ QJ8752 ♡ 4 ◊ 1084 ♣ J42

WEST	NORTH	EAST	SOUTH
—	1◊	1NT	?

Bid 2♠. It isn't forcing so this will end the bidding as far as you are concerned. Your partner opened the bidding promising some high cards so all you are wishing for is that partner will have a spade fit or a spade tolerance. Even the singleton ten of spades would help. NOTE that when you introduce a suit, you have a six card suit. If you have five only, you need to catch partner with at least two cards in your suit. He will have some points for you but he doesn't promise support.

Both Vulnerable
You hold ♠ K4 ♡ QJ863 ◊ 84 ♣ 10763

WEST	NORTH	EAST	SOUTH
—	1◊	1NT	?

Pass. If partner has some heart help for you, it will be useful on defense as well as on offense. If partner has no heart help for you and you bid, you will be down some large number.

Not Vulnerable vs. Vulnerable
You hold ♠ QJ107653 ♡ 43 ◊ 3 ♣ 1083

WEST	NORTH	EAST	SOUTH
—	1♣	1NT	?

Bid 3♠. This is a preempt. Since you are at the three level on a dangerous auction, your partner will play you for a good suit although not much in high cards. If you can't stand to do this, at least bid 2♠. 3♠ has the added attraction that partner may be able to contribute something to the auction.

PASSING

It is legal and often right to pass when the opponents overcall 1NT. You may have a hand that feels like it should be bidding but if you don't have a safe way to show all your messages, it is best to quit.

None Vulnerable

WEST	NORTH	EAST	SOUTH
—	1♦	1NT	?

You hold ♠ J3   ♡ J9752   ◇ 7   ♣ KJ764

You know that 2♡ or 2♣ could be a good spot but there is no way to find out safely. If you bid 2♣ and get doubled, do you run to 2♡? What do you do when they double you there too?

You hold ♠ Q863   ♡ K852   ◇ 3   ♣ QJ72

This is the kind of eight count that should pass. You have no good lead and you have a singleton diamond. It is possible that the opponents are about to run partner's diamonds.

You hold ♠ J76543   ♡ Q7   ◇ J2   ♣ Q64

Let this one go. You have a bad suit and poor high cards. Neither one is fatal but the combination suggests passing.

BIDDING TWO NOTRUMP

In your entire life you may not run into this convention. It is a nice one to have around, though, because if it comes up you get to look very wise. We have seen that you can bid safely with many weak hands after RHO overcalls 1NT. What do you do when you have a rare game forcing hand? Much of the time you can just double 1NT and take your top score that way. But what do you do when you have a hand that wants to force to game but which is afraid to double? Say you have this hand:

♠ QJ10975 ♡ AJ10964 ◇ 4 ♣ None

Partner opens 1♣ and RHO bids 1NT. You want to get to 4♡ or 4♠ but you can't find out which is best without asking partner's opinion. Here are your possible bids.

1. Double is possible, but it has obvious objections. They might make 1NT doubled on a hand where you have a game.

2. Normally you would bid spades and then hearts in order to catch a preference from partner. The 1NT overcall forces changes in your bidding structure. 2♡, 2♠, 3♡, and 3♠ are all weak and nonforcing. You can't bid your suits one at a time and be sure to get another bid from partner.

3. You can jump to 4♡ or 4♠, but may end up in the wrong suit.

The answer? The answer is a funny one. Cue–bid 2NT. The message is that you have a strong hand that wants to go to game but is too distributional to double. It is not likely that you will find a slam if one should exist, but you will always reach a decent game. On this hand, your partner will probably bid 3♣ or 3◇. You will bid 3♠ and will next bid 4♡ over whatever partner does. When you bid 2NT, you create a game forcing sequence so partner, no matter how much he hates it, will keep bidding until you get to game.

WORTHWHILE CONVENTIONS

In practice, there are a lot of conventions. Two of them are worth mentioning here. If I am slighting some favorite convention of yours, it is possible that I just haven't heard of it. No offense intended.

Hamilton Convention

The first convention is the Hamilton Convention. Some people give credit for it to Mike Cappelletti but since I have already discussed one of his conventions in this book, I will refer to Convention One as the Hamilton Convention. It will be less confusing this way. The Hamilton Convention as used here works this way.

Partner opens the bidding in a suit and East overcalls 1NT. South bids as follows.

2♣	Shows a one suited hand. Opener is expected to bid 2♦. Responder will pass if his suit is diamonds and otherwise will bid his suit. Opener is allowed to override the 2♣ bid if he has something he wants to say.
2♦	Shows both major suits. Opener picks his longer major. It might be three cards long. It might in a pinch be only two cards long.
2♡	Shows hearts and a minor. Opener passes if he likes hearts and otherwise can bid 2NT, which asks responder to show his minor suit.
2♠	Shows spades and a minor. Opener passes if he likes spades and otherwise can bid 2NT, which asks responder to show his minor suit.

None Vulnerable

WEST	NORTH	EAST	SOUTH
—	1◇	1NT	?

You hold ♠ QJ8752   ♡ 4   ◇ 1084   ♣ J42

I suggested in the previous section that responder bid

2♠ with this hand. If you use the Hamilton Convention, you will do the same thing except that you have to start by bidding 2♣. This tells partner that you have a one suited hand that wants to compete. North will bid 2◇ and you will correct to 2♠.

You hold ♠ 83   ♡ A3   ◇ J10984   ♣ 8753

You want to raise diamonds, but you can't do it directly. Bid 2♣. North will bid 2◇, waiting to hear your suit. You will pass 2◇, thus achieving your goals.

None Vulnerable
You hold ♠ QJ87   ♡ K10964   ◇ 84   ♣ 104

WEST	NORTH	EAST	SOUTH
—	1♣	1NT	?

Opposite an opening bid, it is probably better to try to play the hand than to defend against 1NT. Your six high card points and your two doubletons make this a decent hand on offense. Bid 2◇, which promises the major suits. You would like to have 5–5 shape but it isn't absolutely necessary when your suits are okay. On a good day your partner has a four card major and everything is wonderful. If partner has a three card major the contract will be reasonable. Especially if his three card major is hearts. If partner has only a two card major to bid, you have made a poor decision. In practice (you will have to trust me for the time being) bidding 2◇ on this hand is a big winner.

None Vulnerable
You hold ♠ Q72   ♡ J109642   ◇ J108   ♣ 3

WEST	NORTH	EAST	SOUTH
—	1♠	1NT	?

2◇ is a possible choice here. Partner will know you have

spade support plus a heart suit you felt was worth offering.

None Vulnerable
You hold ♠ J3 ♡ J9752 ◊ 7 ♣ KJ764

WEST	NORTH	EAST	SOUTH
—	1◊	1NT	?

This hand was discussed earlier in terms of this same sequence. I thought that if responder had to guess a suit, it might be too dangerous to bid. Using the Hamilton Convention, responder can bid 2♡. If North has any kind of heart support he will pass. If he has nothing in hearts, he can bid 2NT to find out which minor South has. In this case South has clubs and will show them if asked.

None Vulnerable
You hold ♠ 1097642 ♡ 4 ◊ 7 ♣ QJ763

WEST	NORTH	EAST	SOUTH
—	1♣	1NT	?

Bid 2♠. If partner doesn't like them, he will ask for your minor and you will show your club suit. In this case, your suit is the suit he opened so you know a fit exists one way or another. A nice feeling.

Bluhm Convention

The second convention was invented, I believe, by the late Lou Bluhm. It has some similarities to the Hamilton Convention. It works this way. When partner opens one of a minor and is overcalled with 1NT, responder bids exactly the same as in Hamilton.

The difference occurs when partner opens a major suit and catches a 1NT overcall. Responder's bids have these meanings.

None Vulnerable

WEST	NORTH	EAST	SOUTH
—	1♡/♠	1NT	?

2♣   Shows clubs and the unbid major.

2◇   Shows diamonds and the unbid major.

2♡   Natural

2♠   Natural

None Vulnerable

WEST	NORTH	EAST	SOUTH
—	1♡	1NT	?

You hold ♠ QJ873   ♡ 8   ◇ 93   ♣ K10872

Bid 2♣, showing clubs and the unbid major, which in this case is spades. NOTE that this convention works out better than the Hamilton Convention in that it shows the suits at an economical level. Whichever suit partner prefers can be played at the two level.

You hold ♠ 1087642 ♡ K3 ◇ K6 ♣ 843

If responder wants to take a chance and bid spades, he has to bid 2♠. In the Bluhm Convention, major suit bids are natural over 1NT overcalls IF the opening bid was one of a major. There is an inference that responder doesn't have a second suit because he could have shown a two–suiter if he wished.

All conventions will haunt you at times. Inevitably you will hold a hand like this one.

None Vulnerable
You hold ♠ 8 ♡ 105 ◇ J543 ♣ KQJ1084

WEST	NORTH	EAST	SOUTH
—	1♠	1NT	?

You would like to bid 2♣ but you can't. 2♣ shows clubs and hearts (the unbid major) and you don't have that. You have just clubs. On this hand, Bluhm does you an injustice. That's the way with most conventions. Sooner or later you hold a hand that doesn't fit your methods. It's all relative. Whatever you do, you will have hands that don't fit. Your task is to choose the combination of conventions that caters to the largest number of important hands. In these terms, both of these conventions are useful. I recommend you adopt one or the other of them.

Chapter Six

THEY MAKE A WEAK JUMP OVERCALL

I DISCUSSED in Chapter Three the situation where your partner opens and your RHO comes in with a two level overcall.

AFTER A WEAK JUMP OVERCALL AT THE TWO LEVEL

You will be pleased to find out that the situation is much the same when your RHO makes a weak jump overcall at the two level. South's considerations will be more or less the same for both of the following auctions.

WEST	NORTH	EAST	SOUTH
—	1♡	2◇	?

WEST	NORTH	EAST	SOUTH
—	1♣	2◇	?

In both cases, East has bid 2◇. In the first auction, 2◇ was a simple overcall and in the second auction, 2◇ was a jump overcall. As noted above, South's actions will be virtually the same in both situations.

I won't spend much time justifying my conclusions because it has been done in earlier chapters. The following situations will serve as reminders.

Responder Raises

None Vulnerable
You hold ♠ 85   ♡ A953   ◇ KJ93   ♣ J64

WEST	NORTH	EAST	SOUTH
—	1◇	2♡	?

Raise to 3◇. A minor suit partscore is worth fighting for. It may not be high on your list of things to do but it must be on your list somewhere. Since the overcall has taken away your bidding room and pushed you higher to boot, your raise will have a wide range of points. You will raise with a good seven points with excellent trumps and you may have to raise with some decent eleven point hands that don't have alternatives. The hand here is about average for the raise.

None Vulnerable
You hold ♠ 74   ♡ J42   ◇ KJ53   ♣ Q763

WEST	NORTH	EAST	SOUTH
—	1♡	2♠	?

This is very close. I think I would pass. Add the ten of hearts and the ten of clubs or diamonds, and I think I would raise. The important issue here is that responder makes an effort to raise. Better to make a little overbid and tell partner you have something for him rather than to make a conservative pass and have your side lose out on the hand entirely.

Responder Jump Raises

None Vulnerable
You hold ♠ K3   ♡ Q1087   ◇ K9642   ♣ J10

WEST	NORTH	EAST	SOUTH
—	1♡	2♠	?

Hard to imagine a hand which would jump raise partner's minor suit. You would surely stop first to look for notrump. It is easy to imagine jumping to four of partner's major suit, however. This jump is semipreemptive but it should show some positive values. This hand would be worth a jump to 4♡. If you had game forcing values, you would cue–bid 3♠ (see next section) or possibly bid a new suit. This jump to game has to show some sort of strength. The opponents have gotten their suit into the auction so there is less reason to use the jump raise as entirely preemptive as you would if East had passed. Because the jump overcall deprived you of bidding room, your raise structure changes a little.

Your simple raise to 3♡ shows a fine seven points up to a crummy eleven. The hands you used to make limit raises on are delicate. A terrible limit raise might content itself with a simple raise. A shapely limit raise might jump to game, as is done with the hand above. Hands worth game forcing raises and even a few super maximum limit raises are handled with a cue bid.

Responder Cue–bids

None Vulnerable
You hold ♠ AQ6 ♡ 983 ◇ AK862 ♣ K4

WEST	NORTH	EAST	SOUTH
—	1◇	2♡	?

South is fortunate that he has a bid available. Bid 3♡.
In the structure I am advocating, a cue bid of an overcall
shows a game forcing raise of partner's suit. If responder
has room to make a jump cue bid, the simple cue bid
carries the inference that responder's hand is balanced.
On this hand South has more than enough to cue–bid
3♡. The cue bid says nothing about a heart control. 3♡
is an artificial noise showing four or more diamonds,
game points, and no interest in the unbid major.

Responder Makes A Jump Cue Bid

None Vulnerable
You hold ♠ Q6 ♡ 7 ◇ AJ1085 ♣ AKJ64

WEST	NORTH	EAST	SOUTH
—	1◇	2♡	?

Bid 4♡. You won't see this hand in the near future. You
might never see it. If the hand does come up, though, you
will be happy to be armed for it. 4♡ shows a monster
hand with a singleton heart and game values for
diamonds. Why else would you go beyond 3NT? The fact
that you are committing to 5◇ suggests a very good
hand, which implies interest in 6◇. You hope partner
will cue–bid 4♠ for you, in which case you will march on
to six or seven diamonds.

Responder Makes A Negative Double

None Vulnerable

WEST	NORTH	EAST	SOUTH
—	1◇	2♡	?

You hold ♠ Q1073   ♡ 43   ◇ 873   ♣ AQ97

Double. This is a minimum hand for a two level Negative Double. Since you are minimum for the bid, you must have four cards in spades. This sequence allows opener to rebid at the two level. If East had bid 2♠, South would need another point or two since a Negative Double would force the bidding to the three level.

You hold ♠ J7532   ♡ 3   ◇ Q8   ♣ K7632

I think you should pass. Do not make a Negative Double. You don't want to hear partner rebid 2NT. Another flaw with double is that if partner doesn't bid spades, you will still feel you have a fifth spade that perhaps should be mentioned somehow. Better to pass.

North is not obliged to reopen. He may pass if he wishes. There is a school of thought that says opener must reopen when an overcall is passed back to him. This is too wretched a method to comment on. If opener wants to pass, he should do so with a clear conscience.

Responder Bids A New Suit
At The Two Level

None Vulnerable
You hold ♠ AJ873 ♡ 83 ◇ KJ3 ♣ J104

WEST	NORTH	EAST	SOUTH
—	1◇	2♡	?

Bid 2♠. It is important to bid with light hands like this one. You may not get another chance. NOTE that the Negative Double won't help. If you double and partner bids, say, 3♣, you will be in the common quandary of wondering whether to show the spades. Bid 2♠ and then pass if partner does nothing useful. According to the discussion in Chapter Two, your 2♠ bid doesn't promise another bid. If North rebids 2NT, 3◇, or 3♠, or if West competes and North doesn't rebid, you can and will pass.

Responder Bids A New Suit
At The Three Level

None Vulnerable

WEST	NORTH	EAST	SOUTH
—	1◇	2♠	?

You hold ♠ 853 ♡ AKJ63 ◇ 73 ♣ Q54

Do not bid 3♡. You can bid a new suit at the two level with hands like these but you can't bid new suits at the three level. If you bid 3♡ with this your partner has little room to make his rebid. He needs the assurance that you will make one more bid. Your best bid is to double. You have ten points so you should be safe at the three level. Double isn't guaranteed to get you to a good spot but it doesn't automatically force you too high. An easy rule is to say that a new suit at the three level is forcing to 3NT or to four of your suit. If you bid three of a major, this becomes a game force and if you bid three of a minor, it is possible to stop in four of your minor.

You hold ♠ 832 ♡ A4 ◇ 8 ♣ KQJ7643

Bid 3♣. If partner can bid 3NT, you will pass and pray. If partner rebids 3◇, you will bid 4♣, which partner may pass. If partner raises clubs, you should treat it as forcing and continue by cue–bidding 4♡ or perhaps just signing off in 5♣.

Responder Jumps In A New Suit

None Vulnerable
You hold ♠ 9762 ♡ AJ97 ◇ KQ109 ♣ 4

WEST	NORTH	EAST	SOUTH
—	1♡	2♠	?

I am not sure what a jump to 4♣ should be. If you play it as a splinter, certainly a reasonable treatment, you can do that with this hand. In support of hearts, you have opening bid strength. The only issue is whether a splinter is the correct interpretation. I think it makes sense to play this as a splinter.

None Vulnerable
You hold ♠ 3 ♡ 873 ◇ KQ10763 ♣ AQ4

WEST	NORTH	EAST	SOUTH
—	1◇	2♡	?

If you keep the splinter treatment, you can bid 3♠ with this hand too. 3♠ will get 3NT from partner any time he has both major suits stopped. NOTE if your hand was:

♠ 83 ♡ 73 ◇ KQ10763 ♣ AQ4

instead, your correct bid would be 3♡ showing a balanced diamond raise.

None Vulnerable
You hold ♠ A73 ♡ 763 ◊ AQJ864 ♣ 9

WEST	NORTH	EAST	SOUTH
—	1◊	2♡	?

A judgment hand. You can bid 4♣ showing a singleton but this gets you beyond 3NT. I would skip the singleton club and would cue–bid 3♡ implying a balanced hand. If we get to 3NT and the defenders beat us with the club suit, I claim bad luck. I would do this at matchpoints and at IMPS. It is silly to assume that this hand is safer in diamonds than in notrump. True, 5◊ may be better than 3NT. It won't be better often enough that I am willing to give up on 3NT by bidding 4♣. NOTE that 5◊ is not out of the question after bidding 3♡. 4♣, on the other hand, is one–dimensional. You get to 5◊ whether you like it or not.

Responder Bids
Two Notrump Or Three Notrump

Both of these bids are natural and nonforcing. One worthwhile point is that the jump to 3NT shows a good eleven up to a so–so sixteen. This is the result of losing bidding room. With good elevens, you usually try to invite 3NT. After RHO's preempt, it is good tactics to take the pressure off partner by bidding game yourself.

None Vulnerable

WEST	NORTH	EAST	SOUTH
—	1♣	2♠	?

You hold ♠ K93 ♡ J73 ◊ QJ8 ♣ K1064
This is your typical 2NT bid. It shows nine good points

to a terrible twelve, promises a spade stopper, and implies no interest in hearts.

You hold ♠ AQ ♡ 104 ◇ KJ954 ♣ J873

This eleven points has tricks and it has two spade stoppers. Go ahead and shoot it out in 3NT.

You hold ♠ KJ ♡ QJ4 ◇ KQ543 ♣ 652

With one spade stopper, a wasted honor in spades, no spots in particular, and no fitting honor in clubs, I wouldn't criticize 2NT. I wouldn't criticize 3NT either. I think I would bid 2NT at matchpoints and 3NT at IMPS.

Responder Passes

A Negative Double promises only eight points but it also promises that you are ready for partner's rebid. Responder can have some nine or ten point hands that don't have a safe bid.

None Vulnerable

WEST	NORTH	EAST	SOUTH
—	1♡	2♠	?

You hold ♠ 7643 ♡ Q8 ◇ AQ ♣ J5432

Awkward. I would pass. 3♣ is obviously out of the question. The only choice is to double and that won't work if North rebids 3◇. Fortunately, there won't be many unbiddable nine or ten point hands so this headache will be rare.

You hold ♠ 765 ♡ Q8 ◇ AQ8 ♣ J8752

Double. A flawed Negative Double, but better than passing. The worst thing partner can do is to bid 3◇. With AQ8 instead of AQ doubleton, it won't be as traumatic for you if partner bids them.

AFTER A WEAK JUMP OVERCALL AT THE THREE LEVEL

The auction is getting out of hand here. The opponents are jacking up the bidding and as a consequence are running us out of room to use our methods. Even so, some agreements are possible. Here are some thoughts on possible bids by responder after RHO makes a three level overcall. Note that these three level overcalls can be a single jump (1♠–3♣) or a double jump (1◊–3♡). Your judgment will be similar in both cases.

Responder Raises

None Vulnerable
You hold ♠ KJ642 ♡ J84 ◊ 873 ♣ K7

WEST	NORTH	EAST	SOUTH
—	1♡	3◊	?

Bid 3♡. If you would have been happy to raise to 2♡, you can raise to 3♡ when under pressure. You should not make a Negative Double when you have support for North's major suit. What will you do if partner rebids 3♡? Will you pass thinking he has a minimum hand or will you bid 4♡ hoping he has a maximum hand? Bidding 3♡ is by far the easiest way to get partner back into the decision.

None Vulnerable
You hold ♠ 74 ♡ 1083 ◊ AQ864 ♣ K104

WEST	NORTH	EAST	SOUTH
—	1♡	3♠	?

I hate to hear the magic words 'Skip Bid' which warn that the auction is taking off. I especially hate to hear that the opponent's suit is spades. The 3♦ bid on the previous hand was annoying, but it was relatively a pleasure to hear when the alternative was 3♠. Spade overcalls always cost you a level of bidding. Sometimes you have the values to bid after a preempt but sometimes you have a hand like this one, which is too good to pass but which isn't really full strength for a bid. I would bid 4♥ on this hand, taking an overbid. This isn't too terrible a decision. The problem is that I have to bid 4♥ with better hands such as this next one.

None Vulnerable
You hold ♠ K73 ♥ AQ32 ♦ Q1096 ♣ A4

WEST	NORTH	EAST	SOUTH
—	1♥	3♠	?

You have to bid 4♥ since there is nothing else available. What you would LIKE to do is make a bid that shows sixteen support points, but you can't. All you can do is raise to 4♥, leaving partner to guess whether you have a ten point hand that pushed or a sixteen point hand that wishes to bid 4⁺♥. An aside here. When you have spades, you should bid them. Your opponents will like you less for it.

None Vulnerable
You hold ♠ J75 ♥ 87 ♦ 762 ♣ AKJ94

WEST	NORTH	EAST	SOUTH
—	1♣	3♦	?

Bid 4♣. You can experiment with Negative Doubles but it all gets back to how many clubs you want to bid. If you double, the only thing partner can do to cheer you up is bid 3NT. Maybe that one possibility should encourage you to try double. But I doubt it.

Responder Jump Raises

None Vulnerable
You hold ♠ 92   ♡ J4   ◇ KJ   ♣ AJ109642

WEST	NORTH	EAST	SOUTH
—	1♣	3♡	?

Oh my! There is no answer. 3NT might be right. 5♣ might be right. 6♣ might be right. 3♡ doubled could be the top spot and even 4♣ could be the limit on these cards. This is what preempts are supposed to do. They are supposed to give the opponents problems. This one is a lulu. Accept that you are hurting and try to find the best bid you can under the circumstances. Consider this one point. If everyone else has this problem, you haven't lost anything yet. You may yet guess yourself out of this mess. I guess to bid 5♣. It gets us to a game and it keeps open the small hope that partner can bid a slam. Because you didn't start with a cue bid, North will play you for a good hand that wasn't worth a cue bid.

Responder Cue–bids

None Vulnerable
You hold ♠ QJ74   ♡ QJ84   ◇ Q8   ♣ AQ4

WEST	NORTH	EAST	SOUTH
—	1♡	3◇	?

Bid 4◇. The cue bid remains a game forcing raise of partner's suit. Because you can't make a simple cue bid and a jump cue bid without getting beyond 4♡, you have to cue–bid on all hands that have game forcing strength with a fit. You can be balanced, as you are here, or you can have a singleton or void in diamonds. You may have a high card control in diamonds or you may have no control in diamonds. Your cue bid expresses that you have a hand with game points and heart support and carries no further message. Don't make the mistake of bidding just 4♡ with this hand. You would bid 4♡ with some weaker hands. 4◇ is not a slam try per se. It is a bid telling partner your raise to game is for real and not a stretch pushed on you by the preemptor.

None Vulnerable

WEST	NORTH	EAST	SOUTH
—	1♣	3♠	?

You hold ♠ 83　♡ AK　◇ Q73　♣ KQ7542

Stuck again. Cue–bid 4♠. Be sure you and partner know this is a generic cue bid and not a control–showing cue bid. This is the only way to tell partner you have this good a hand with support. The rest of the bidding will be hard but that is the result of the preempt. Your cue bid does as much for your side as can be done under the circumstances.

You hold ♠ K3　♡ 83　◇ AKJ8　♣ AJ1064

I recommend Blackwood if that is in your methods here. You can't afford to cue–bid 4♠ because partner won't have a good enough hand to do anything but rebid 5♣. 4NT is a gamble forced on you by the preempt. If partner has an ace, you will bid 6♣, which should have some sort of play. The ace of spades is likely to be with East and if there is a heart finesse to take, it should be on side too. Preempts are hard to contend with but they have been known to haunt the preemptor. You may bid to a poor slam which you wouldn't normally bid and then make it as a result of the information given to you by the preempt.

Responder Jump Cue–bids

Both Vulnerable
You hold ♠ KJ974   ♡ 842   ◇ None   ♣ AKQJ6

WEST	NORTH	EAST	SOUTH
—	1♠	3◇	?

Bid 5◇. A splinter bid at the five level is rare. I can't recall making one and I had a hard time constructing a hand that would do so. This one looks possible. What South wants to do is to get North to cue–bid the ace of hearts. South will follow with 5NT (the Grand Slam Force) asking opener how good his spades are. If South had a doubleton heart and a singleton diamond and the same hand otherwise, I would just bid Blackwood as on the previous hand. It's possible that five level splinters should guarantee a void suit. This is not the kind of question that deserves a lot of thought.

Responder Jumps In A New Suit

None Vulnerable
You hold ♠ KQJ10764   ♡ Q8   ◇ 82   ♣ K3

WEST	NORTH	EAST	SOUTH
—	1♡	3◇	?

Does 4♠ show this hand or does it show a splinter in spades with heart support? Seems to me that this should be natural. A small point but useful to be on the same wavelength.

None Vulnerable
You hold ♠ Q10 ♡ KQJ10763 ◇ K4 ♣ 93

WEST	NORTH	EAST	SOUTH
—	1♠	3♣	?

Could 4♡ be a splinter? Or is it natural? Here is a rule I play with many partners.

RULE: Jumps to major suit games are always natural unless the opponents have bid the suit.

It is a useful rule to have. If it is in effect here, you can bid 4♡ without fear of having a misunderstanding.

None Vulnerable
You hold ♠ AQJ8 ♡ KJ532 ◇ 7 ♣ 763

WEST	NORTH	EAST	SOUTH
—	1♠	3♣	?

Another systemic discussion. Is 4◇ a splinter or is it natural? Since 3◇ would be forcing and since a jump to 4◇ as natural doesn't make a lot of sense, it is correct to use the jump to four of an unbid minor suit to show a singleton.

Responder Makes A Negative Double

None Vulnerable

WEST	NORTH	EAST	SOUTH
—	1♣	3◇	?

You hold ♠ K762 ♡ 10743 ◇ K3 ♣ J83

Back to more normal situations. I would pass this. Three level Negative Doubles need more than this. Ten working points is par for the bid.

You hold ♠ AJ75 ♡ Q104 ◊ 874 ♣ A94

Make a Negative Double. At the three level you won't always have four cards in the unbid majors. In fact, it is possible to have only three cards in the unbid majors. The reason you promises four card support for one level Negative Doubles is that at the one level you usually have room to make some other bid. As the opponents' bidding gets higher, your alternatives diminish. Sometimes you are forced to use an imperfect Negative Double as the best choice of a bad lot. When you do double with less than perfect shape, you need extra points to make up for distributional blemishes. This hand has only three hearts but it has eleven good points.

None Vulnerable
You hold ♠ J107 ♡ J3 ◊ 873 ♣ AKQ64

WEST	NORTH	EAST	SOUTH
—	1♡	3◊	?

This is a nightmare. You don't want to bid 4♣ and get beyond 3NT. You can't raise hearts with only two. And you don't want to pass with this good a hand. The solution, uncomfortable perhaps, is to make a Negative Double with only three spades.

Responder Bids A New Suit At The Three Level

None Vulnerable
You hold ♠ AJ652 ♡ 72 ◊ 1063 ♣ A106

WEST	NORTH	EAST	SOUTH
—	1♡	3◊	?

A new suit at the three level is game forcing (forcing to game or forcing to four of responder's suit). This hand is not strong enough to bid 3♠. Your compromise bid is to double. It is not guaranteed. If partner bids 3♡, you have to guess whether to bid 3♠. And if you do bid 3♠, your partner has to guess whether you have five or six of them. A crummy situation all around.

None Vulnerable
You hold ♠ QJ9875   ♡ 7   ◇ KJ3   ♣ K82

WEST	NORTH	EAST	SOUTH
—	1♣	3♡	?

Bid 3♠. You don't have a game forcing hand in theory. It is still closer to being a game forcing hand than it is to a Negative Double. Both bids are a fib. Better to make a descriptive fib (3♠) than to make an undefined bid (Negative Double).

Responder Bids A New Suit at The Four Level

Vulnerable vs. Not Vulnerable
You hold ♠ 6   ♡ QJ764   ◇ KJ4   ♣ AJ87

WEST	NORTH	EAST	SOUTH
—	1◇	3♠	?

Whose idea was it to bid 3♠? East has found a heck of a time to preempt. Your hand normally takes three or more bids to describe and East has reduced the rounds of bidding to one or two. Your choices are to bid 4♡ or to make a Negative Double. Both carry risk. 4♡ may leave you in a 5–1 or 5–2 fit. Double will work if you can follow it up with 4♡ but if West bids 4♠ in the meantime, you will lose the heart suit.

There are so many questions to ask here and not enough answers to go around. For starters. What is the difference between bidding 4♡ right away and doubling first and then bidding 4♡? Does one sequence show five hearts and the other six? Or should the difference be that one sequence is stronger than the other?

My guess is that the direct 4♡ bid should show pretty good hearts and the Negative Double and then 4♡ sequence should show five hearts but no certainty that hearts is the right place to play. If you have this treatment, you can double with this hand and then convert partner's bid to 4♡, if possible. If the opponents have bid 4♠ in the meantime, you have enough to double them.

Vulnerable vs. Not Vulnerable
You hold ♠ A5 ♡ KJ8643 ◇ Q73 ♣ 82

WEST	NORTH	EAST	SOUTH
—	1◇	3♠	?

Bid 4♡. It is clear to bid hearts if you choose to bid. The question is whether to bid or pass. If East had passed 1◇, you would have invited with this hand but you would not have forced to game. The preempt stole your bidding room so you have to make a committal decision and it is a big one. If you bid 4♡ and are wrong, you are talking about going –800 when they couldn't make anything. If you pass 3♠ and are wrong, you are talking about missing a game or a slam in return for which you are getting +50 or +100. The price for the wrong guess is high.

Responder Bids 3NT
Or Four Of A Minor

Vulnerable vs. Not Vulnerable
You hold ♠ Q52 ♡ J4 ◇ 93 ♣ AQJ963

WEST	NORTH	EAST	SOUTH
—	1◇	3♠	?

Bid 3NT. On the previous two hands, the problem was whether to bid four of a major. On this hand and the next few hands, the problem is whether to bid 3NT or four of a minor suit.

There is a big difference between the two situations. When you are bidding four of a major, you are in a game contract, which partner may pass. When you are bidding four of a minor, you are not in a game contract and since your bid is forcing, your side will have to continue. If you bid 4♣ on this hand, you will end up in game. If you bid 4♣ and partner rebids 4♢, you owe him another bid. If you pass 4♢, you will have violated just about every rule of bidding that I know. When you bid four of a minor, your side is committed to game and if it turns out to be a minor suit game, that will take eleven tricks.

For this reason, the following rule has been developed. It is a little like the rule I offered in the book on bidding against preempts in my *Topics on Bridge* series. If the opponent's preempt has forced you to the three level and you are wondering whether to raise partner's minor suit or bid the other minor, you should reflect back on this rule.

RULE: On any auction where you are thinking of bidding four of a minor, bid 3NT instead if it makes any sense at all.

The hand above is the perfect example of this rule in action. You have a possible 4♣ bid. Before making the bid, you look to see if 3NT is reasonable. It is. You have a spade stopper and you have a source of tricks. If you bid 4♣, the bidding will continue to the five level. This hand isn't worth it. 3NT, on the other hand, requires only nine tricks and should be your choice.

Vulnerable vs. Not Vulnerable

WEST	NORTH	EAST	SOUTH
—	1♣	3♡	?

You hold ♠ AQ3   ♡ K2   ◇ AQ10874   ♣ 73

Bid 3NT again. This hand is good enough to think of slam. The trouble is that bidding 4◇ gets you beyond 3NT, which is your most likely game. What you have to weigh here are the chances of getting to and making a slam versus the chances of making 3NT. 3NT should be makeable most of the time. A slam will be makeable some lesser amount. I will guess 20% or less of the time. It is true that if you bid 4◇, you may end up in a game only, but it will be a minor suit game and that will punish you in matchpoints and it will cost you an IMP or two in team games. Really. The rule above works well in these situations. If you see 3NT is an okay spot and that bidding higher than 3NT is both speculative and possibly dangerous, you should take the easy way out.

You hold ♠ A3   ♡ A2   ◇ AQ9863   ♣ QJ5

Here, the chances of a slam are too great to bid only 3NT. Six clubs, diamonds, or notrump are in the game as well as some occasional grand slams. Bid 4◇ and see this hand through to the end.

You hold ♠ J53   ♡ K   ◇ K732   ♣ KQJ83

This may not be for the weak of heart, but 3NT rates to be the winner. The question is simple. Why should East have been dealt the ♡AQJ10xxx? Nowadays, the average 3♡ bid looks something like ♡ Q1087653. There is a good chance that your partner has some help in hearts. If this doesn't work for you, please feel free to blame it on me. (I doubt you will need this encouragement.)

Vulnerable vs. Not Vulnerable
You hold ♠ 64   ♡ 93   ◇ AKJ975   ♣ AJ4

WEST	NORTH	EAST	SOUTH
—	1♣	3♠	?

If you must bid four of the unbid minor, you must. Bid
4◇. This hand hasn't a whiff of a spade stopper for
notrump and the heart holding doesn't permit a Negative
Double. Your 4◇ bid will force your side to game, but it
is more or less a necessary action.

More Possible Hands Which Can Bid Three Notrump

In the previous section I showed a few hands which had
to choose between 3NT and four of a minor. There are
some additional hand types which may fall back on 3NT.

Vulnerable vs. Not Vulnerable
You hold ♠ AJ3   ♡ KJ9   ◇ QJ7   ♣ AJ63

WEST	NORTH	EAST	SOUTH
—	1♣	3◇	?

If you happen to play that 4NT is a quantitative bid, you
can bid that. If you are like most of us, you don't have
that bid available. The point here is that you have a hand
that wants to invite a slam but you can't do so easily. Bid
3NT and take your plus score. A fair rule of thumb is to
pretend that your partner has a decent fourteen point
hand. If you need more than that for a slam, you should
consider 3NT if it is an alternative. A lot of points get lost
because someone holding this hand decides they have
something. I have seen players bid Blackwood with this
hand. The usual result is that partner shows an ace or
two and the Blackwooder, hardly wiser than before, now
continues to 6NT. When opener has a minimum opener,

6NT goes down and everyone agrees it was unlucky. When opener has a little extra and 6NT happens to make, declarer looks pleased and accepts plaudits for his brave bid. When opener has a lot extra and 7♣ or 7NT is cold, declarer acts aggrieved as if North wasn't supposed to have all those points.

Listen to this rule and accept it as gospel.

RULE: If the opponents preempt and give you an impossible problem, take the cash in front of you. Do not be hustled into making a rash decision.

Another way of stating this is to look twice before you leap. Make sure you know what you are leaping into. I can phrase this in yet another fashion. If you think you may have a slam but you have no clear way to find out, just stop the auction as soon as you can. STAY FIXED.

Vulnerable vs. Not Vulnerable
You hold ♠ J4   ♡ J85   ◇ K108   ♣ AJ1096

WEST	NORTH	EAST	SOUTH
—	1♠	3◇	?

Vulnerable versus not, this isn't an unreasonable shot at 3NT. If you don't feel like it, I understand. There is an important point to make here regardless of your decision on this specific hand. When the opponents preempt at the three level, your 3NT decisions are under pressure. A 3NT bid can't be defined as 11–13 points with a stopper in the opponent's suit. A 3NT bid is defined as any hand that thinks 3NT could be the best contract. Pointwise, it can range from ten points (I have seen 3NT bid on less) up to eighteen points. You will find that the number of points is not the only variable factor in your decision. For instance.

Vulnerable vs. Not Vulnerable
You hold ♠ AQ9864 ♡ KJ6 ◇ K2 ♣ J8

WEST	NORTH	EAST	SOUTH
—	1♣	3♡	?

3♠ is the obvious bid. Plan ahead for a second. If you bid 3♠, what will North do? Hopefully, he will bid 4♠. What if he doesn't have spade support? He won't be able to bid 3NT. You are the one with all the heart stoppers. What he will do a lot of the time is rebid clubs. You can continue with 4♠, but are you sure this is the best contract? The solution is to bid 3NT the first time. At least consider it. On this hand your six card spade suit gives you some protection in that you can always rebid the suit at the four level. What if you had only five spades instead of six? Give yourself this hand instead.

♠ AQ964 ♡ KJ6 ◇ K82 ♣ J8

Now 3NT is the only acceptable call. Plan ahead!

Responder Passes

Bad hands are easy to pass. There are some good hands, though, that have to be passed too. The usual reason for passing a good hand is that you want partner to reopen with a double so you can make a penalty pass. The second reason is that you have a good hand up to ten or eleven points with unbiddable shape.

Vulnerable vs. Not Vulnerable
You hold ♠ K ♡ Q8 ◇ Q7653 ♣ QJ652

WEST	NORTH	EAST	SOUTH
—	1♠	3♡	?

Probably a pass. A Negative Double maybe.

Vulnerable vs. Not Vulnerable
You hold ♠ Q8   ♡ KJ87   ◇ KQJ4   ♣ K82

WEST	NORTH	EAST	SOUTH
—	1♣	3♡	?

Bid 3NT. You will make it. The reason you don't pass is that your partner may not reopen the bidding. He will try to do so but he is not required to. If he has a minimum opening bid or if he has the wrong shape for a double, he may pass it out.

Here are some hands that North can pass out in 3♡.

Vulnerable vs. Not Vulnerable

WEST	NORTH	EAST	SOUTH
—	1♣	3♡	Pass
Pass	?		

1. ♠ J73   ♡ 93   ◇ A103   ♣ AQJ73
2. ♠ KJ3   ♡ Q4   ◇ A5   ♣ Q97653
3. ♠ AJ   ♡ Q4   ◇ A985   ♣ AQJ104
4. ♠ J52   ♡ A   ◇ A1073   ♣ QJ642

All of these hands would pass 3♡. Hand One is a minimum and has only so–so spade support. If North doubles, he will survive ONLY if South has a penalty pass. Hand Two is worse than minimum. It has the wasted queen of hearts, only three spades, and only two diamonds. Hand Three has lots of points but it has no reason to think South has a penalty pass. North should pass this hand out in 3♡. Remember, if North doubles, he will hear 3♠ a lot of the time. How will North escape from that? The alternative is 3NT. The eighteen points are nice but there are no tricks. Hand Four is a third minimum hand. North's ace of hearts isn't wasted so he has a full minimum (as compared with Hand Two) but the ace of hearts also suggests that South doesn't have a penalty pass.

Not all of opener's reopening bids will be doubles. There may be reasons why opener would do something besides double. Here are some hands where opener will reopen by bidding something.

Vulnerable vs. Not Vulnerable

WEST	NORTH	EAST	SOUTH
—	1♣	3♡	Pass
Pass	?		

	♠	♡	◇	♣
1.	♠ AQJ4	♡ 83	◇ 9	♣ AKJ872
2.	♠ 73	♡ AJ	◇ K103	♣ AKQ873
3.	♠ 84	♡ 8	◇ AQJ	♣ KQJ9876
4.	♠ A10	♡ A3	◇ A873	♣ AQJ93

Hand One clearly wants to reopen but can't double for fear that South will bid 4◇. Instead, North bids his spades. Because he is doing so at the three level, he is showing a good hand. Hand Two knows that partner is not waiting with a penalty double of hearts. Partner is still allowed, however, to have seven or eight points, in which case 3NT will make. Hand Three suspects that partner is waiting with a heart stack, but doesn't double for two reasons. The first reason is that you don't want to defend against 3♡ doubled with this hand. It is offensive, not defensive, in strength. The second reason is that a double by opener suggests some spades and these are missing. I suggest reopening with 4♣. The last hand is unclear. I would bid 3NT and hope. Knowing where the high cards are may allow opener to play the hand more intelligently than if the opponents had passed throughout.

Vulnerable vs. Not Vulnerable
You hold ♠ J63   ♡ Q1063   ◇ A1083   ♣ K4

WEST	NORTH	EAST	SOUTH
—	1♣	3♡	?

This is a fine pass. If North passes it out, there won't be a game for North–South. But if North reopens with a double, and the signs are good for this to happen, 3♡ doubled will go down a satisfying number.

Vulnerable vs. Not Vulnerable
You hold ♠ 64   ♡ 93   ◇ Q84   ♣ AKJ542

WEST	NORTH	EAST	SOUTH
—	1♠	3♡	?

This is a very good hand opposite an opening bid. Still, it should pass 3♡. 4♣ would be game forcing and there is no chance game will make unless North has a good enough hand to reopen. I would pass this hand and hope North can do something. If he reopens with a double, I will jump to 5♣. If he reopens with 3♠, I will raise to game.

If you are reading these examples carefully, you will note that I suggested that North pass it out in 3♡ with:

♠ AJ   ♡ K4   ◇ KJ83   ♣ AQ764

If North can pass 3♡ with this eighteen count and South is supposed to pass with hands as good as:

♠ 64   ♡ 93   ◇ AQ8742   ♣ Q87

it is clear some games will be missed. Try not to let it bother you.

Chapter Seven

THEY SHOW
A TWO SUITER

BRIDGE IS CHANGING and it shows signs of continuing to do so. Until the mid–sixties, a cue bid of opener's suit showed a huge hand, usually defined as game forcing. Then Mike Michaels introduced the Michaels Cue Bid where a cue bid of opener's minor suit showed 5–5 in the majors. It didn't take long for this cue bid to catch on. It was useful and it had the advantage of coming up a lot more frequently than the strong cue bid. Somewhere along the line, someone had the idea that if Michaels Cue Bids worked over a minor suit, why shouldn't they work over a major suit? It became endless. One convention led to another. Variations appeared as fast as new conventions themselves. Few things cause me to grab an opponent's convention card as quickly as a cue bid. And with good reason. There are so many conventions in play that you have to look in self defense.

Even knowing what convention is in use isn't always enough. Your partner bids 1♣ and RHO bids 2♣. The opponents' card says it's Michaels. That's a good start. But what does it promise besides both majors? Does it promise 5–5 distribution? How about 5–4 or 4–4 distribution? How many points does it show? Etc.

I looked at the index in Amalya Kearse's *Bridge Conventions Complete*. It certainly is. There was an entire column of entries under 'Cue Bids', many of which were appropriate to this chapter. The following list includes most of the common cue bids. Do you know how your partnership bids when one of these is used against you?

Michaels Cue Bids
Astro Cue Bids
Colorful Cue Bids
Top and Bottom Cue Bids
Strong Cue Bids
Natural Cue Bids
Light Takeout Cue Bids
Unusual Notrump
Notrump Asking Cue Bids

It is not so easy to say that you will use a particular defense against these conventions. According to what the cue bid shows, your goals will differ from convention to convention. For example, if your partner opens 1◇ and RHO bids 2◇ showing the majors, your side will have these objectives:

1. Doubling the opponents.
2. Untangling major suit stoppers for notrump.
3. Competing in one of the minor suits.

You will note that playing in a major suit is not one of your goals. RHO showed the major suits so you won't want to play in one of them after this start. Also finding a 4–4 club fit isn't a goal. It may be achieved, but it isn't a priority.

Now let's say that your partner opens 1◇ and RHO bids 2◇ showing spades and clubs. Your side will have different objectives.

1. Doubling the opponents.
2. Untangling stoppers in their suits for notrump.
3. Competing in partner's diamond suit.
4. Showing partner a five card heart suit.
5. Finding out if there is a 4–4 heart fit.

The first three goals are common to each auction. Goals four and five are different. In this case there is a missing major suit for your side to discover. A 5–3 fit would be acceptable but so would a 4–4 fit. The differences in goals after these two different 2◇ bids means you need more than one method to handle the interference.

DEFENDING AGAINST MINOR SUIT MICHAELS

There are a couple of methods you can use to defend against the Minor Suit Michaels Cue Bid showing the majors. I will look at both of them because the ideas used here may be adopted in some other situations.

Method One vs Michaels

This method stresses looking for notrump and includes some help in competing in the minor suits. It works this way.

None Vulnerable

WEST	NORTH	EAST	SOUTH
—	1◇	2◇	?

2♡   A cue bid of one of the opponent's majors shows a stopper, suggests weakness in the other major suit, and promises ten or more notrump points. You may have a lot more but that will come out later. For now, only ten points are implied.

Your side isn't interested in playing in hearts after East's 2◇ bid. It is more important to find out if your side can play in notrump. 3NT is much more likely to make than five of a minor so you cater your bidding accordingly.

It is possible that South has a big diamond raise. If this happens, he starts with a cue bid and then raises diamonds. This will show that 2♡ was a real cue bid and not just a stopper cue bid. These hands would all bid 2♡ over 2♢ using these methods.

You hold ♠ 75 ♡ KJ6 ♢ QJ74 ♣ KJ83

You have a heart stopper, 10–11 points and notrump shape. You happen to have four card diamond support. You might have five card support. You might have only two or three.

You hold ♠ 972 ♡ AQ ♢ AQJ53 ♣ 843

You have enough points to insist on game but the spade suit is nervous. NOTE that your 2♡ bid doesn't promise anything in clubs. Your bidding is focusing on the major suits. Club stoppers tend to be lost in the shuffle.

You hold ♠ K2 ♡ A2 ♢ KJ653 ♣ AJ108

Start with 2♡ and then attempt to catch up. It isn't clear that you will be able to bid this hand perfectly, but you are off to a start that gives you a chance.

2♠   A 2♠ cue bid has the same meaning as 2♡. Partner will play you for a 10–11 point hand with a spade stopper. If you have more than this, it will become apparent later.

2NT   This is natural and nonforcing. It shows ten or eleven high card points with stoppers in both major suits. There is an inference that you don't have very good holdings in the majors because you didn't double.

202

None Vulnerable

WEST	NORTH	EAST	SOUTH
—	1◇	2◇	?

You hold ♠ K3 ♡ Q93 ◇ J1054 ♣ KQ42

2NT is a possible bid. It shows stoppers in both majors and 10–11 high card points. 2NT is not forcing so the meaning is precise.

There are some inferences available from your choice of bids. When you bid 2NT, you show that you have a pretty good hand, yet you didn't try to double the opponents. That suggests your major suit stoppers aren't overwhelming. Another inference is that you have support for partner's minor suit. Without support, you might double 2◇ hoping that partner could double the opponents' major suit bid. Length in partner's suit is a historical warning against making low level penalty doubles. It is logical that length in partner's suit is one of the reasons you decided to bid 2NT.

You hold ♠ J82 ♡ A10 ◇ KQ862 ♣ J73

One choice is to raise to 3◇. Another choice is to bid 2NT, which gives a more precise definition of your shape and values. Since the opponents may run the spades, I won't say this is a perfect bid, but it is one that a lot of players would try. There is a very useful rule which you should know. IF POSSIBLE, you should bid notrump whenever it is a reasonably descriptive bid UNLESS there is something better. The reason this is true is that a notrump bid is more descriptive than the alternatives. I am willing to take mild risks in order to follow this rule. On the hand above, I can bid two slightly imperfect notrumps or I can raise to three diamonds. Assume you were my partner and your kibitzer asked you what the difference was between 2NT and 3◇.

You would say that 2NT showed 10–11 points, a balanced hand, stoppers in the majors, and probably some diamond support. There are a few fuzzies in this description, but overall, it is accurate.

Now define for your kibitzer what 3♦ shows. You would say that it shows diamond support. It says nothing about stoppers in either major suit. And you aren't sure how many points it shows. Partner might be pushing with seven points and very good support, but partner might also have eleven points and nothing else to bid.

There is a lot of room to the definition of 3♦ and opener will be guessing much of the time. Since 2NT is descriptive and since 3NT is the logical game for your side after they use Michaels, it behooves you to get notrump mentioned ASAP.

3♣   Bidding the other minor suit is invitational and passable. 1♦–2♦–3♣ and 1♣–2♣–2♦ are both nonforcing. You should have something like a good weak two bid in the suit.

None Vulnerable

WEST	NORTH	EAST	SOUTH
—	1♦	2♦	?

You hold ♠ A62   ♡ 53   ♦ J3   ♣ KJ9764

Bid 3♣. 3♣ is not forcing, contrary to most rules, if you play METHOD ONE against Michaels. Partner can pass.

You hold ♠ 4   ♡ 843   ♦ 73   ♣ AK107643

A good hand for this method. Bid 3♣ and get your say heard immediately. If you played 3♣ as forcing for any length of time, you couldn't risk bidding with this hand or the previous hand.

You hold ♠ 7532 ♡ Q9 ♢ 63 ♣ AQJ42

You should probably pass. 3♣ isn't forcing but getting to the three level with only a five card suit, some wasted values, and balanced shape is nervous. It's frustrating. I would feel guilty about passing this but I would be apprehensive about bidding too. Change the queen of hearts to the queen of diamonds, and 3♣ would be fine.

3♢   Raising partner's minor suit. This is natural. It shows a hand that would have been happy to raise 1♢ to 2♢, if there had been no overcall, up to some so–so eleven counts. You have to be a little aggressive on auctions like these because you may not get a second chance.

None Vulnerable

WEST	NORTH	EAST	SOUTH
—	1♢	2♢	?

You hold ♠ AJ3 ♡ 83 ♢ Q10764 ♣ 984

Bid 3♢. This hand is worth a raise to 2♢. Unfortunately, you have to raise to 3♢. One of the most important things you have to tell partner is that you have support. You have to press to raise when the bidding is competitive or you lose the chance. One thing you should not do is double just because the opponents have bid your partner's suit. Noises like this are incredibly expensive. Not only do they do nothing for your side, they deprive you of an important weapon. Use the double wisely. (Double will be discussed shortly.)

You hold ♠ 72 ♡ 9432 ♢ AK104 ♣ KJ3

3♢ is an acceptable bid because there is nothing else that fits. At least partner will learn you like his suit.

3♡, 3♠   The jump cue bid of either of their major suits is a rare but very useful bid. These jumps show game forcing splinter raises of partner's minor suit.

The splinter raise isn't common but just having it on your convention card gives you a useful hidden benefit. If you double a Michaels Cue Bid and later show game forcing support for partner's minor suit, your partner will work out that you have a balanced raise. If you had a singleton in one of the major suits, you would have started with a splinter. This negative inference will help on your high level decisions when the opponents can jack up the bidding.

None Vulnerable

WEST	NORTH	EAST	SOUTH
—	1♣	2♣	?

You hold ♠ 4   ♡ 843   ◇ K82   ♣ AKJ752

Jump to 3♠. Your sixth club makes this hand worth a game forcing response. If West bids 4♠, North will be able to make a wise decision.

You hold ♠ A54   ♡ 4   ◇ AQ53   ♣ Q10963

Bid 3♡. The splinter raise again. This time you have an alternative bid of 2♠ showing a spade stopper. I prefer the splinter bid because it shows your shape and game forcing values all at once. There won't be any of the ambiguity that occurs after a double or a cue bid.

You hold ♠ A102   ♡ 3   ◇ J542   ♣ KJ875

Bid 2♠. An in–between hand. It is too good to raise to 3♣. It isn't good enough to splinter. What you have is a limit raise but no more. 3♡ would show the shape but it is game forcing. You don't have the values. Sorry, but you can't do everything.

3NT   This is a value bid showing some eleven counts with a source of tricks up to a fifteen or sixteen count. In all cases, you don't have heavy major suit stoppers else you would double first, looking for a penalty. The inference is that 3NT includes some support for partner's suit. It is not guaranteed though.

None Vulnerable

WEST	NORTH	EAST	SOUTH
—	1♣	2♣	?

You hold ♠ K3   ♡ K9   ◇ J53   ♣ KJ9653

Try 3NT. You have a source of tricks and you don't want to be involved in looking for penalty doubles. If the opponents insist on bidding four of a major, you can double that on the basis of your two tricks, assuming North hasn't done something in the meantime.

You hold ♠ QJ3   ♡ K2   ◇ QJ2   ♣ AQ963

I'd bid 3NT with this one too. You lose a little in your slam bidding but you gain by getting the hand off your chest quickly. You also gain a little by getting in West's way. He might have been willing to compete to the three level but not the four level. If they have a real fit, you might not get a big penalty against 4♡. There is something to be said for stealing a little of their bidding room, which is what they are attempting to do to you.

DOUBLE   Double is a catchall bid for decent hands that don't have another way to be bid. It is somewhat like a redouble when RHO doubles your partner's opening one bid.

At the point that you double, your partner will know only that you have ten or more points. Many hand types qualify for a double.

1. You may have a fair hand that is looking to double the opponents for penalty.

2. You may have a limit raise or better in partner's minor suit.

3. You may have a forcing bid in the unbid minor.

Hands Interested
In Doubling The Opponents

None Vulnerable

WEST	NORTH	EAST	SOUTH
—	1♣	2♣	?

You hold ♠ J10   ♡ KQ83   ◇ A10642   ♣ J3

Double. You will double hearts and if partner can double spades, that will be fine with you. One issue you have to address is this. If you double and LHO bids 2♠ and it is passed to you, are you forced to bid? Since this is analogous to a redouble, I can't imagine passing 2♠. If you make a strong noise, you owe it to partner to do something.

I have played with a lot of excellent players who are far better theoreticians than me. I called one of them (Kit Woolsey) with this exact hand and asked what I should do. (Kit has about 600 pages of notes that he plays in his regular partnerships and when I played with him, we used about 200 of them.) He said he would double 2♣ as I suggested, and when I told him that West bid 2♠, passed back to me, there was a silence. "Kit? Are you still there? Kit?"

We sorted it out. We agreed that we were in a forcing auction and we agreed we didn't like it. I suggested his system needed another 100 pages to cater to situations like this.

So what was the recommended action after a twenty minute call? The solution was to double as was done and to bid 2NT when 2♠ was passed back to me. The idea is twofold. A forcing situation has been created so something must be done. Since double and 3◊ are out, the only leftover bid is 2NT. You owe partner a spade stopper, but since this hand didn't double 2♠, your hand is marked for weak spades.

One last note on this very hard hand. It was agreed that if you doubled 2♣, you have created a forcing sequence. How high does this force go? If the opponents bid 2♠, the force is on. But what if they bid 3♠ or 4♠? I suggest that you play a force is established if the opponents bid 2♡ or 2♠ but that you don't have to keep the bidding open if West jumps to 3♡ or 3♠. This means that your partner will have to bid something if they jump to 3♡ because he won't have the luxury of a forcing pass. This is one of those areas that deserves much more space than it is getting. Eddie Kantar wrote a book on forcing passes and I know he felt like writing more. I leave you with the problem and some simple suggestions about how to handle it.

None Vulnerable
You hold ♠ KJ4   ♡ QJ4   ◊ A764   ♣ 753

WEST	NORTH	EAST	SOUTH
—	1♣	2♣	?

You can try 2NT or you may decide to play for a penalty. One approach is to play that a pass here followed by a double of 2♡ or higher shows a decent hand with a trick in their suit and is cooperative. You will have at least a ten count with three cards in the doubled suit and very probably three cards in the other major. Partner can sit if he likes your double and he can bid something else if he hates it. Definitely, you should talk to partner to see if he likes this idea.

What Do You Do If You Have A Limit Raise Or Better Of Partner's Suit?

This was touched on in the earlier discussion of cue bids. If you are lucky, you can cue–bid and then show support or raise notrump if the auction goes well. If you have nothing to cue–bid, you more or less have to start with double and hope.

None Vulnerable
You hold ♠ 72   ♡ A8   ◇ Q1043   ♣ A10973

WEST	NORTH	EAST	SOUTH
—	1♣	2♣	?

Start with 2♡. If North bids notrump, return to 3♣, which shows a limit raise. With a tad more, you would just raise to 3NT and forget the club support. NOTE that you will have troubles with this specific area of bidding. It isn't easy to bid against two suited overcalls if the opponents are able to find a fit and speed up the sequence. What you are hoping for is the ability to show most of your hands and to guess through a few. With no method at all, you are guessing more often than not.

None Vulnerable
You hold ♠ 73   ♡ 1094   ◇ AKJ4   ♣ AQ73

WEST	NORTH	EAST	SOUTH
—	1♣	2♣	Double
2♡	Pass	Pass	?

I'm stumped. You can't bid diamonds because that shows game forcing diamonds. You can't raise to 3♣ because that shows a limit raise. I would choose 2♠ and hope that partner can work out the inference that I don't have a major suit stopper because I didn't show it earlier.

None Vulnerable
You hold ♠ 1073   ♡ 973   ◇ K4   ♣ AK874

WEST	NORTH	EAST	SOUTH
—	1♣	2♣	?

This is your limit raise hand. Double 2♣ and try to catch up. Ideally, West will bid 2♡ or 2♠ and you will bid 3♣ showing these invitational values.

None Vulnerable

WEST	NORTH	EAST	SOUTH
—	1♣	2♣	Double
3♠*	Pass	Pass	?

*Preemptive

If West bids 3♡ or 3♠, and it gets back to you, you should raise to 4♣. It isn't what you wanted to do but it is reasonable. Remember, your partner would have bid something if he could have. He didn't bid 3NT and he didn't double. The hands he is likely to have will include real clubs and some modest shape. It may in fact turn out that they can make 3♠ and that you are saving in 4♣. That, of course, is the pessimistic view. It is still possible for you to be cold for 5♣ at this point in the auction.

As an aside, you should note West's 3♠ bid. It is a standard expert treatment to play this jump as showing a weak hand. If South hadn't doubled, the jump to 3♠ would be invitational. But, when South announces strength, West uses the jump to show a hand like:

♠ Q874   ♡ 43   ◇ J9863   ♣ 83

His intention is to get in the opponents' way. It does this nicely. That 3♠ bid makes it hard for North–South to

211

sort out their notrump stoppers, as well as taking away important bidding room. If North–South decide to double 3♠, West's fourth trump and the doubleton heart will hold the penalty to down one or down two. This will usually be good for West.

None Vulnerable
You hold ♠ J3 ♡ 832 ♢ AQJ3 ♣ AQ106

WEST	NORTH	EAST	SOUTH
—	1♣	2♣	Double
2♠	Pass	Pass	?

Whatever you do, you have to consider these points.

1. A double shows much better spades. It is a penalty double, usually showing four trumps.

2. 2NT shows 10–11 points and you have game forcing values, to say nothing of having no spade stopper. One lie, maybe. Two lies, no.

3. 3♣ shows a limit raise strength only.

4. 3♢ shows a game forcing bid with diamonds.

I think I would bid 3♢. If partner can bid 3NT, we will make it. If partner raises diamonds, I will go back to clubs. Since North didn't bid 3NT, it is likely that 5♣ is the only possible game. An alternative bid is 3♡ or even 3♠ but I would hesitate to try these. No matter how much time you spend on these auctions, there is always something undiscussed. I hate to hit partner with unclear bids when I can fake a reasonable one that won't be misunderstood.

What Do You Do If You Have The Other Minor Suit And Game Forcing Values?

None Vulnerable

WEST	NORTH	EAST	SOUTH
—	1◊	2◊	?

You hold ♠ 72 ♡ 832 ◊ AQ8 ♣ AKQJ7

This hand doesn't have an easy answer. 3♣ is not forcing so bidding 3♣ rates to end the auction. You will make it but your partner won't be impressed. Bidding hands with forcing values in the unbid minor suit is difficult in this method. You have to bid something which is forcing and later convert it to a forcing club bid. There are two ways you can do this.

With this hand, I would start with double. (You might choose to read the section on doubles first to see what double usually means.) Hopefully, you will be allowed to bid clubs at the three level. You don't want to hear West bid 3♠ or 4♠. Whatever happens, you will have a heavy decision.

The other thing you can do with hands of this nature is bid 2♡ or 2♠ and then show your minor suit. The reason you might choose double instead of 2♡ or 2♠ is that the double followed by a club bid denies a prime major suit holding. Bidding 2♡ or 2♠ and then bidding the minor suit shows a control in that major suit.

You hold ♠ A6 ♡ 72 ◊ Q7 ♣ KQJ9652

Start with 2♠ and then bid clubs. If partner bids notrump along the way, you will raise to 3NT and give up on clubs. What you really hope is that this hand type doesn't come up. Fortunately, it is rare.

None Vulnerable

WEST	NORTH	EAST	SOUTH
—	1♣	2♣	?

When the bidding starts 1♣–2♣, you have a lot of room to show diamonds. You can bid 2♦, which is nonforcing. You can bid 3♦, which is forcing. And you can double (or cue–bid if appropriate) and then bid diamonds, which is also forcing.

When the bidding starts 1♦–2♦, you have less room to show your club hands since you don't have the two level available. You can bid 3♣, which is not forcing, but since you are at the three level, you need a pretty good suit to do this. The harder hands are the ones where you want to make a forcing bid in clubs. You can bid 4♣, which is surely forcing, but that takes up a lot of room and gets past 3NT. Similarly, you can double or cue bid and then bid clubs, which will be forcing.

Here is a table of ways you can show the other minor.

WEST	NORTH	EAST	SOUTH
—	1♣	2♣	?

2♦	Natural and not forcing. It shows a good five card suit or a decent six card suit and 8–11 high card points.
3♦	Natural and forcing. It shows a six card suit and game forcing points.
DOUBLE	Followed by a diamond bid shows game forcing points but implies a five card suit and tends to deny a stopper in either major.
CUE BID	Followed by a diamond bid shows game forcing points, implies a five card suit, and shows a stopper in the major suit cue–bid.

A very strong suggestion is that you bid an appropriate number of notrump if you can. If you have stoppers and the right number of points, a notrump bid will make the auction easier for you than any indirect bid.

WEST	NORTH	EAST	SOUTH
—	1◇	2◇	?

3♣ — Invitational showing 9–11 points. You want a very good five card suit or better for this bid. Six cards is more the norm than not.

4♣ — Forcing, showing game values. This is an odd bid. It gets you beyond 3NT so it must show a distributional hand with no interest in notrump.

DOUBLE — Followed by a club bid shows a good hand with clubs and probably no major suit stopper. It is game forcing. It does not promise more than five clubs.

CUE BID — Followed by a club bid shows a good hand with clubs and a stopper in the major suit cue–bid. This sequence does not show more than five clubs.

None Vulnerable

WEST	NORTH	EAST	SOUTH
—	1♣	2♣	?

You hold ♠ 6 ♡ KJ54 ◇ AJ6543 ♣ 73

Bid 2◇, which is nonforcing. A relatively easy problem which depends on having agreements in place. You could try for a penalty but getting it would be lucky. The opponents have an eight card or better spade fit. Better to get your suit in now.

You hold ♠ 74 ♡ 942 ◇ AKJ1064 ♣ K10

Bid 3◇. This is forcing to game unless you have some
rule that lets you stop in 4◇. I admit 3◇ is an overbid
but the suit is good and your side card is in partner's suit.
If 3NT is biddable, this is the bid that will get you to it.
At the table, you will find that aggressive opponents will
respond to 3◇ by overbidding themselves. You may get
to double 4♡ or 4♠ for down one when you didn't have
much yourself. NOTE that this overbid rests in part on
the ten of diamonds. If it wasn't there, 2◇ would be
enough. Partner will know from your bidding that you
probably do not have a major suit stopper.

None Vulnerable

WEST	NORTH	EAST	SOUTH
—	1♣	2♣	?

You hold ♠ QJ83 ♡ 73 ◇ KJ763 ♣ AQ

Start with 2♠. If North bids 3♣, you will bid 3◇. If
North can bid notrump, you will raise to 3NT. It would
not be terrible to double with this since you are willing
to defend against hearts if partner can double and you
certainly want to double spades.

You hold ♠ 53 ♡ 8652 ◇ AKQ73 ♣ AJ

Double and then bid 3◇. You need a six card suit to jump
to 3◇, which would also be forcing.

None Vulnerable

WEST	NORTH	EAST	SOUTH
—	1◇	2◇	?

You hold ♠ 74 ♡ None ◇ KQ63 ♣ AKQJ642

I'm not sure what a jump shift to 4♣ should look like.
This hand feels about right. It is a hand that wants to
force and doesn't want to try notrump. Notrump may be

the best place for this hand but there is no way you can get to 3NT and know it is right. If you bid 4♣, North will know you have something special with twisted shape.

You hold ♠ 84   ♡ 74   ◇ J2   ♣ AKQ10874

Awkward. With seven likely tricks, you want to force to game. With bad shape, a partscore might be enough. Which way do you go? I would double 2◇ and then bid clubs. There is risk here but it is also risky being cowardly. Perhaps the opponents will misjudge and not double if this sequence doesn't work out.

You hold ♠ AJ3   ♡ K3   ◇ J54   ♣ KJ842

Bid 3NT. Don't look for clubs unless you have real interest in them or are unable to bid notrump.

Method Two vs Michaels

The second method of bidding when your opponents use a Michaels Cue Bid is to emphasize natural bidding and to hope that notrumps will take care of themselves. In Method One, cue bids of 2♡ and 2♠ were used to show stoppers in that major. In Method Two, cue bids of 2♡ and 2♠ are artificial. Here is a list of what your bids will mean using Method Two.

None Vulnerable

WEST	NORTH	EAST	SOUTH
—	1♣	2♣	?

If the auction starts as above, South's bids have the following meaning.

2◇	Natural, invitational, and not forcing. 2L shows the same thing in both methods.
2♡	This always shows clubs. When the opening bid was 1♣, the 2♡ bid shows a limit club raise or better.
2♠	This always shows diamonds. When the opening bid was 1♣, the 2♠ bid shows a game forcing hand with diamonds.
2NT	Natural, showing both major suits stopped, and 10–11 points. Since you didn't try to double the opponents, you probably have a fit for partner's minor suit.
3♣	Raising clubs shows a 7–10 point hand with club support. If East hadn't cue–bid, you would have been happy to raise to 2♣. You might even have a poor limit raise hand.
3◇	Since you can bid 2◇ to show a nonforcing diamond bid and 2♠ to show game forcing diamond bid you can do any one of a number of things with this 3◇ bid. You can play 3◇ is very encouraging with a good six card or better diamond suit and 2♠ is forcing with a five card suit. You can play 3◇ is very encouraging and 2♠ is game forcing. You can play 3◇ is fit showing with diamonds and club support and is forcing. Heck. You can do anything you want. For the purpose of this discussion, I will treat 3◇ as being forcing with a very good suit.
3♡ , 3♠	These are both splinter raises of partner's suit. Exactly the same as in Method One.

DOUBLE   Remains the black sheep of this family. It shows at least ten points and is probably head–hunting. Because Method Two has a way to show minor suits immediately, the double doesn't have as much work to do as it did in Method One.

When the bidding starts 1◇–2◇–? responder's bids have more or less the same meaning with a couple of variations.

2♡   Still shows clubs as always. It is game forcing and natural. Responder can't do as many things with clubs so the 2♡ bid has a broad range of club hands.

2♠   Shows a limit raise or better in diamonds.

2NT   Natural, balanced 10–11 point bid implying some support for diamonds.

3♣   Invitational and can be passed. It shows something like a good weak two bid in clubs. 8–11 points is typical for this bid.

3◇   Natural raise. Responder usually has a 7^+–11^- support points.

3♡ , 3♠   Splinter bids showing a stiff plus support plus game forcing values.

DOUBLE   Same no matter which minor suit was opened and cue–bid. It shows the ten or more point hands that don't fall in to any of the previous categories.

Here are some examples of Method Two. Let me say before the letters come pouring in that there are more complex methods available. I could show you another two or three treatments and they all have various levels of intricacies.

None Vulnerable

WEST	NORTH	EAST	SOUTH
—	1♣	2♣	?

You hold ♠ 763 ♡ AQ8 ◇ AQ984 ♣ J7

Bid 2♠. This is artificial, showing a game forcing hand with diamonds. 2♠ says nothing about spades. You may or may not have a spade stopper. This is the big difference between the two methods. In Method One you would bid 2♡ telling partner you had a heart stopper and you would continue by showing your diamonds. In Method Two, you don't get to look for notrumps until the next round.

You hold ♠ 763 ♡ K4 ◇ AQJ974 ♣ K2

Bid 3◇. This is an optional treatment. You can, when the opponents are cue–bidding clubs, bid diamonds in a number of ways. You can bid 2◇, 3◇, or cue–bid 2♠. If you play 2♠ as forcing with diamonds, you can also play 3◇ as forcing with diamonds but showing a good six card suit or better. This is an important distinction since the bidding will include an occasional preemptive bid from the opponents.

You hold ♠ 943 ♡ AJ ◇ 652 ♣ KQ765

Bid 2♡. This shows at least a limit raise in clubs. If North bids 3♣, you should accept his decision and pass.

You hold ♠ 843 ♡ AJ ◇ 843 ♣ AK1053

Bid 2♡. You will cue–bid your heart stopper if you can do so. The one thing you can't do is to return to 3♣. You have a game forcing hand and a return to 3♣ would show a limit raise.

You hold ♠ KJ5 ♡ 76 ◇ K1032 ♣ A642

In Method One, you would bid 2♠ showing, usually, a spade stopper and 10–11 points. In Method Two, you can't bid 2♠ because it is game forcing. You have to find another call. Choose from these bids.

2♡   Showing a limit raise in clubs.

3♣   Showing a pretty good club raise but not good enough for a limit raise.

2NT   Showing the values but owing partner a heart stopper.

DOUBLE Intending to do something later. This raises a few questions. If you double and LHO bids 2♡, you are in forcing auction. You will raise to 3♣ if possible, but what will partner think you have? More importantly, how will you get to 2NT if that was your best spot?

My inclination is to bid 2♡ showing a limit raise in clubs. The advantage is that I get the hand out of the way in a hurry. This is no small accomplishment. When the opponents are likely to compete, it is an excellent policy to get the nature of your hand into the bidding as soon and as safely as possible.

None Vulnerable

WEST	NORTH	EAST	SOUTH
—	1◇	2◇	?

You hold ♠ QJ6 ♡ 72 ◇ J3 ♣ AKQ652

Bid 2♡, an artificial bid showing game forcing strength with clubs and saying nothing about hearts. Partner won't know if you have a good suit such as here or a so–so five card suit like A10863. One possibility is that on some of your strong club hands, you may be able to jump to 4♣ if you have a hand that wants to look for a slam and which has no interest at all in 3NT.

THEY BID THE UNUSUAL NOTRUMP

The Unusual Notrump has been with us for so long that I can't remember being without it. I can state this for a fact. When I was just learning bridge at the University of California card room, my LHO bid 1♠ and my partner overcalled 2NT. To me, this was supposed to be a fistful of points and since I had eleven points of my own, I put it into 6NT without ado. My LHO had something to ado about it, though. He doubled. I can still hear it. My partner gave me great credit when he passed and since I didn't have the courage of my convictions, I didn't redouble. It didn't matter. We were down a lot. We weren't playing for anything, but don't think for a second that no one cared. My LHO cared enough to tell us we had just set a personal record and my partner cared enough to tell me his opinion of my judgment. Actually, I had a pretty good idea what he thought about the time he saw my dummy.

Bridge has advanced a bit from those times. People still abuse the convention, but there aren't many abusers who use it with an unsuspecting partner. After forty or so years, most players know how to use the Unusual Notrump (I say this cautiously), but very few are comfortable when it is used against them. This failure is one of the reasons that the Unusual Notrump remains as popular as it is. Maybe this inequity can be removed.

There is a convention called Unusual vs Unusual which also appears under the name 'Invisible Cue Bids'. I will call it UVU for the rest of this discussion. It works in one of two ways. Notice as you read the two treatments how similar they are to the two treatments used against the Michaels Cue Bid.

Method One vs Unusual Notrump

WEST	NORTH	EAST	SOUTH
—	1♡	2NT	?

South's bids in both Methods One and Two are artificial. Starting with Method One, here is how they work. Given the above auction, this is what South's bids mean.

3♣   This always shows hearts. If North opens the bidding with 1♡, 3♣ shows a limit raise in hearts. This does not promise four card support. If North opens the bidding with 1♠, 3♣ shows a game forcing heart bid.

3♢   This always shows spades. If North opens the bidding with 1♡, 3♢ shows a game forcing spade bid. If North opens the bidding with 1♠, 3♢ shows a limit raise in spades. This does not promise four card support.

3♡   This is always natural and shows a weaker hand than 3♣, which also shows hearts. If North opens the bidding with 1♡, 3♡ shows a 7–10 point heart raise. If you do this with seven point hands, make sure they are good ones. If North opens the bidding with 1♠, 3♡ shows a good five or six card heart suit with 9–11 points. 3♡ is not forcing. If you wished to force in hearts, you would start with 3♣.

3♠   This is always natural and shows a weaker hand than 3◇, which also shows spades. If North opened the bidding with 1♡, 3♠ shows a good five or six card spade suit with 9–11 points. 3♠ is not forcing. If you wished to force in spades, you would start with 3◇. If North opened the bidding with 1♠, 3♠ shows a 7–10 point spade raise. If you do this with seven point hands, make sure they are good ones.

3NT   Bidding 3NT is a useful trick which you better tell partner about in advance. 3NT shows: A game forcing raise of partner's major suit, a balanced hand, and at least four card support. If you have a natural 3NT bid, you double first and then either double them or bid 3NT.

4♣, 4◇   These are splinter raises of partner's major suit showing: A game forcing raise of partner's major suit. You are allowed to fudge a little on your values since you are otherwise giving partner a perfect description of your hand. A singleton in that minor suit. At least four card support.

4♡   If North opened the bidding with 1♡, this raise is preemptive but not suicidally so. The bidding is likely to continue so you need some minimum promised values for your partner, who will often be forced to bid again. If North opened the bidding with 1♠, the jump to 4♡ shows a preemptive hand with a good suit. If you had normal game forcing values, you would start with 3♣. Again, don't do this with nothing.

4♠	If North opened the bidding with 1♡, the jump to 4♠ shows a preemptive hand with a good suit. With normal game forcing values, you would start with 3◊ showing spades. This jump to 4♠ should show a little something since you can be doubled if you are wrong. If North opened the bidding with 1♠, the jump to 4♠ shows a decent preemptive hand. North can count on you for something.
DOUBLE	You can use double on a variety of hands. If you have a game forcing raise with only three trump, you can double first and then raise partner's suit. Knowing you have three trump and not four or more will help partner decide what to do in the bidding. If you have three trump and a limit raise, you have to make the limit raise immediately. If you have a hand that wants to double the opponents, you can double, which invites partner to act. Maybe he can double them too.

As an aside here, you may choose to use this idea which was shown in the discussion on the Michaels Cue Bid. If you pass and then double the opponents, this can show a ten point hand or better with only three cards in the suit you are doubling. This double is for penalty but it is not binding. Your partner can yank it if he has the wrong hand.

Use this auction for all of the following discussion hands.

None Vulnerable

WEST	NORTH	EAST	SOUTH
—	1♠	2NT	?

You hold ♠ K102   ♡ A8752   ◇ 1093   ♣ 72

Raise to 3♠. You can't have less than this. The reason you raise to 3♠ on a hand that would have raised 1♠ to 2♠ only is that there is a big price to pay for being quiet. Telling partner about your fit is the most important message you can give him in competitive auctions. It is okay to overbid a little to tell him something he may wish to know and which he can't learn any other way.

You hold ♠ J8   ♡ AQ984   ◇ K542   ♣ 93

You can bid 3♡ since it is not forcing. Whether it is safe will depend on whether you find a fit. This hand is a little better than average for this bid. If you had a sixth heart, you could bid 3♡ with a point or two less.

You hold ♠ 1095   ♡ KJ853   ◇ AQ   ♣ 872

Bid 3◇, which is artificial promising spades. Since the opening bid was 1♠, the 3◇ bid promises a limit raise. This is one of the rare times that you can make a limit raise with only three trump. Only because 2NT took away a lot of bidding room can you do this. NOTE that it would confuse the issue to bid 3♡. Partner can pass that. Much better to show support.

You hold ♠ A6   ♡ AJ874   ◇ AQ   ♣ 8543

Bid 3♣, which is artificial promising hearts. Since the opening bid was 1♠, 3♣ shows a game forcing heart bid. You may have five or more hearts. You will never have four. If you have four hearts and the strength to bid at the three level, you have to double. Hopefully, it will be possible for someone on your side to show hearts later.

You hold ♠ AQJ73   ♡ K43   ◇ K3   ♣ 1084

Bid 3NT. 3NT is an artificial bid showing four or more trumps for partner's major, game points, and a balanced hand.

You hold ♠ K1062　♡ AQ10853　♢ 93　♣ 5

Bid 4♣. This splinter bid shows four trumps, game values, and a stiff club. You are a little light for this bid in theory, but it is still closer to the truth than any other AVAILABLE bid.

You hold ♠ Q2　♡ KJ108642　♢ K8　♣ 72

Bid 4♡. The jump to game in the unbid major suit shows a very good suit and not enough points to start with 3♣ (the corresponding minor suit). It is a mildly gambling bid.

You hold ♠ Q8752　♡ KJ752　♢ 7　♣ 82

Bid 4♠. You have a good playing hand with a few high card points. It is not a hopeless hand but it is not a forward going hand either.

You hold ♠ J8642　♡ 732　♢ 4　♣ Q962

It is hard not to do something but it may be best. If you insist on bidding, 3♠ is enough. 4♠ will get your side in trouble one way or another.

You hold ♠ QJ7　♡ AJ75　♢ AJ73　♣ 83

Double and later raise to 4♠. This shows a game forcing raise with three trump. It is possible you have a singleton, but if you do, it can't be helped. In fact, a singleton isn't worth as much when you have only three trump, so the loss may not hurt you. What is important is that partner knows you have three trump and not four or five.

You can use double on a variety of hands. If you have a game forcing raise with only three trump, you can double first and then raise partner's suit. Knowing you have three trumps and not four or more will help partner decide what to do in the bidding. If you have three trump and a limit raise, you have to make the limit raise immediately. If you have a hand that wants to double the opponents, you can double, which invites partner to act. Maybe he can double them too.

Method Two vs Unusual Notrump

In Method Two, 3♣ and 3♢ are still artificial but the emphases of the bids are switched. Here are the differences.

3♣   This always shows a limit raise for partner's suit regardless of which major he bid.

3♢   This always shows a game forcing bid in the unbid major suit.

Other than these two small changes, the rest of the two methods are the same. Bidding three of either major shows less strength than bidding the corresponding minor suit. Splinters are on, as is the artificial 3NT bid showing a balanced game forcing raise with four trump.

DEFENDING AGAINST CUE BIDS IN GENERAL

If you use some amount of the material in the preceding chapters, you should be able to handle many otherwise awkward hands. The ideas in this chapter are proven and used by a large number of players. That is the good news. The down side is that the opponents sometimes use one or another of the myriad cue bids that I didn't get a chance to look at. Fortunately, you can usually adapt the ideas shown. Here is how it might work.

You are in the middle of a nice game when something occurs that you haven't discussed. Your partner opens 1♡ and RHO cue–bids 2♡. There are two things that may happen.

1. You don't need to know what the cue bid means because you aren't interested in bidding. DO NOT ASK what it means. Your opponents may be about to have a misunderstanding and your question will help them get their act together. This sounds like it might be unethical, but it is not. If someone uses one of the less known conventions, they do so at their own risk.

2. If you have a hand that needs to know what is happening, you should ask. If you prefer, you can refer to their convention card if you are playing in a tournament.

In this case, you are told that they are using Hi–Lo Cue Bids which show the higher and the lower unbid suits. The 2♡ cue bid here means that your RHO has spades and clubs. What do you do? Look at the following two tables. Compare the methods for bidding versus an unusual notrump with the methods for bidding versus a high–low cue bid.

Versus An Unusual Notrump

WEST	NORTH	EAST	SOUTH
—	1♡	2NT*	?

* Shows the minors

3♣	The lower cue bid shows a limit raise in hearts.
3♢	The higher cue bid shows a forcing bid in spades.
3♡	Shows a 7–10 point heart raise.
3♠	Shows a nonforcing spade bid.
3NT	Shows a balanced forcing heart raise.

229

4♣	Shows a singleton with game forcing heart values and four card heart support.
4♦	Shows a singleton with game forcing heart values and four card heart support.
4♡	Shows a preemptive raise to 4♡ with a few decent points.
4♠	Natural and preemptive.

It is possible to do almost the same thing with the opponents' Hi–Lo Cue Bids. This structure works for you when you know both of the opponents' suits as you do here.

Versus A High Low Cue Bid

WEST	NORTH	EAST	SOUTH
—	1♡	2♡*	?

* Shows spades and clubs

2♠	The lowest cue bid shows a limit raise in hearts.
2NT	Natural showing 10–11 high card points with stoppers.
3♣	The higher cue bid shows shows a forcing bid in diamonds.
3♦	Nonforcing showing 8–11 points and a suit worth showing at the three level.
3♡	Shows a 7–10 point heart raise.
3♠	A jump in one of their suits is a splinter with game forcing heart values and four card heart support.

3NT	Shows a balanced forcing heart raise with four or more trumps just like after the Unusual Two Notrump.
4♣	Shows a singleton with game forcing heart values and four card heart support.
4♦	Can be treated as a splinter bid, too. Makes perfect sense.
4♥	Shows a weakish raise to game showing a little defense.
DOUBLE	Usually a penalty double against one of their suits and invites partner to double if he can. If you later jump to 3NT, that shows a 13–15 point hand with stoppers, and if you jump to four of partner's major, it shows a game forcing hand with three trumps.

WEST	NORTH	EAST	SOUTH
—	1♠	2♠*	?

* Shows hearts and clubs

2NT	Natural showing 10–11 high card points with stoppers.
3♣	The lower cue bid shows a limit raise in spades.
3♦	Nonforcing showing 8–11 points and a suit worth showing at the three level.
3♥	The higher cue bid you can make shows a forcing diamond bid.
3♠	Shows a 7–10 point spade raise.
3NT	Shows a balanced forcing spade raise with four or more trumps just like after the Unusual Two Notrump.

4♣	The jump in one of their suits shows a splinter with four trumps and game values.
4♦	Can be treated as a splinter bid, too.
4♥	The jump in one of their suits shows a splinter with four trumps and game values.
4♠	Shows a preemptive jump to game.
DOUBLE	Usually a penalty double against one of their suits and invites partner to double if he can. If you later jump to 3NT, that shows a 13–15 point hand with stoppers, and if you jump to four of partner's major suit, it shows a game forcing hand with three trumps.

NOTE. You might wish to say that the 3♣ cue bid shows a forcing diamond hand and that a cue bid of their major shows a limit raise. This gives you a little more room to develop the bidding when you like partner's minor suit.

The whole idea here is that if you have a defense you can use against one convention, you may be able to transfer that defense to similar conventions.

DEFENDING AGAINST A CUE BID THAT SHOWS A SPECIFIC SUIT AND AN UNKNOWN SUIT

Some opponents play cue bids that do not have the courtesy to show both suits. This makes it harder for you to show your hand because you have only one suit to cue–bid. For example, your partner opens 1♥ and RHO bids 2♥. You find out that 2♥ shows spades and either clubs or diamonds. No one knows now except RHO what he really has.

This makes things difficult for you. It isn't all that bad because your LHO doesn't know what is going on any more than you do. It is possible that a bid by you will quiet LHO from bidding. After all, if LHO doesn't know what his partner has, he will bid more cautiously. Perhaps fatally so. The following structure is imperfect. I admit it immediately and without apology. If you wish a more complete structure, you will find one in Amalya Kearse's *Bridge Conventions Complete*. Or, if you have access to the magazine *Bridge Today*, you will find a write up in issue #1. Why not put the full method in this book? If you get your hands on either of the above sources, you will understand my reservations about presenting it here. Let me assure you that as complex as the following material may seem to be, it stands up very comfortably in the comparison.

WEST	NORTH	EAST	SOUTH
—	1♡	2♡*	?

*Spades and an unknown minor

PASS	And Double later is a cooperative double. You have three of their trumps and 10–11 points.
DOUBLE	Head–hunting or looking for 3NT.
2♠	Shows a limit raise.
2NT	Natural, shows 10–11 high card points.
3♣	Natural and forcing.
3♢	Natural and forcing.
3♡	Shows a 7–10 point heart raise.
3♠	Shows an unknown splinter.
3NT	Shows a balanced forcing heart raise.
4♣	Shows a game forcing three card raise.

4♦	Shows a semipreemptive raise.		
4♥	Shows a preemptive raise.		

WEST	NORTH	EAST	SOUTH
—	1♠	2♠*	?

*Hearts and an unknown minor

PASS	And Double later is a cooperative double. You have three of their trumps and 10–11 points.
DOUBLE	Head–hunting or looking for 3NT.
2NT	Natural, shows 10–11 high card points.
3♣	Natural and forcing.
3♦	Natural and forcing.
3♥	Shows a limit raise.
3♠	Shows a 7–10 point spade raise.
3NT	Shows a balanced forcing four card spade raise.
4♣	Shows an unknown splinter.
4♦	Shows a game forcing three card raise.
4♥	Shows a semipreemptive raise.
4♠	Shows a preemptive jump to game.

There are very few differences between these two structures. You have to be aware of one or two quirks though. In both structures, the jump to game is preemptive. The jump to the suit under game shows a semipreemptive raise. The jump to the suit two under game shows a game forcing three card raise. NOTE these two sequences:

WEST	NORTH	EAST	SOUTH
—	1♡	2♡*	3♠

WEST	NORTH	EAST	SOUTH
—	1♠	2♠*	4♣

* Michaels—The other major and an unknown minor

Both of these jumps show game forcing values plus an unknown singleton. Opener has to bid the next suit if he wants to find out where responder's singleton is. (See end of section for explanation.)

This structure deserves some examples.

None Vulnerable

WEST	NORTH	EAST	SOUTH
—	1♡	2♡*	?

*Spades and an unknown minor

You hold ♠ Q73 ♡ 73 ◇ KJ72 ♣ KJ108

Pass and then double. It is likely that you will get to double 2♠. Because you passed first and then doubled, you imply only three trump and 10–11 points. If the opponents bid 3♣ or 3◇, you will double that too, but there is some chance that partner will pull the double.

You hold ♠ Q1074 ♡ Q ◇ AJ83 ♣ QJ107

You won't get this dream hand very often. If you do get it, you can double 2♡ and then double anything they bid. When you double the cue bid and later double their bid, you imply a four card holding. Partner will sit for it most of the time. If you double and then bid 3NT, you rate to have a game going hand of some sort or another.

You hold ♠ K2 ♡ 83 ◇ J10753 ♣ AQ87

Bid 2NT. It is natural and not forcing. You probably do not have too strong a holding in spades else you would try to double them one way or another. Perhaps you should try anyway. I think the easy way out is best. Keep the auction simple and you may miss some plums but you will avoid some disasters too.

You hold ♠ 74   ♡ Q5   ◇ KQ10974   ♣ Q72

Pass. This structure does not let you show competitive minor suit hands. It only lets you show forcing minor suit hands. This is a loss. It would be nice to be able to show this hand without getting beyond 3 ◇. Fortunately, there are some gains too.

You hold ♠ K32   ♡ A4   ◇ 83   ♣ AQ8643

3♣. This is easy. 3♣ is forcing, which is what you want it to be.

You hold ♠ Q9653   ♡ QJ2   ◇ A83   ♣ 72

Raise to 3♡. It shows around 7–10 points. There are many reasons for raising. First, you want to tell partner you have something for him, which is commendable enough. Secondly, you are blocking their chances of getting their minor suit shown. This isn't a big deal, but it has some merit.

You hold ♠ A832   ♡ KJ4   ◇ 10953   ♣ Q9

This is close. If you feel you have limit raise values, you should bid 2♠. Cue–bidding their major shows limit raise values regardless of how the auction started. NOTE that you can't distinguish between three trump and four or more trumps.

You hold ♠ J853   ♡ KQ93   ◇ 3   ♣ AJ107

Bid 3♠. This is definitely an alert. This is completely artificial showing an unknown singleton, four or more trumps, and game values. (See the end of this section for how opener continues.)

You hold ♠ 932   ♡ K1064   ◇ AKJ4   ♣ Q8

Bid 3NT. This is also an alert. 3NT, regardless of which major suit partner opened, shows a balanced game forcing raise with four or more trumps.

You hold ♠ AJ53   ♡ K104   ◇ KJ52   ♣ 83

Bid 4♣. Another alert. 4♣ is two bids under partner's heart suit. This two–below jump says you have a game forcing heart raise with only three trumps. You may or may not have a singleton. The purpose of this sequence is to get the nature of your hand across to partner. If you don't show your general intentions immediately, the auction can get away from you in a number of ways. Remember. If possible, keep it simple.

You hold ♠ 3   ♡ QJ73   ◇ 83   ♣ A107532

Bid 4◇. Yet another alert. The jump just below four of your trump suit shows a preemptive raise but one with some merit. You don't object if partner bids on or if he doubles them. Usually, you have four trump for this bid.

You hold ♠ 843   ♡ J9652   ◇ Q10964   ♣ None

Bid 4♡. After either 1♡–2♡ or 1♠–2♠, the jump to game shows a weak hand. Nothing is promised except some trumps and some shape.

None Vulnerable

WEST	NORTH	EAST	SOUTH
—	1♠	2♠*	?

*Hearts and an unknown minor

You hold ♠ 86542   ♡ 8   ◇ AJ3   ♣ AJ83

Bid 4♣. This is one of the differences between auctions starting 1♡–2♡ and auctions starting 1♠–2♠. On this sequence, responder is forced by method to jump to 4♣ to show an unknown singleton.

When Responder Splinters

WEST	NORTH	EAST	SOUTH
—	1♡	2♡*	3♠

*Spades and an unknown minor

3♠ shows four or more hearts, game forcing values, and a singleton SOMEWHERE. If the next player passes, opener bids 3NT to ask where the singleton is.

WEST	NORTH	EAST	SOUTH
—	1♡	2♡*	3♠
Pass	3NT	Pass	?

* Spades and an unknown minor

4♣   Shows a club splinter.

4♢   Shows a diamond splinter.

4♡   Shows a spade splinter with 12–16⁻ support points.

4♠   Shows a spade splinter with 16+ support points.

If you open 1♠, they cue–bid 2♠, and partner bids 4♣ your task is more difficult. You can ask for the singleton with a 4♢ bid but because responder's answers go beyond four of your trump suit, there is the risk you will get too high for naught. Here are the responses.

WEST	NORTH	EAST	SOUTH
—	1♠	2♠*	4♣
Pass	4♢	Pass	?

*Hearts and an unknown minor

4♡	Shows a heart splinter.
4♠	Shows a club splinter with 12–16⁻ support points.
4NT	Shows a diamond splinter.
5♣	Shows a club splinter with 16+ support points.

This looks awkward, and it is. Believe me, if opener has to ask for the singleton, you may get into trouble. The real benefit of using 4♣* as an unknown splinter is that you tell partner so much about your hand in general. If partner doesn't have to ask for your singleton, you are in good shape. Usually, partner will know your singleton without having to ask. If you get in trouble with this part of the structure, I apologize. The greater difficulty you will experience with this method is that you won't be able to show those 8–10 point hands with a decent minor suit. That is a loss which may haunt you. If you get bothered too much by this flaw, you can look up an alternative structure in one of the references mentioned above. I predict you will wish to stay with this one.

* For the scientist—play the 1♠–2♠–3NT shows an unknown splinter and 4♣ shows a balanced four card raise with game points. You gain one extra bid by doing so.

Chapter Eight

SUPPORT DOUBLES AND REDOUBLES

OPPONENTS HAVE LEARNED to get into the auction quickly and to raise the level of the bidding even faster. That is bad news because it takes away important bidding room. Here's a sample hand.

As South, you hold ♠ A763   ♡ Q983   ◊ 73   ♣ KQ4

WEST	NORTH	EAST	SOUTH
—	1♣	Pass	1♡
2◊	2♡	Pass	?

What does partner have over there? Admit it. You are more worried about a little thing like the two of hearts than anything else at this moment. Here's what I mean.

YOU	PARTNER
♠ A763	♠ 82
♡ Q983	♡ AK7
◊ 73	◊ 962
♣ KQ4	♣ AJ952

YOU	PARTNER
♠ A763	♠ 82
♡ Q983	♡ AK72
◊ 73	◊ 962
♣ KQ4	♣ AJ92

How many hearts do you want to be in with the first pair of North–South hands? The answer is that you want to see how hearts split before committing yourself.

241

How many hearts do you want to be in with the second pair of North–South hands? The answer is that you want to be in 4 ♡. What makes 4 ♡ a good contract on one hand and not on the other? It is that little two of hearts that North acquired in a trade for the five of clubs. It makes an enormous difference to how well the North–South hands will play in hearts. Now go back to the bidding. What is South supposed to bid over 2♡? On values, South wants to make a game try of some sort. The trouble is that there is no game try that doesn't risk your sure partscore. If North has four hearts, you can afford to make a game try because 3♡ should be a pretty good spot if North can't go on to 4♡. If North has three hearts, 4♡ won't be a pretty spot and more importantly, your sign–off contract of 3♡ will also be ugly. NOTE that on this hand, North has the good taste to put down three hearts with two top honors. If he puts down lesser hearts, say, K104, any number of hearts will be risky. This is where the Support Double becomes useful.

How Do Support Doubles And Redoubles Work?

WEST	NORTH	EAST	SOUTH
—	—	—	1♣
1♢	1♡	2♢	?

In standard bidding, it is correct for South to raise on many hands with only three hearts. No apologies to the pundits. It is correct to raise with three trumps. There are many very good things that come of this but there are some poor things too. When opener raises with three trumps, responder has to go slowly when he has a so–so four card suit. If there was a way for responder to know how many trumps opener had, life would be much easier. Now there is a way. It only works in one situation, but it is the most important situation you can face. It works when your partner responds in a suit at the one level and your RHO does something that leaves you room to raise partner to the two level. NOTE these two auctions.

WEST	NORTH	EAST	SOUTH
—	—	—	1♣
1♦	1♠	2♦	?

Assume opener wants to show spade support.

1. Opener shows three card support by doubling 2♦ (the Support Double).
2. Opener shows four card support by raising to 2♠.

WEST	NORTH	EAST	SOUTH
—	—	—	1♣
Pass	1♠	Double	?

Assume opener wants to show spades support.

1. Opener shows three card support by redoubling 1♠ (the Support Redouble).
2. Opener shows four card support by raising to 2♠.

There are a number of guidelines which go with this convention. Most of them are logical so you don't have to remember much beyond the fact that the double is no longer a penalty double.

The Support Double and Redouble are on no matter how the bidding has gone as long as there is room for opener to raise to the two level.

When opener makes a Support Double or Support Redouble, he shows three trumps but he does not necessarily promise a minimum opening bid. Opener's usual hand will be a 12–15 point hand with three trumps. NOTE. Opener may have some good hands which wish to show trump support first before showing other assets.

When opener raises responder's suit, promising four trumps, he will always have the 12–14 point raise.

None Vulnerable

WEST	NORTH	EAST	SOUTH
—	—	—	1♣
Pass	1♡	2◇	?

You hold ♠ Q872   ♡ A872   ◇ 72   ♣ AQ9

Raise to 2♡. This promises four card support and 12–15 support points.

You hold ♠ AJ73   ♡ Q72   ◇ 82   ♣ KQJ9

Double. You are confirming three card support. The double has no penalty connotations. NOTE that you can't bring the spade suit into the bidding. At least you can raise hearts descriptively.

Does Opener Have To Show Three Card Support?

You have to decide this in your own partnership. I think that if your hand was good enough to open, you should show three card support unless something about the auction made your hand go downhill in value. For example:

None Vulnerable

WEST	NORTH	EAST	SOUTH
—	—	—	1♣
Pass	1♡	2◇	?

You hold ♠ KQJ5   ♡ 973   ◇ Q7   ♣ KQ42

I don't think you could be faulted for passing this. I guess that opener should show support over 90% of the time that he has it.

You hold ♠ A62 ♡ KJ3 ◇ K3 ♣ AK862

Double showing three hearts and then bid again. For instance, if North returns to 2♡, you will bid 2NT showing an 18–19 point raise with three trumps.

You hold ♠ AK2 ♡ QJ84 ◇ 3 ♣ AJ1084

Jump to 3♡. Your single raise promises a minimum hand. The Support Double or Redouble may have extra values, but not the simple raise.

None Vulnerable
You hold ♠ 953 ♡ AQ4 ◇ 73 ♣ AQ1083

WEST	NORTH	EAST	SOUTH
—	—	—	1♣
1◇	1♡	1NT	?

If you wish to raise hearts, you can do so by doubling, showing three trumps. North can pass for penalty if he wishes. NOTE that you are not obliged to show three trumps on this auction. With East volunteering 1NT, you might decide not to show three little hearts.

None Vulnerable
You hold ♠ K73 ♡ J108 ◇ 832 ♣ AKQ8

WEST	NORTH	EAST	SOUTH
—	—	—	1♣
1◇	1♡	2♣*	?

*Cue Bid—Usually showing diamond support.

Double to show support. Remember the rule. If there is room for you to raise partner to the two level, a double by you shows three card support.

Both Vulnerable
You hold ♠ AJ3 ♡ QJ8 ◇ 3 ♣ AKJ1054

WEST	NORTH	EAST	SOUTH
—	—	—	1♣
1◇	1♡	Double*	?

*Snapdragon—Spades plus some diamond support.

Before looking at the right bid, decide for yourself what
you would bid if not using Support Doubles and
Redoubles. Your choices would include 3♣, 2♣, 2♡, 3♡,
and Redouble. Using Support Redoubles, you can
redouble and then bid some number of clubs. This will
show three card support and, because you are bidding
again, a good hand. This is a difficult family of hands. It's
curious. If the opponents didn't bid, you would have a
hard rebid problem over North's 1♡ bid. For once, the
opponents' bidding makes your life a little easier.

You hold ♠ 1062 ♡ KQJ ◇ 62 ♣ AK984

WEST	NORTH	EAST	SOUTH
—	—	—	1♣
1◇	1♡	3◇	?

You have to bid 3♡ if you are willing to raise with three
card support or you pass. Those are your options. You
can't use the Support Double because the opponents' bid
is higher than two of your partner's suit.

You hold ♠ KJ2 ♡ KJ3 ◇ 732 ♣ AQ104

WEST	NORTH	EAST	SOUTH
—	—	—	1♣
1◇	1♡	2♡*	?

*Cue Bid showing a big diamond raise

You may not see this auction but it is possible so I have included it here to help you with your definitions. Whatever you do is tempered by the fact that Support Doubles don't apply. The rule is that if you are unable to bid two of partner's suit, Support Doubles are off. Since you can't bid 2♡, the Support Double is off. In fact, I would double anyway. But only to tell partner I had something in hearts.

Both Vulnerable
You hold ♠ A8   ♡ 4   ◇ AJ763   ♣ AQ1084

WEST	NORTH	EAST	SOUTH
—	—	—	1◇
Pass	1♡	2♣	?

You have to pass. Even though there is an 1100 waiting for you, you can't go for it. Double would show three hearts. Your partner would bid something and your 1100 would lose one of its naughts.

Corollary To Support Doubles And Redoubles

As a result of Support Doubles, you lose the ability to make penalty doubles. This won't often be serious but once in awhile, you will pay a price. The previous hand shows the typical problem that comes from using Support Doubles. There is a way around these problems but it is a delicate one. I will show you a possible solution. Let's switch you around to the North seat for a moment.

You hold ♠ 83   ♡ AJ763   ◇ Q62   ♣ QJ3

WEST	NORTH	EAST	SOUTH
—	—	—	1◇
Pass	1♡	1♠	Pass
Pass	?		

What would you do with this? You have enough points to want to bid. Your ten and partner's twelve or more is enough to argue for a partscore. How do you continue? Here are your choices.

1. Bid 2♡. You have a pretty good five card suit.

2. Raise to 2◇.

3. Bid 2♣, which is a new suit and is therefore forcing.

4. Double.

In order, I rate these bids thusly.

The worst bid is 2♡. Rebidding five card suits is usually a bad tactic. Partner didn't make a Support Double so there is a good chance he has a singleton heart. Even if he has two, 2♡ isn't going to be wonderful.

The next worst bid is 2♣. It's true that the 'Fourth Suit' only shows ten points, but it should at least show a good ten points. If there was no better bid, 2♣ might survive. But here, there are two much better bids available.

I like 2◇ a lot. Partner didn't raise hearts and he didn't bid 1NT. He is almost a certainty to have five diamonds and a minimum hand.

But the winning bid is double. IF YOU ARE USING SUPPORT DOUBLES, it is possible, even likely, that South has a penalty double of 1♠ and has passed since he can't double for penalty. North has a hand that would have accepted a penalty double so he reopens with a double himself saying that he has a ten point hand with no clear way to express it.

I don't intend to expand on this aspect of the Support Double. If you choose to play the convention, though, you must think through the repercussions it creates in your bidding.

Chapter Nine

THEY BID AFTER PARTNER RESPONDS

CHAPTERS NINE THROUGH TWELVE will discuss auctions where you open and the opponents get into your sequence. Here are the topics for these chapters.

CHAP.	SOUTH	WEST	NORTH	EAST
9	Opens	Passes	Bids	Bids
10	Opens	Bids	Bids	Bids
11	Opens	Bids	Passes	Bids or Passes
12	Opens	Passes	Passes	Bids

If you look at each of the four situations in turn, you will sense different degrees of competitiveness creeping into the auction. Take the third situation. You opened with the usual optimistic feelings that come with having an opening bid but nothing came of it. West got into the auction and East also had something to say and your partner? Your partner is sitting there with his head in the sand doing nothing. In this situation, it is easy to imagine that the opponents are taking the hand away from you. It won't be easy to retrieve ownership of the hand after this start.

Conversely, look at sequence one. You opened the bidding and West passed. That's always a nice start because it allows North to bid anything he wants. Whatever he does will not be under duress which is what often happens when West has bid. Believe me. Being able to open and respond with no intervention is a big deal when you compare it to the alternatives.

The differences you feel here are representative of differences that do in fact exist between each of the four bidding areas to be covered. For this reason, each is getting coverage.

All four areas will be discussed in terms of the changes opener has to make in a contested auction as opposed to an uncontested auction.

THEY OVERCALL AT THE ONE LEVEL

If East, opener's RHO, overcalls at the one level, you will usually be able to make your normal rebid. One change which you may already have made is the Support Double. You will find that using the Support Double gives you a nice feeling of comfort. For instance.

None Vulnerable
You hold ♠ A762 ♡ Q104 ◇ 63 ♣ KQJ4

WEST	NORTH	EAST	SOUTH
—	—	—	1♣
Pass	1♡	1♠	?

If you don't use Support Doubles, you have to decide whether to bid 2♡ or pass. Whichever you do, you will have moments of doubt. If you use Support Doubles, you get the best of both worlds. You can double, showing three card support, and you don't have to worry that you have overbid your hand. Showing support for partner's major suit has to be the number one objective for opener. Being able to show partner not only that you have support but to show partner at the same time how many you have is a real bonus.

None Vulnerable

WEST	NORTH	EAST	SOUTH
—	—	—	1◇
Pass	1♡	1♠	?

You hold ♠ 10642　♡ 4　◇ AKJ984　♣ A8

Rebid 2◇. Does a 'Free Bid' show extra values? No. A free bid does not show extra values. It shows some extra distributional feature. In this case South is showing an extra good diamond suit. It is conceivable that South has five diamonds, but six will be expected. It is more important to emphasize the good diamond suit than it is to emphasize an extra point or two. Distributional assets are often worth more than high card assets.

You hold ♠ 74　♡ 32　◇ AQJ43　♣ KQJ7

Bid 2♣. This is not much more than a minimum but it is still worth bidding with. As long as your suits are good and you don't object to being preferenced back to your first suit, it is correct to bid with hands like these.

You hold ♠ J52　♡ 53　◇ AKJ74　♣ AJ3

Pass. Do not bid 2◇. Almost never rebid five card suits. I said earlier that it was conceivable to do so, but in fact, it is closer to being a rare exception. You don't have extra values and a fifth diamond, while nice, is nothing so special that you have to rave about it. Save your 2◇ rebids for six card suits.

None Vulnerable
You hold ♠ K92 ♡ 83 ◇ AQ6 ♣ K10852

WEST	NORTH	EAST	SOUTH
—	—	—	1♣
Pass	1♡	1♠	?

The only thing South can bid is 1NT. If South does bid 1NT, it is not a 'Free Bid' showing a good hand. It still shows 12–14 points. Whether South should bid 1NT with a minimum hand with only one spade stopper is a moot point. I am inclined to pass with this hand. If South does pass, there is a mild inference that he has something like this hand. If South had three hearts, he would show them and if he had some other good feature, he would show that. If South had either an extra value or a second spade stopper, I would accept 1NT.

None Vulnerable
You hold ♠ Q872 ♡ K3 ◇ 94 ♣ AQJ32

WEST	NORTH	EAST	SOUTH
—	—	—	1♣
Pass	1◇	1♡	?

Bid 1♠. The need to get your suits bid overrides the comfort of having something extra for the so called 'Free Bid'. If you don't bid 1♠, you are giving away too much.

None Vulnerable
You hold ♠ 84 ♡ A6 ◇ Q8 ♣ AKQJ642

WEST	NORTH	EAST	SOUTH
—	—	—	1♣
Pass	1♡	1♠	?

Bid 2♠. The simple cue bid tends to show one of two hands. You may have a big balanced hand with three card support that isn't able to raise directly. Though, if you use Support Doubles, this interpretation won't apply. Or you may have a hand like this which is just too good to rebid 3♣. Your intention here is to get North to bid notrump if he can. You will show this hand by rebidding clubs later. I think this cue bid should be forcing to game or to 4♣ if you determine that game doesn't exist.

None Vulnerable

WEST	NORTH	EAST	SOUTH
—	—	—	1♣
Pass	1♡	1♠	?

You hold ♠ 852   ♡ AKJ   ◇ K4   ♣ AKJ43

Bid 2♠. You intend to bid 3♡ later, showing a big hand with only three hearts. 3♡ will be forcing at this point. If partner goes back to 4♣, though, you should be able to pass. If you chose to reverse to 2◇ instead, that would be an acceptable effort subject to the rules you use for your reverses.

This is another good hand for Support Doubles if you use them. You can double 1♠, showing three hearts, and later do something to show your extra values. For instance, if North rebids 2♡, you will bid 2♠. This approach gives you the ability to show your three card support and your strength. You still have to sort things out, but you are off to a good start.

You hold ♠ 7   ♡ KQ73   ◇ K32   ♣ AKQ82

Bid 3♠. Do not overlook the splinter raise. This is game forcing, shows four trumps, and promises a singleton spade.

You hold ♠ A   ♡ KQ73   ◇ K32   ♣ KQ832

Bid 3♡ only. Bid 4♡ if you hate bidding only three. Do not bid 3♠. There are two reasons for this. Singleton aces are not worth three distributional points as are small singletons. This hand just isn't worth bidding 4♡. If you doubt this, just look at the hand and the previous one and ask yourself which hand is better. It is obvious that the first hand, with the identical high card points, is better. Its ace is in clubs which means the club suit is ready to run. You have three immediate club tricks and may have five. The second hand has no fast source of tricks and the club suit isn't good enough to guarantee a slow source of tricks.

The second reason is that your partner will treat your splinter bid as showing a small singleton spade. He will expect your points to be elsewhere and will evaluate his hand on that assumption. Experts have learned the hard way that singleton aces are fetching sirens luring you into overbidding. You will notice that I suggested 4♡ as a possibility. There is a lot to be said for treating hands with singleton aces as balanced hands. You will have to believe me on this one. Keep notes for awhile and you will agree.

WEST	NORTH	EAST	SOUTH
—	—	—	1♣
Pass	1♡	1♠	?

You hold ♠ A ♡ KQ73 ◊ AQ5 ♣ KQ832

Bid 3♠. This hand has enough extra values that it can splinter and still not be a disappointment to partner.

You hold ♠ K7 ♡ KQ104 ◊ A4 ♣ AQJ63

Cue–bid 2♠ and then force the issue to 4♡. Partner will work out that you have a spade control along with a good balanced hand. Remember, if you had a hand with a singleton, you would have started with a splinter bid.

You hold ♠ K43 ♡ AQJ7 ◊ 3 ♣ KQJ83

If your system defines 3◊ as a splinter, you can make that bid. Splinters don't have to be in the opponent's suit. You can splinter in any of the other suits.

You hold ♠ K43 ♡ AQJ7 ◇ None ♣ KQJ832

If your partnership agrees that 3◇ is a splinter, what would it mean in your partnership if you bid 4◇ instead? A reasonable treatment is to play that if a jump bid is defined as a singleton, a jump one level higher shows a void. With this understanding, you can bid 4◇ and tell partner you have no diamonds as opposed to a singleton.

You can show voids only when room and safety permit. Say the bidding went:

WEST	NORTH	EAST	SOUTH
—	1♠	2♡	?

In the methods I suggest in this book, 3♡ would be a balanced game forcing spade raise. 4♡ would be a splinter bid showing a singleton heart with four trumps and game values. If you have a heart void, you can bid 5♡ if you are safe at that level. But if you are worried that the five level is too high, you have to bid 4♡. Most splinter bids are made with singletons. Occasionally, you do have a void which will be a surprise to partner unless you are able to make further definition on the next round of the bidding.

WEST	NORTH	EAST	SOUTH
—	—	—	1♣
Pass	1♡	1♠	?

You hold ♠ 74 ♡ AQ107 ◇ 4 ♣ AQJ532

Another possible trick for you. You can play that a jump to 4♣, rebidding your original minor suit, shows a 6–4 hand with good suits but not enough points that you want to make a splinter bid.

You hold ♠ 84 ♡ KQJ6 ◇ AK ♣ KQ1073

Bid 4♡. This shows a balanced hand with twenty support points. You may have 4–3–3–3 shape or you may have up to 5–4–2–2 shape. There is an inference that you don't have a control in their suit (in this case, spades) because you didn't cue–bid 2♠ on the way to 4♡.

THEY OVERCALL
AT THE TWO LEVEL

As before, adding Support Doubles to your methods will help you immensely. Still, they will solve only a few of your rebid problems. You will still have irritating hands to bid. As discussed in the previous section, opener should strive to rebid whenever he has something new to show. Remember this rule. If you have extra points, it is not as imperative to rebid as it is when you have extra shape to show. Some examples.

None Vulnerable
You hold ♠ A2 ♡ AQJ6 ◇ KJ542 ♣ 82

WEST	NORTH	EAST	SOUTH
—	—	—	1◇
Pass	1♠	2♣	?

Pass. Your diamonds aren't good enough to rebid and reversing to 2♡ shows a lot more. Compare this hand with the next hand.

None Vulnerable
You hold ♠ AQJ8 ♡ A3 ◇ KJ873 ♣ 43

WEST	NORTH	EAST	SOUTH
—	—	—	1◇
Pass	1♡	2♣	?

I have misgivings about this hand. 2◇ is out. You need a better suit. But 2♠ strikes me as tempting. I had intended to rebid 1♠ but now I can't. East's 2♣ bid is an irritation which is definitely getting my attention.

One school of thought says you should pass because 2♠ shows more. Another school of thought says that you should bid 2♠ but that it shouldn't be considered a true reverse. This school says that it shows a couple of points more than a minimum and it guarantees good distribution and is passable. A third school says that you should double to show four spades. That is going too far in my opinion. Double is better used to show support for partner's suit.

And finally, a fourth school says that South should pass it around to North. If North has anything at all, he will make an 'Action Double' showing at least nine otherwise unbiddable points. This double is not for penalty. It is a statement saying that North thinks we own the hand but he doesn't have a good bid available. NOTE that this treatment is much different from the first treatment mentioned above. If your partnership uses these reopening doubles, you are in a totally different contest than the partnership that isn't using them. Much more on these doubles in their own chapter to come.

I am not at all sure what to tell you to do here. I think it is reasonable to play that opener's reverse to 2♠ is okay with hands like this and that it can be played as not forcing. If you do play this way, there are a couple of cautions you need to be aware of.

1. Responder has to bid the value of his hand if opener reverses to 2♠. If responder has a ten point hand, he can't bid 3♣ or 3♠ and expect opener to go on. Responder must jump to game or make a cue bid or bid a new suit to guarantee the auction will go on.

2. This is important. The only time these light reverses come up is when the overcall deprives you of the ability to bid one of the suit you are reversing into. Compare these two auctions.

WEST	NORTH	EAST	SOUTH
—	—	—	1♦
Pass	1♠	2♣	2♡

WEST	NORTH	EAST	SOUTH
—	—	—	1♦
Pass	1♡	2♣	2♠

On the first auction, South needs full reversing strength to bid 2♡. If South wanted to bid hearts, he was obviously prepared to do so at the two level.

On the second auction, South clearly would have bid 1♠ if given the chance. East's 2♣ bid got in the way so South had to bid spades at the two level or not at all.

3. If opener has a real reverse, he can't bid 2♠ because it may be passed out. If opener has:

♠ AKJ2   ♡ A53   ◇ AQ1095   ♣ 4

he will have to bid more than 2♠. 3♣ is a possibility. It is an overbid. But at least it keeps the bidding going. This is not a situation to be enjoyed. Hopefully, you will have a lot more 'nonforcing' reverses on this sequence than you do the really big ones. Incidentally, those reopening 'Action Doubles' mentioned earlier may help. Don't rush to use them though unless you are sure they are agreed upon.

None Vulnerable
You hold ♠ J2   ♡ AKQ73   ◇ Q54   ♣ Q102

WEST	NORTH	EAST	SOUTH
—	—	—	1♡
Pass	1♠	2♣	?

Pass. 2♡ is a huge overstatement and 2NT is worse. For

starters, North already knows about your five hearts. If he has support, he can raise hearts. If he has a stiff heart, you will have four potential tricks, which translates into nine potential losers. 2♡ shows six hearts at least. 2NT is wrong for a different reason. What were you going to rebid if East passed 1♠? You were going to bid 1NT showing 12–14 balanced points. There is no reason that a 1NT rebid should suddenly be worth a 2NT rebid just because East bid 2♣. 2NT by you shows the same 18–19 points that you would show had you jumped to 2NT, auction permitting. If you play Support Doubles, you can't double 2♣ for penalty.

None Vulnerable
You hold ♠ AK3   ♡ 43   ◇ 94   ♣ AKQJ73

WEST	NORTH	EAST	SOUTH
—	—	—	1♣
Pass	1♡	2◇	?

With little confidence, I suggest you cue–bid 3◇. You are obviously hoping to hear 3NT. This is imperfect, to say the least. Your only alternative is to bid 2♠ and that opens up a different can of worms.

NOTE. If you play that 2♠ is a nonforcing reverse here, you may run into this problem. Let's say you bid 3◇ on the hand above and partner rebids 3♡. If you now bid 3♠, North will think you are showing a full reverse and are finally showing your second suit. He will raise spades if he feels like it.

None Vulnerable
You hold ♠ 92   ♡ KQ7   ◇ AKQ109   ♣ AJ4

WEST	NORTH	EAST	SOUTH
—	—	—	1◇
Pass	1♡	2♣	?

Bid 3♣. You would like to hear partner bid 3♡ so you

259

can raise. If he bids 3◊, you will bid 3♡, giving him a say. He will play you for only three trumps unless you later show you really have four of them.

Opener's RHO Makes A Takeout Double After Partner Makes A One Level Response

Most of your bids will be as if East hadn't bid. The one major change is that you can use the Support Redouble here to show three trump. With four trumps, you just raise to the appropriate level.

You should usually make your normal rebid. Do not be so impressed by the double that you forget to bid when you should.

None Vulnerable
You hold ♠ AJ62 ♡ 732 ◊ AQ106 ♣ J4

WEST	NORTH	EAST	SOUTH
—	—	—	1◊
Pass	1♡	Double	?

Go ahead and bid 1♠. You could redouble if you wished to show three card heart support, but showing these spades is preferable. It is not mandatory to show three card support. Sometimes there are other things to do. One thing you shouldn't do is pass. If you pass, West will bid 2♣ and you will have lots of unstated messages and no room to make them. Incidentally, you should not feel automatically that East's double says you don't have a spade fit. You may have a 4–4 fit even if East has four of them. Also possible is that East has doubled with only three spades. It wouldn't be the first time. To paraphrase another popular expression, "Bad bids happen."

None Vulnerable
You hold ♠ 743   ♡ AJ105   ◇ 3   ♣ AQ1094

WEST	NORTH	EAST	SOUTH
—	—	—	1♣
Pass	1♡	Double	?

Bid 3♡. In competition, the jump raise can be made a
little lighter than normal. West might be quieted by a
raise to 2♡, but a raise to 3♡ has a better chance yet of
hushing him. When you jump to 3♡, you show a hand
that normally would have raised to 2♡ and would have
bid to 3♡ if pushed. Your bid is not entirely preemptive.
It is quasi–preemptive and quasi–invitational. If 3♡ is
bid on this hand, you have to overbid a little bit on the
upper ranges too. For instance, if you had:

♠ J103   ♡ AKJ4   ◇ 3   ♣ AQ982

you should bid 4♡ or you should splinter to 3◇ over
East's takeout double.

They Bid A Strong Notrump
After Partner Responds
At The One Level

What is there to say here? You still have the option of
using Support Doubles. It is possible you don't want to
use them since a penalty double also makes sense. Be
sure to decide.

There is another issue here. When RHO overcalls 1NT,
you should not be cowed to the extent that you quit
bidding. With a shape hand, you should rebid. Rebids
don't show high cards. Rebids show winning tricks. It
is to your advantage to rebid with light, shape hands
because it stops LHO from using Stayman or any of the
myriad other available conventions.

None Vulnerable
You hold ♠ K3   ♡ A86   ◇ KJ10974   ♣ 52

WEST	NORTH	EAST	SOUTH
—	—	—	1◇
Pass	1♠	1NT	?

Bid 2◇. You might be beating 1NT, but maybe not. 2◇ stirs the pot, so to speak. Whatever else happens, 2◇ won't be an awful contract and it does stop West from looking for a 4–4 heart fit.

They Overcall After Partner Responds One Notrump

This is a situation that lends itself to penalty doubles. Opener can count on his partner to have some range of points and something resembling a balanced hand. If RHO overcalls in a suit lower than opener's suit, opener can count on responder having some length in that suit. If RHO overcalls in a suit higher ranking than opener's suit, it is possible that partner is short in that suit. Opener can therefore be quicker to double a suit lower ranking than his opened suit.

None Vulnerable
You hold ♠ A863   ♡ A1052   ◇ A95   ♣ Q3

WEST	NORTH	EAST	SOUTH
—	—	—	1◇
Pass	1NT	2♣	?

North didn't bid 1♡ or 1♠ so he is a favorite to have four clubs. You can double 2♣ with good expectations. You still have to contend with partner's putting you back in 2◇, but the possible gain from doubling is worth it.

None Vulnerable
You hold ♠ Q3   ♡ A863   ◇ A1052   ♣ A95

WEST	NORTH	EAST	SOUTH
—	—	—	1◇
Pass	1NT	2♠	?

I suppose you could double but it isn't the same thing at all as when you doubled 2♣ with the preceding hand. On this hand, North has a maximum of three spades and two isn't impossible. I would pass and accept down one if I got it.

None Vulnerable

WEST	NORTH	EAST	SOUTH
—	—	—	1♡
Pass	1NT*	2◇	?

*Forcing Notrump

You hold ♠ AQ7   ♡ AQ1095   ◇ 73   ♣ Q84

Pass. Your slight extra values don't make up for having only five hearts. Bidding 2♡ is fairly awful.

You hold ♠ AQ7   ♡ AQ1095   ◇ 87   ♣ KJ6

Bid 2NT. In competition, this is a little bit lighter than it would be if East had passed. There is an evolving school of thought that suggests opener's best bid is a takeout double. This alertable treatment needs work and at this moment, I hesitate to suggest it. The possibility is mentioned here because there are some pairs using this style. If you encounter it, you need to realize that you are being doubled with a hand like this one.

You hold ♠ AQ7   ♡ AQ10974   ◇ 84   ♣ 53

Bid 2♡. As long as you have something useful to show in terms of shape or in terms of a very good suit, go ahead and show it. NOTE that since you are really minimum, you need your suit to be both six cards long and good quality.

You hold ♠ 73 ♡ AQ873 ◇ 3 ♣ AKJ42

It looks automatic to bid 3♣. You have two good suits plus excellent high card structure. Everyone would bid 3♣ with this hand.

You hold ♠ 73 ♡ AQ743 ◇ 5 ♣ KQ832

Would you bid 3♣ with this hand too? Many would. This presents North with a problem. If South will rebid 3♣ with this eleven points and with the fourteen point hand above and also some sixteen point hands, how is North to know if he is supposed to bid again?

THE FUNNY 2NT REBID

There is a newish treatment on the market today which lets you distinguish between good hands and bad hands. If you have a good hand, you bid 3♣ as you did on the good 5–5 hand above. If you have a weak hand, you bid 2NT, which asks partner to bid 3♣. You will pass this, of course.

None Vulnerable
You hold ♠ 3 ♡ KJ763 ◇ AQ973 ♣ K2

WEST	NORTH	EAST	SOUTH
—	—	—	1♡
Pass	1NT	2♠	?

This 2NT treatment works here too. Opener rebids 2NT, gets North to bid 3♣, and then converts it to 3◇. This shows a weakish heart–diamond hand. With a good heart–diamond hand, opener bids 3◇ over East's 2♠.

I'm not sure I recommend this treatment. It has merit and on paper, it looks great. At the table, it is likely to cause problems. I mention it because it is out there in the hands of many of your opponents. If one of them bids this way and you hear opener bid 2NT followed by an alert, you should know what they are doing.

There is an expanded discussion of this bid in the final chapter along with a discussion of 'Action Doubles'. I've alluded to these conventions in various places in this book.

They Make A Takeout Double
After Partner Responds One Notrump

A couple of minor items on this one. First. If opener has a good hand, he can redouble. Good hands will usually start at about sixteen high cards with shape (else why not open 1NT?), and go upwards.

If you are using forcing notrump responses to one of a major, opener does not have to rebid when East doubles. If opener has a balanced hand, he can pass, which says he doesn't have a natural rebid to make thus implying a 5–3–3–2 shape.

They Make An Overcall
After Partner Raises Opener's Major

Before going into specific hands, I need to define what it means when opener rebids three of his suit in competition.

WEST	NORTH	EAST	SOUTH
1♡	Pass	2♡	2♠
3♡			

It used to be that this 3♡ bid was a game try asking responder to bid game with a maximum. This method worked alright when it came to bidding games, but it sacrificed a lot of partscores. Partscores are too valuable to ignore. If you cater your bidding to games and concede the partscore fights, you will be a loser. You've heard the expression "being nickled and dimed to death." That's what happens when you go quietly. Fighting back against thieves requires that you adopt this rule.

RULE: In competition (opener is raised and RHO overcalls), if opener rebids his suit, it is competitive. It is NOT invitational.

The following discussion assumes that opener wants to compete only.

This is one of the most common competitive problems you will have. You open a suit, partner raises, and RHO bids something. When should you bid again, and when should you double, and when should you just give it up?

I see many players overbid in this situation with the wrong hands. If you have a balanced hand with scattered values, it is seldom right to continue. If you have some shape, it is often right to continue. If you have an extra trump, it is usually right to continue.

THE LAW OF TOTAL TRICKS

There is a guideline practiced by many experts known as the 'Law of Total Tricks'. Hard–core cult members refer to it as the LAW. When it works, they speak of the LAW in reverent terms. When it fails they light another candle to remind the LAW of their devotion. Never will you hear a follower of the LAW complain in other than hushed whispers. Louder cries could displease the LAW and it might cease to provide for its doubters.

The Law of Total Tricks works in this fashion. You add the number of trumps that the other side has to the number of trumps that your side has. This number represents the number of tricks that can be taken by both sides. For instance. Let us assume that your side has nine spades and the other side has nine hearts. The LAW tells you that the number of tricks you can take in spades plus the number of tricks they can take in hearts will equal eighteen. If the opponents take ten tricks in their heart contract, the LAW says that you will have eight tricks in your spade contract. If you can make exactly three spades, the LAW says the opponents will make exactly three hearts. If the opponents can make twelve tricks in hearts, you will be able to make six tricks in spades.

Both Vulnerable
You hold ♠ 973 ♡ J1064 ◇ A1085 ♣ 109

WEST	NORTH	EAST	SOUTH
—	1♡	1♠	2♡
2♠	Pass	Pass	?

You assume your side has nine hearts given you are playing five card majors. The opponents are likely to have eight spades. This totals seventeen, which translates to seventeen tricks. If they can make eight tricks in spades, your side can make nine tricks in hearts. If you can make only eight tricks in hearts, they can make nine tricks in spades. It is true that if you bid 3♡ and get doubled and go down one, you will get a bad board, but for that to happen, they have to double you and they have to beat you. Assuming you don't get doubled, the LAW dictates that you compete to 3♡.

If you don't want to do all this adding and subtracting, you can do something less complicated. In the simplest of all terms, you should bid more when you have an extra trump and you should go quietly when you don't. Extra quality points or useful distribution will sway some of your decisions. But if you have normal values for your

auction and it gets competitive, it is often right to concede
when you don't have the magic fourth trump.

WEST	NORTH	EAST	SOUTH
—	—	—	1♡
Pass	2♡	2♠	?

You hold ♠ QJ4 ♡ KJ985 ◇ AQ ♣ Q53

Pass. The LAW doesn't help you here because you can't
judge how many trumps they have. Sometimes, you are
forced to rely on judgment. Your judgment should tell you
to pass. You have fifteen points but the good news stops
there. You have five only hearts and you have 5–3–3–2
shape. If you can make 3♡, it will mean that the high
cards are working well for you. If they work well for you,
they are working poorly for them. You don't really want
to be in 3♡ unless North votes for it. Passing is not
conceding. Partner still has a second chance.

Here are two possible hands for North to have. NOTE
how well each plays opposite your opening bid.

♠ QJ4 ♡ KJ985 ◇ AQ ♣ Q53

1. ♠ 82	♡ Q764	◇ 863	♣ KJ104
2. ♠ 1082	♡ Q76	◇ J86	♣ KJ104

The first hand has a fourth trump and a doubleton spade
and six high card points. Hand One will make 3♡ for you
if the diamond finesse is onside or if the defenders fail to
lead a diamond through your AQ in time.

The second hand has only three trumps and it now has
a third spade and the jack of diamonds to make it worth
a raise to 2♡. On this hand, 3♡ is down one off the top
after the defenders get their spade ruff and it can go
down two against many defenses.

The main difference between these two hands is that
the first hand has one more trump than the second. That

extra trump reflects its value in many ways. If your side has nine trumps:

1. The defense can't lead trump to easy advantage.

2. The defense won't be able to run you out of trump.

3. You will have time to set up and use your side suits.

4. You will be able to execute some end plays that you couldn't execute with only eight trumps.

5. The opponents won't have many trump stacks so you won't be doubled.

None Vulnerable
You hold ♠ AQ7   ♡ J87542   ◇ 3   ♣ KJ4

WEST	NORTH	EAST	SOUTH
—	—	—	1♡
Pass	2♡	3◇	?

An easy 3♡ call. Your sixth heart is worth tons. That, plus your good shape and quality points, makes this a clear bid. But only if your partner will pass. Few things are more agonizing than to bid 3♡ on this hand and then have to stew while your partner thinks. Every second of waiting hurts more than the one before. Whatever partner comes up with, regardless of whether it is right or wrong, you will have lost some years off your life.

None Vulnerable
You hold ♠ 963   ♡ AKJ83   ◇ 63   ♣ KQ8

WEST	NORTH	EAST	SOUTH
—	—	—	1♡
Pass	2♡	2♠	?

The quality of your trump suit and the concentration of strength gives you reason to compete to 3♡ even though it will go down as often as not. Vulnerable, you can bid

3♡ with this hand, but you are subject to a penalty double. Down one will be terrible for you. My bid if vulnerable? I bid 3♡ and hope I look confident.

None Vulnerable
You hold ♠ 7   ♡ AQ874   ◇ A10964   ♣ J3

WEST	NORTH	EAST	SOUTH
—	—	—	1♡
Pass	2♡	3♣	?

Bid 3♡ with this, too. This hand doesn't have an extra trump, but it does have fine distribution with playing potential. It's minimum in high cards, but they are in your long suits which is a plus.

How Does Opener Make A Game Try After An Overcall?

In competition, it used to be that opener's rebid was a game try. If you have decided to play it as competitive, as suggested here, you will need another way to make a game try. The current trend is to play as follows.

None Vulnerable

WEST	NORTH	EAST	SOUTH
—	—	—	1♠
Pass	2♠	3♣	?

DOUBLE	Penalty.
3◇	A game try which suggests something in diamonds.
3♡	A game try which suggests something in hearts.
3♠	Competitive only.

In this auction, opener had room to bid 3♦ and 3♥ as game tries. Sometimes there is less room.

None Vulnerable

WEST	NORTH	EAST	SOUTH
—	—	—	1♠
Pass	2♠	3♦	?

DOUBLE   Penalty.

3♥   An ambiguous game try. Because it is the only bid opener can make to try for game, it will be coincidental if opener has anything in hearts.

3♠   Competitive only.

You hold ♠ AQ842   ♥ J3   ♦ K2   ♣ AQ106

South wants to invite game but has only one way to do it. He has to bid 3♥. North evaluates his hand in general terms and tries to come up with the right decision. NOTE that North does not play South for heart strength. If you use this technique, your 3♥ bid is alertable. Don't forget!

What Happens If Opener Has No Room?

None Vulnerable

WEST	NORTH	EAST	SOUTH
—	—	—	1♠
Pass	2♠	3♥	?

What does South do now? There should be a way to invite a game here but in the current scheme, there is no way to do so. The answer is inevitably a bid of science. You have to make a change to cater to the one situation where you don't have a free bid available. There are two ways you can handle this.

1. You can play double is a game try (Alert this!) and that bidding 3♠ is still competitive.
2. You can play that double is for penalty and that 3♠ is your game try.

In fact, there is a third variation which uses both of the above methods. The third variation depends on whether your RHO is bidding his suit by himself or whether he is raising his partner. IF THE OPPONENTS HAVE A FIT—If East is raising West's overcall or if East is responding to West's takeout double, DOUBLE is a game try and 3♠ is competitive. IF THE OPPONENTS DO NOT HAVE A FIT—If East is bidding the suit totally on his own, DOUBLE is for penalty. 3♠ is your game try.

None Vulnerable
You hold ♠ KQJ63   ♡ 73   ◇ AK83   ♣ K6

WEST	NORTH	EAST	SOUTH
—	—	—	1♠
2♡	2♠	3♡	?

The opponents have a fit. It is not likely that you will want to double them for penalty. In this case, it is acceptable to say that double is a game try and that 3♠ is competitive. Here, West overcalled 2♡. If West had made a takeout double instead, your bids would be the same because they have a known fit.

None Vulnerable

WEST	NORTH	EAST	SOUTH
—	—	—	1♠
Pass	2♠	3♡	?

On this sequence, East is bidding with no assurance that

he is doing the right thing. He could be speculating. Speculating should not be free. It is possible that you will want to double East for penalty. In this case your bids will mean:

DOUBLE   Penalty. (They don't have a fit.)

3♠   Your game try. Whatever you do, you will have to give up something. In this case you give up on the competitive 3♠ bid.

NOTE that the above discussion also applies when your side is bidding hearts and the opponents start bidding diamonds.

Opener's RHO Doubles After Partner Raises Opener's Major

When East doubles for takeout, South has an extra bid to play with. Redouble is the new option and it comes in handy.

None Vulnerable

WEST	NORTH	EAST	SOUTH
—	—	—	1♡
Pass	2♡	Double	?

2♠   Your normal game try.

3♣   Your normal game try.

3♢   Your normal game try.

3♡	Competitive. You are hoping to buy the hand or to push the opponents up to the three level. North must pass. If you wanted to invite you would start with redouble.
REDOUBLE	Either a game try or it is head–hunting. Redouble asks North to double the opponents if he can do so. North is also invited to bid a game if he has a maximum. It should be agreed that the redouble forces the partnership to three of the trump suit. If opener redoubles on the example auction and West bids something, North does not have to bid. He can pass and be assured that South will bid something.
2NT	A funny bid. If you had a good balanced hand, you would redouble. 2NT doesn't make a lot of sense unless you have some special meaning for it. I have nothing worthwhile to offer.

None Vulnerable
You hold ♠ 82   ♡ KQ1084   ◇ AQJ7   ♣ 93

WEST	NORTH	EAST	SOUTH
—	—	—	1♡
Pass	2♡	Double	?

Bid 3♡. Over a takeout double, this is competitive. If you pass, West will bid something like 2♠ or 3♣. If this is passed back to you, you will have to pass or plunge back in with 3♡. I would bid right away because of the good shape and concentration of high cards. If you agree that you will probably bid 3♡ later, it is better to bid it now. As long as it is understood to be preemptive, you can bid 3♡ which forces West to come in at the three or four level.

You hold ♠ 3   ♡ K10753   ◇ AKQ4   ♣ K102

Not quite good enough to bid a game yourself. You will have to ask partner for his opinion. There are two bids you can make to this end. Either 3♣ or 3◇ are game tries which ask partner to evaluate his hand. Partner will view help in your new suit as being especially useful. Redouble shows a balanced hand and 3♡ shows a preemptive hand so neither of these bids will get the job done. You have to choose between 3♣ or 3◇. There are all kinds of game tries you can make. I am going to assume you are using natural game tries. In this light, the following rule will help.

RULE: When you make a game try, make the game try in a suit where partner can have some useful cards.

On this hand, you have solid diamonds. There is nothing partner can have in diamonds to help you. Partner will be discouraged by his diamond holding. Clubs, however, are a different story. Any club honor will help. The ace, the queen, and the jack will all be useful. If partner has one of these honors, he will upgrade them appropriately.

None Vulnerable
You hold ♠ A   ♡ AKJ83   ◇ 8754   ♣ KJ5

WEST	NORTH	EAST	SOUTH
—	—	—	1♡
Pass	2♡	Double	?

South should bid 3♣. Not 3◇. South wants North to like club honors. The queen of clubs will be nice, as will the ace. Whatever North has in diamonds won't be worth much since they will be in front of the doubler. If North has the queen of clubs, that's good. If North has the queen of diamonds, it's almost worthless. The only useful high card North can have in diamonds is the ace and if that is the case, North will appreciate it whatever game try

275

South makes. Don't make game tries in honorless suits if at all avoidable.

They Overcall After Partner Raises Opener's Minor

When responder raises a minor and RHO competes, opener's most likely game will be 3NT. This is in contrast to when responder raises a major suit. Opener may bid himself to five of a minor, but early in the bidding, his partner will assume opener is looking for 3NT unless it is clear that he is just competing.

None Vulnerable
You hold ♠ AJ82 ♡ 732 ◇ A6 ♣ KQ108

WEST	NORTH	EAST	SOUTH
—	—	—	1♣
Pass	2♣	2♡	?

The whole point of bidding is to find an eight or nine card fit and then to decide how high to go or whether to transfer to notrump. This hand isn't interested in a game but it is good enough that it doesn't want to sell out to 2♡. I suggest you bid 3♣. North's raise promises four or five clubs so there are adequate trumps. The rest of South's hand is good enough that competing is worthwhile. NOTE that 3♣ is competitive just like it is in the major suits. North must pass. Competing with just a four card suit is not a well known strategy. If you do it at the right times, it has merit.

Not Vulnerable vs. Vulnerable
You hold ♠ J8   ♡ 732   ◇ KQ7   ♣ AQ1095

WEST	NORTH	EAST	SOUTH
—	—	—	1♣
Pass	2♣	2♡	?

If you have a five card minor and get raised, it is hard to imagine not competing to the three level. 3♣ doesn't show anything except a desire to steal some bidding room from the opponents. Bidding 3♣ with this hand does two important things.

1. West may have a hand with heart support but not enough values to raise. When you bid 3♣, West is obliged to bid 3♡ even though he doesn't really want to. East may misjudge West's intentions when you put West under pressure.

2. Your 3♣ bid keeps West from cue–bidding 3♣. West may have a good enough hand that he wants to bid 3⁺♡. The way he would do this is by cue–bidding 3♣. If you take his cue bid away, West has to guess.

They Make A Takeout Double After Partner Raises Opener's Minor

This start is the beginning of some furious auctions. RHO is showing three suits so the chances are that they have a suit to compete in. Opener should rebid aggressively.

None Vulnerable

WEST	NORTH	EAST	SOUTH
—	—	—	1♣
Pass	2♣	Double	?

You hold ♠ 32   ♡ KJ63   ◇ A92   ♣ KQ75

I would bid 3♣ here. The opponents have eight spades and adequate points to make eight to ten tricks. Bidding 3♣ may cause them to end up in hearts and in any event, you shouldn't be hurt. When you have good trump honors, you can get away with a fair amount.

None Vulnerable

WEST	NORTH	EAST	SOUTH
—	—	—	1♣
Pass	2♣	Double	?

You hold ♠ 743   ♡ 3   ◇ KQJ5   ♣ AKJ73

If you think you would save against 4♡ or 4♠, you should do so right away. I think that is a little pessimistic. I would, however, be willing to compete to 4♣. You have good clubs, a good side suit, and good shape. 4♣ sticks it to West. He will have a few points and he surely has a major to bid. He may decide he is being pushed around (he is) and take an overbid. The down side to this action is that they may bid a game that no one else will bid and then proceed to make it. More likely, if they overbid to game, it will go down.

You hold ♠ AJ6   ♡ A97   ◇ Q10   ♣ AQJ84

Bid 2NT. This is no big deal other than to recognize that 2NT is invitational. It is reasonable to hope for North to have a diamond card for you. He didn't bid a major so there is an inference that he has length in diamonds.

You hold ♠ AJ2   ♡ K3   ◇ 103   ♣ AJ8753

3NT is a reasonable gamble here. It is safe to bid like this because North won't be taking any more bids. The only down side is that they will kill you with diamonds. If they can't run diamonds, you have eight potential tricks available and hopes for a ninth. This is a two way bid. You hope 3NT will make. If it goes down, it may turn out to be a save against three or four of a major. If you get doubled, that is a different story. Sit for it if you dare. I don't.

Opener's RHO Overcalls After Partner Makes A Two Over One Response

Finally! An area of bidding which isn't put out too much by an opponent's bidding. When your side is able to start with an opening bid and a two over one response, you are in a strong situation. If you play your two over one responses as game forcing, or nearly so, an overcall needn't bother you. If you play your two over one responses require only a fair nine count, you will not be as well placed. I am going to assume that your two over one responses show a good hand.

None Vulnerable

WEST	NORTH	EAST	SOUTH
—	—	—	1♡
Pass	2♢	2♠	?

When North bid 2♢, he started a strong sequence. In effect, he said that the partnership was going to game. Or, if not a game, the partnership was committed to discussing it until 4♢ was reached.

This means that opener is not obliged to rebid over 2♠ unless he has something worthy to add to the auction. A number of players who are just getting into Two Over One bidding hear this sequence and rush to bid something. This sequence offers your side the potential for a quick top. If East has come in at the wrong time, you may be able to double him. Your side has so many points that East won't find much help in his dummy. This is one reason why you shouldn't bid without reason over 2♠. If you have nothing to say, pass it to partner, who may double 2♠ himself. If you do pass, North will not take it as a sign of weakness. He will take it to mean you had nothing you wanted to say. South can pass with an eighteen count if appropriate because North has guaranteed the bidding will continue.

None Vulnerable

WEST	NORTH	EAST	SOUTH
—	—	—	1♡
Pass	2♢	2♠	?

You hold ♠ K7   ♡ AKQ63   ♢ 73   ♣ Q1083

What is the right bid? Mull it over for a moment. Should you bid 2NT? Should you rebid those very nice hearts? How about showing the clubs? The answer is none of the above. The right bid is pass with no other bid deserving mention. If North can double 2♠, you will be happy. If North bids 3♡, you will go on to game. If North bids 2NT, you will raise that. Whatever North wants to do, he can do it just as well without a bid from you. If you have nothing SPECIAL to show, don't bother.

You hold ♠ 3   ♡ AQ97543   ♢ K3   ♣ K93

Rebid 3♡. You have a suit you want to show plus you aren't interested in defending against 2♠ doubled. 3♡ does not show extra values. It shows an extra good feature.

You hold ♠ 8   ♡ AKJ1075   ♢ A8   ♣ KJ83

Bid 3♡. Rebidding 3♡ does not show extra values but it does not deny them either. You don't have to jump to 4♡ to show this hand. Partner is going to bid again. I promise.

You hold ♠ 73   ♡ KQJ10763   ♢ Q3   ♣ A8

You can bid 4♡ with this one. The jump to game shows

a super suit but it also shows no slam interest. If you had more than this, you would rebid just 3♡.

You hold ♠ 72 ♡ AQJ105 ◇ KJ3 ♣ K32

Raise to 3◇. This shows a touch more than a minimum. You have quality points, which makes up for the lack of a lot of them. There is no reason to rebid these hearts. 3◇ creates a game force.

None Vulnerable

WEST	NORTH	EAST	SOUTH
—	—	—	1♡
Pass	2◇	2♠	?

You hold ♠ K3 ♡ QJ762 ◇ KQ7 ♣ QJ3

2NT. You have poor defensive values and you have a diamond fit. Since you didn't make any effort to double 2♠, North won't play you for super spades. It is unlikely you have more than one spade stopper.

You hold ♠ 32 ♡ AK843 ◇ AQ83 ♣ K3

Raise to 3◇. When you raise to 3◇, you are now in an official game force. You hope to get some cue–bidding from partner. If he can show a spade control, you will look for 7◇ and will settle for 6◇ if that is all there is. If North bids 3NT over your 3◇, you will bid 4◇. You are already in a game force so the bidding is going on. The fact that you took it out of 3NT does not show weakness. It shows slam interest.

You hold ♠ 3 ♡ AKJ83 ◇ AQ632 ♣ J4

Bid 4♠. This is a splinter bid showing diamond support, a stiff spade, and a sensational hand. You hope North can bid Blackwood, but a club cue bid will be almost as nice.

You hold ♠ Q963   ♡ A9863   ◇ J3   ♣ AJ

DOUBLE. When your partner makes a two over one response and East bids your side four card suit, you should think double and then look to see why you shouldn't double. Double is not a strong bid. You might double with a very weak opening bid. One of the conditions of double is that you don't have much in partner's suit. This fact should help him judge how to continue.

None Vulnerable
You hold ♠ KJ753   ♡ 3   ◇ K104   ♣ KQ63

WEST	NORTH	EAST	SOUTH
—	—	—	1♠
Pass	2♡	3◇	?

You opened a dog and partner made a response you didn't want to hear. Here comes East with his 3◇ bid. What now?

I gave this hand to a panel of sixteen experts from around the world. Thirteen of them agreed on what they would bid. I'll give you one hint. No one in the panel bid 3NT. The near unanimous choice was to double 3◇. Everyone said things along these lines. "We have a misfit and partner has enough points to go to game. If partner passes my double, we should kill them." The three panelists who didn't double all passed. Two of them hoped that North would be able to double. One of these passers had misgivings and hinted that he should have doubled.

I think there is something important here. If sixteen of the top opinions in the world think only of doubling 3◇, there must be something to it. I wonder if I put this problem to sixteen players who had played bridge for only a year or two, how many of them would double. What is your opinion?

282

I would not suggest doubling a two level overcall with only three trumps, but at the three level, when the signs are right, you can do so.

YOU	PARTNER
♠ KJ753	♠ 104
♡ 3	♡ AQ1054
♢ K104	♢ 95
♣ KQ63	♣ AJ54

None Vulnerable
You hold ♠ KJ753   ♡ 3   ♢ K104   ♣ KQ63

WEST	NORTH	EAST	SOUTH
—	—	—	1♠
Pass	2♡	3♢	?

Your hand is on the left and a possible hand for partner is on the right. In defense against diamonds, your side has the potential for one or two spade tricks, two or three heart tricks, one or two club tricks, and one diamond trick with the additional potential of getting an overruff with the ten of diamonds. This adds up to down five if it all happens. The key is that your side has a misfit plus you likely have more than sixty percent of the high cards. These two hands have no sure game. In fact, partner's hand is minimum for the 2♡ bid. Some would say it isn't strong enough. If this is true, it means that North will have more than the example hand above.

One last reminder. North doesn't have to pass the double. He can still rebid hearts or raise spades if he wants.

Chapter Ten

EVERYBODY BIDS

WHEN YOU ARE IN THE MIDDLE OF A SEQUENCE where everyone is bidding, you are going to be faced with all kinds of decisions. As you can imagine, there are probably one hundred or more kinds of sequences that I could discuss under this chapter heading. The most frequent decisions revolve around hands where their side has found a fit. This can happen when RHO answers a takeout double or when RHO raises his partner's overcall. These auctions tend to be busy auctions in that when fits exist, there is more bidding than when they don't.

The hands in this chapter will do more than present problems. They are intended to remind you of some of the possible agreements that were discussed in earlier chapters. Many of these hands will include defensive conventions you are likely to encounter at the table.

OPENER'S LHO DOUBLES
FOR TAKEOUT

None Vulnerable

WEST	NORTH	EAST	SOUTH
—	—	—	1◇
Double	1♠		

The point of this auction is to remind you that a new suit by North at the one level is forcing when West doubles. This is what North's bids mean:

1♡ or 1♠	Both forcing. Partner may have a four card suit but it rates to be a pretty good one. South should rebid as he would have if West's double didn't happen.
1NT	Shows a good seven up to a poor ten count. Responder doesn't have to bid 1NT with six point hands and poor seven pointers. If you play 1NT forcing to one of a major, it does not apply over a takeout double.
2♣	Not forcing. A new suit at the two level over a takeout double shows a good five or six card suit and 5–8 points (assuming you are not using the Cappelletti Convention or the 2♣ Constructive Raise discussed in Chapter 4).
2♢	A raise, is weaker than normal. It can be made on 4–7 points.
2♡, 2♠	Weak jump shifts showing six card suits and 3–5 points not vulnerable and a little more when vulnerable.
2NT	In response to a major suit shows a limit raise with four trumps.
	In response to a minor suit shows 10–11 points with diamond support and some stoppers on the side. Opener can pass 2NT.
3♣	Means whatever you have decided .
3♢	Preemptive.
REDOUBLE	Shows the ten point hands or bigger that don't fall into any of the above categories. Denies four card support for a major. Three card support for a major and four or more card support for a minor are possible.

None Vulnerable
You hold ♠ J73   ♡ AQ63   ◇ 10986   ♣ AJ

WEST	NORTH	EAST	SOUTH
—	—	—	1◇
Double	1♠	2♣	?

Double if using Support Doubles and raise to 2♠ if not. You should believe North's 1♠ bid and not West's double. West's double can be correct even if holding only three spades. His double does not promise 4–4 in the majors. West might double with:

♠ Q94   ♡ KJ106   ◇ A4   ♣ K1084

That hand won't be too menacing against a spade contract by North.

None Vulnerable
You hold ♠ QJ6   ♡ J3   ◇ AQ873   ♣ A64

WEST	NORTH	EAST	SOUTH
—	—	—	1◇
Double	1♡	1♠	?

Bid 1NT. North's 1♡ bid promises sixish points and he can have more than an opening bid. It is not necessary for North to redouble with all ten point hands. Bid 1NT now before the auction gets cluttered up.

Not Vulnerable vs. Vulnerable
You hold ♠ QJ763   ♡ 4   ◇ AJ2   ♣ KQ94

WEST	NORTH	EAST	SOUTH
—	—	—	1♠
Double	1NT	Pass	?

Rebid 2♣. Your natural rebid. This promises four clubs. Forcing notrump responses to one of a major are off over doubles. If you have a balanced hand, you can pass 1NT.

None Vulnerable
You hold ♠ 874   ♡ A72   ◊ KQ964   ♣ K3

WEST	NORTH	EAST	SOUTH
—	—	—	1◊
Double	2◊	2♡	?

Bid 3◊. You aren't going to buy this hand but you may be able to change the tenor of their bids. If you pass, West may raise to 3♡. If you bid 3◊, West will certainly bid 3♡ but it won't be so clear to East that West is raising and not competing.

WEST	NORTH	EAST	SOUTH
—	—	—	1◊
Double	2◊	Double*	?

* Responsive Double showing the majors

The Responsive Double requires a few words of introductory advice. There is a tendency to be impressed by this double. Don't let it bother you. The Responsive Double IS NOT FOR PENALTY. It is for takeout. In this case, it shows the major suits. East may have as little as six high card points with 4–4 in the majors. If you have anything to say, you should say it now before the opponents get an extra round of free conversation. For example.

Not Vulnerable vs. Vulnerable
You hold ♠ 73   ♡ J3   ◊ KQ87   ♣ AK842

WEST	NORTH	EAST	SOUTH
—	—	—	1♣
Double	2♣	Double*	?

* Responsive Double showing the majors

Try the effect of bidding 5♣. It is likely they can make a game. If you can make 2♣ your way, you will have a good save. Bidding 5♣ is consistent with the strategy that says to let them make the last guess.

Not Vulnerable vs. Vulnerable
You hold ♠ K4   ♡ J7642   ◇ AQJ4   ♣ Q8

WEST	NORTH	EAST	SOUTH
—	—	—	1♡
Double	2♡	Double*	?

* Responsive Double showing the minors

Pass. The only point here is that you be aware of what
East's double is. Here, it is the Responsive Double. You
will note that on this hand East's double shows the
minors. On the previous hand, it showed the majors. It's
not magic. The Responsive Double works that way. If
your partner doubles a major suit and next hand raises,
a double by you shows the minor suits. Conversely, if your
partner doubles a minor suit and next hand raises, a
double by you shows the major suits. On this hand, East
wants West to pick between clubs and diamonds. You
don't have to worry that East–West are about to get to a
spade fit. What is probably happening is that your
partner has four spades along with his heart raise. You
don't need to do anything heroic. Pass and let them do
what they want. Who knows? They may try to play in
diamonds. Incidentally, if you remember the earlier
discussion, you will reflect on how light a hand North
may have for his 2♡ bid over the double.

Not Vulnerable vs. Vulnerable
You hold ♠ AQJ63   ♡ 763   ◇ AK6   ♣ J4

WEST	NORTH	EAST	SOUTH
—	—	—	1♠
Double	2♣*	2♡	?

* Decent raise to 2♠

That 2♣ bid by partner as used here is artificial showing
a decent raise to 2♠ (see Chapter Four). This is a reasonable
convention to use. You can bid 2♣ to show a normal 6–9

point raise and you can raise directly with appropriate 3–6 point hands. With the hand here, You can rebid 2♠, which shows a sound opener but no real interest in bidding on. With a game invitational hand you would bid 3♠.

Not Vulnerable vs. Vulnerable
You hold ♠ AJ32   ♡ Q4   ♢ Q106   ♣ AJ54

WEST	NORTH	EAST	SOUTH
—	—	—	1♣
Double	3♣	3♡	?

How do you play 3♣? Earlier, I suggested you play it as preemptive. If so, you should pass. If the opponents bid 4♡, you should pass again.

Not Vulnerable vs. Vulnerable
You hold ♠ Q10763   ♡ AJ3   ♢ 3   ♣ KQ42

WEST	NORTH	EAST	SOUTH
—	—	—	1♠
Double	2NT*	3♢	?

* Limit spade raise

Bid 4♠. Your hand has revalued nicely after North made his limit raise. NOTE that North has promised four trumps not . He can't make this bid with only three. Which is just as well. If you bid 4♠ with this and North puts down K52, the combined hands will play much worse for you than you anticipated.

Not Vulnerable vs. Vulnerable
You hold ♠ K82   ♡ KQ752   ♢ 82   ♣ AQ6

WEST	NORTH	EAST	SOUTH
—	—	—	1♡
Double	Redouble	1♠	Pass
2♠	3♡	Pass	?

It's marginal. You may pass or go to 4♡ according to how lucky you feel. There is one important piece of information you have to help you with your decision. What might that be?

You should be consciously aware that your partner has exactly three hearts. If he had four, he would have bid 2NT instead of redouble. If he has three hearts, the hand will play at least a half trick worse than if he had four of them. The takeout double warns you about a possible bad split in hearts which makes things worse yet.

Both Vulnerable
You hold ♠ AK ♡ KJ1054 ◊ QJ2 ♣ Q102

WEST	NORTH	EAST	SOUTH
—	—	—	1♡
Double	3♡	4◊	?

Probably right to pass. If you play it as preemptive with a vengeance, you were high enough in 3♡. Take into account North's style and bid accordingly. Some Norths I know will bid 3♡ with:

♠ 10643 ♡ Q983 ◊ 4 ♣ J985

4♡ has no play at all and 4◊ is a favorite to go down.

Both Vulnerable
You hold ♠ 1062 ♡ AJ73 ◊ KQJ4 ♣ J8

WEST	NORTH	EAST	SOUTH
—	—	—	1◊
Double	Redouble	1♠	Pass
2♠	3♣	Pass	?

What you bid is less important than the fact that you do bid something. North redoubled and then bid a suit. That is forcing. Absolutely. South should, I think, rebid 3♡. This will be interpreted most likely as showing a heart stopper.

Both Vulnerable

WEST	NORTH	EAST	SOUTH
—	—	—	1◇
Double	Redouble	Pass	Pass
1♠	2♡	Pass	?

Is this auction possible? It sounds sensible enough but it is, if you think about it, most unusual. What is wrong with it?

The answer is that North apparently wasn't looking to double spades. If North has a good hand with just hearts or with hearts and support for diamonds, he shouldn't redouble, he should bid 1♡. 1♡ is forcing and may lead to game auctions and even slam auctions. I can not imagine a sensible hand which would redouble and then bid 2♡. In my opinion, this auction is impossible unless it is a conventional treatment. None comes to mind. Maybe in my next book?

OPENER'S LHO OVERCALLS
PARTNER BIDS A SUIT
AT THE ONE LEVEL

There are many things that RHO can do and even more things that opener can do in response. I will show a few of the more common actions by RHO and how opener can react to them.

Both Vulnerable
You hold ♠ A652   ♡ J72   ◇ 103   ♣ AKJ8

WEST	NORTH	EAST	SOUTH
—	—	—	1♣
1◇	1♡	1NT	?

What do we know here? How many hearts does North have? How many spades? At this point, his heart length is unknown. He may have ♡ 8643, which doesn't look much like a suit. It is reasonable to assume North doesn't have four spades since he didn't make a Negative Double. If he does have four spades he has his reasons for not showing them. Pointwise, North doesn't show much. He can bid with five or six decent high card points. If you can make a support double, that is probably best. It is possible that North will choose to pass for penalty if he has decent points.

Both Vulnerable
You hold ♠ Q72   ♡ A86   ◇ 73   ♣ AQ842

WEST	NORTH	EAST	SOUTH
—	—	—	1♣
1♡	1♠	Pass	?

Raise to 2♠. This is the right bid regardless of how many spades North has. This sequence is special in that you know North has five of them, making the raise more comfortable for you. You know North has five spades because with just four he would make a Negative Double. This inference is available only when West overcalls 1♡ and North bids 1♠. (Some partnerships play that a Negative Double denies four spades. In this case, North's 1♠ bid only shows a four card suit. This is an unusual treatment but it is out there.)

Both Vulnerable
You hold ♠ AQ5   ♡ K83   ◇ 5   ♣ AKQJ43

WEST	NORTH	EAST	SOUTH
—	—	—	1♣
1◇	1♡	1♠	?

With Support Doubles, you can double first, showing three card heart support, and then show your extra values. If you can't do this, you have a tough rebid.

Both Vulnerable
You hold ♠ 9   ♡ Q1084   ◇ AJ3   ♣ AKQ64

WEST	NORTH	EAST	SOUTH
—	—	—	1♣
1♡	1♠	2♡	?

This is a hard hard problem. It is tempting to double for penalty. (This assumes you do not play Support Doubles.) There is a huge reason not to do that though. One of the least rewarding things you can do is to double the opponents in a fit sequence when you are in front of the original bidder. You have ♡ Q1084. It is possible that these will take no tricks. If you were sitting North with the Q1084 of trumps OVER the heart bidder, you would have two potential tricks. Really, doubling when you are in front of the bidder when they have a fit is a hard way to make a living. I would hope you could learn this lesson the easy way by reading about it here. It's less painful than learning it at the table. Going back to the hand, you have good values. I would rebid 3♣, which shows six clubs. I don't have them but I do have a super five card suit, extra values, and enough hearts that I know North is short. If North has two or three clubs, 3♣ will survive. NOTE that North can expect a six card suit. Five will be a surprize. That's why you need extra values along with the reasonable hope that North doesn't have a bunch of heart losers.

Using Support Doubles offers a subtle benefit. If you can't double 2♡ for penalty because of system, you will be spared from making some bad decisions.

Both Vulnerable
You hold ♠ KQ   ♡ J3   ◇ 74   ♣ KQJ7532

WEST	NORTH	EAST	SOUTH
—	—	—	1♣
1◇	1♡	2◇	?

You have the tricks to bid 3♣ but you don't have the values. If you bid 3♣, North will bid 3NT a lot of the time. Your hand is too thin to want to hear that. Probably better to pass. You can bid 3♣ later if the auction permits.

Both Vulnerable
You hold ♠ 843   ♡ QJ4   ◇ A6   ♣ AK953

WEST	NORTH	EAST	SOUTH
—	—	—	1♣
1◇	1♡	3◇*	?

* Preemptive

That 3◇ bid is annoying. If East had bid 2◇ only, you could have raised to 2♡ or made a Support Double. East bid 3◇, though, so you have to reconsider. NOTE that asterisk by 3◇. A popular method used today is to play that jump raises of an overcall are preemptive. If you have a good raise, you have to start with a cue bid and then raise. East's 3◇ bid shows something as weak as:

♠ K1076   ♡ 3   ◇ J1083   ♣ J1072

This is often effective, as it seems to be here. South doesn't like hearing 3◇ at all. Since Support Doubles don't apply at this level, you have to decide if the hand is good enough to bid 3♡. I would say yes. Be aware that North's 1♡ bid does not promise five cards. 3♡ might work poorly. Conversely, it might be necessary to get us to some good games. I can easily make up a few hands where we can make 4♡ and North has to pass it out in 3◇. If this is partner's hand:

♠ 1092   ♡ A10862   ◇ 93   ♣ Q62

there are ten tricks with a successful heart finesse. In fact, if the defense doesn't take its three spade tricks, North may end up with eleven tricks.

Both Vulnerable

WEST	NORTH	EAST	SOUTH
—	—	—	1♣
1♦	1♡	Double*	?

*Snapdragon showing spades and diamond tolerance

East's double is one more in a never ending parade of strange doubles. First there was the penalty double. Then the takeout double. Then came the Lightner Double, the Negative Double, the Responsive Double, the lead directing double, and about ten more etcs.

The Snapdragon Double is a semi–takeout double. The East hand is showing spades and some amount of diamond support. According to how the partnership defines the requirements, East can have either of these two hands.

1. ♠ A10764   ♡ 7542   ◇ K8   ♣ 74
2. ♠ KQ104   ♡ 64   ◇ K83   ♣ 10542

You will note that there is no hint of penalty in this double. East wants West to choose between the unbid spade suit and West's overcall suit, diamonds.

Both Vulnerable

WEST	NORTH	EAST	SOUTH
—	—	—	1♣
1♦	1♡	Double*	?

*Snapdragon showing spades and diamond tolerance

You hold ♠ A874   ♡ K73   ◇ Q8   ♣ A1075

If using Support Doubles and Redoubles, you should redouble to show three card heart support. When you have four spades, it is usually right to show them before showing three card support for partner but in this case it is right. East showed four or five spades with his double. No need to bid them ourselves.

You hold ♠ 10653 ♡ AKQ5 ◇ 4 ♣ A1098

When you have super trumps and working values, you can afford to overbid a little. Bid 3♡. 2♡, even using Support Redoubles, would not show this solid a hand. You have the three top trumps so you know partner will be worried about them. You have a stiff diamond. And you have the ace of clubs. The ♣ 1098 may be valuable too. Give partner the ♣ J43 and you are a favorite to take three club tricks.

You hold ♠ QJ74 ♡ Q873 ◇ K ♣ KQJ6

Two hearts is enough. You have four trumps, which partner knows about (Support Redoubles), but that is the last good thing you have. Your spade cards are soft, the king of diamonds is a big minus and your clubs, even as good as they are, will take time to establish if North doesn't have the ace.

On both of the last two hands, you ignored East's double. One of the difficulties with all these doubles is that you need to know which ones to pay attention to and which ones to ignore. Usually, they are ignorable.

OPENER'S LHO OVERCALLS PARTNER BIDS A SUIT AT THE TWO LEVEL

None Vulnerable

WEST	NORTH	EAST	SOUTH
—	—	—	1♦
1♠	2♡	Pass	?

Before looking at any of the hands in this section, ask yourself how long 2♡ is forcing for. This question is addressed most strongly at Two Over One players.

The answer is that it is forcing for now but does not promise a rebid. If opener makes a minimum rebid, it may end the auction. (Refer to Chapter Two.)

Both Vulnerable
You hold ♠ J863 ♡ AQ3 ♦ AK84 ♣ 32

WEST	NORTH	EAST	SOUTH
—	—	—	1♦
2♣	2♡	Pass	?

South should bid 4♡. Even in Two Over One bidding, 2♡ does not promise game values. If South rebids 2NT, 3♦, or 3♡, North can pass. In these situations, South has to bid the full value of his hand. Nice slow inferential forcing sequences no longer exist.

You hold ♠ AQ7 ♡ 4 ♦ AKQ1042 ♣ 954

Because 3♦ wouldn't be forcing, you have to find a stronger bid. One possible bid is 2♠. You should be able to survive this small lie because North seems to have denied spades with his 2♡ bid. But it could lead to trouble. The other possible bid is 3♣. It is a cue bid without immediate direction. All North knows now is that you have a good hand. He will try to bid 3NT but he might be tempted into bidding a good six card heart suit again. If he does, you can continue the torment by bidding 3♠. Partner will surely bid notrump now if he has a club stopper.

This aspect of Two Over One in competition isn't very nice. I included this hand to show you this method at its not very best, and to show you how you might wriggle out of it.

None Vulnerable
You hold ♠ KQJ4 ♡ J ◇ AQ3 ♣ KJ763

WEST	NORTH	EAST	SOUTH
—	—	—	1♣
1◇	2♡	Pass	?

This hand is a test. If 2♡ is weak showing three to five points, you should pass. Weak jump shifts preempt the opponents, but they also serve to warn opener to be quiet on hands like this. Pass. Responder's hand is something like:

♠ 83   ♡ Q98643   ◇ 542   ♣ Q4

It might be a touch less. Your seventeen high card points may keep you from being doubled. It is unlikely that they will be enough to make 2♡. North would happily trade both of your black jacks and the queen of diamonds for one more little trump.

Both Vulnerable
You hold ♠ AQ107 ♡ K43 ◇ 5 ♣ KJ964

WEST	NORTH	EAST	SOUTH
—	—	—	1♣
1♠	2◇	2♠	?

Double. A few hands back I suggested you shouldn't double the opponents when they have a fit and you are in front of the bidder. In this case, it is closer to being an acceptable double because partner showed you two over one strength. That, plus the misfit, suggests defending. North may have ten points, but that is still only a minimum. He may have more. If you double and North passes, you should beat 2♠ a few. North doesn't have to pass. He is allowed to bid.

One other observation here. When partner bids his suit at the two level, it is impossible for you to use Support Doubles. These only apply if you double below two of his suit and that can't happen under these circumstances.

Both Vulnerable
You hold ♠ QJ73 ♡ 65 ◇ AKQ3 ♣ 953

WEST	NORTH	EAST	SOUTH
—	—	—	1◇
2♣	2♡	Pass	?

Bid 2♠. You have been forced to the two level. 2♠ shows the same values you would have for the 1♠ rebid on this uncontested sequence:

WEST	NORTH	EAST	SOUTH
—	—	—	1◇
Pass	1♡	Pass	?

Both Vulnerable
You hold ♠ AQ763 ♡ Q ◇ KQ8 ♣ 9832

WEST	NORTH	EAST	SOUTH
—	—	—	1♠
2◇	2♡	Pass	?

Bid 2NT. This sequence is not a normal two over one auction. If West had passed and North had responded 2♡, you would rebid 2♠. Rebidding 2NT with a stiff in partner's suit should be avoided. After West's 2◇ overcall, though, North does not promise a rebid if you bid 2♠. Better to bid 2NT than to risk bidding 2♠ and playing it there. All in all, it is a close decision. It is important to know when a sequence can stop and to cater to it.

OPENER'S LHO OVERCALLS PARTNER BIDS A SUIT AT THE THREE LEVEL

When partner bids a new suit at the three level after an overcall, he needs a good hand. Responder can't come in with those ten point hands that he was able to bid with at the two level. Since you have lost bidding room, it is necessary to wait for good hands to bid new suits at the three level. Opener can rebid with less pressure because he knows responder has enough for game. Usually, a new suit at the three level will lead to a game contract. Only if responder repeats a minor suit at the four level is the bidding allowed to stop short of game.

Both Vulnerable
You hold ♠ AQ4   ♡ KQ7642   ◇ 86   ♣ AJ

WEST	NORTH	EAST	SOUTH
—	—	—	1♡
2◇	3♣	Pass	?

Bid 3♡. You don't have to worry that North will pass 3♡. 3♣ was forcing to game (or to 4♣ if you wish). This agreement must be in place or South will have an impossible decision. If 3♡ isn't forcing now, South would have to bid 4♡ on a crummy suit, raise clubs with a doubleton, or manufacture a 3◇ or 3♠ bid. I know that funny cue bids have their places, but they should be last gasp choices. If there is a good natural bid available, it is better.

Other that knowing that new suits at the three level are forcing, there isn't that much to discuss here. The situation is rare fortunately. The greatest difficulty you will have at the three level is that North may not be able to restrain himself from bidding on too weak a hand.

Not Vulnerable vs. Vulnerable
You hold ♠ KQ762 ♡ J1084 ◇ Q7 ♣ KQ

WEST	NORTH	EAST	SOUTH
—	—	—	1♠
2♡	3◇	3♡	?

With junk and with wonderful vulnerability, you can double for penalty. Even if you don't take a trump trick, your side has so many points that they won't have many tricks outside of the trump suit. Again, remember that North can and will pull this double on some hands.

Not Vulnerable vs. Vulnerable
You hold ♠ AQJ32 ♡ 84 ◇ 72 ♣ KQ42

WEST	NORTH	EAST	SOUTH
—	—	—	1♠
2♡	3◇	Double*	?

*Penalty

Highly unusual. East probably has a poor hand with a lot of diamonds. They may have you. They may not. But it is not your decision to make. Pass doesn't say you like diamonds. In fact, if you had much reason to want to play in diamonds, you might redouble. No. Pass is a noncommittal bid. Here's hoping North has good diamonds or that he has spade support to show you.

Not Vulnerable vs. Vulnerable
You hold ♠ K10763 ♡ KJ653 ◇ None ♣ A43

WEST	NORTH	EAST	SOUTH
—	—	—	1♠
2♡	3◇	Pass	?

I'm open to suggestions. You started with a nice hand that had all kinds of potential. It was terrible for you when West bid 2♡, but North's 3◇ bid was even worse news. I have seen hands like these in various solvers' clubs. The panel of experts all agree that 3◇ is forcing and they all agree that they would rather be in Philadelphia.

I offer no real suggestion. It might be right to pass a forcing bid. But since that isn't good for the partnership, I would bid 3NT. We might survive. I can give you one good piece of advice. When you bid 3NT, don't roll your eyes or otherwise show how unhappy you are. You haven't been doubled yet. Why tell the opponents that you are ripe for whacking?

OPENER'S LHO OVERCALLS PARTNER MAKES A NEGATIVE DOUBLE

By now, the large majority of serious bridge players use Negative Doubles in one form or another. I am assuming that you use them. In the following examples, Negative Doubles will be used through a 3♠ overcall. There are a few questions of judgment which will be addressed and there is a new extension of the Negative Double that you may not be familiar with. In principle, it works this way. You open the bidding, LHO overcalls, your partner makes a Negative Double, and RHO raises LHO's overcall. In this bidding situation, a double by opener is what is referred to as an 'Action Double'. What this means is that opener has a good enough hand to bid with but doesn't have a clear suit to bid. Responder is asked to bid something knowing that opener "kinda sorta" has support of sorts for the suits that responder showed by the Negative Double. I won't leave you with this definition. There will be examples shortly.

Not Vulnerable vs. Vulnerable

WEST	NORTH	EAST	SOUTH
—	—	—	1♣
1♦	Double*		

* Negative Double

A quick quiz. What is the fewest number of points North can have? What is the most points North can have? How many hearts does North have? How many spades does North have? Answers. North can make a Negative Double at the one level with six high card points. There is no upper limit to North's high card points. Presumably, North has four hearts and four spades. It is possible he has 5–4 distribution although that would be rare.

Not Vulnerable vs. Vulnerable
You hold ♠ 83   ♡ Q984   ♢ KQ4   ♣ AJ104

WEST	NORTH	EAST	SOUTH
—	—	—	1♣
1♦	Double*	1♠	?

* Negative Double

Assuming you opened this hand, you should DEFINITELY bid 2♡. North's double is the equivalent of bidding hearts. If you heard partner bid 1♡ instead of double, wouldn't you raise him? This is the same thing. You must let partner in on the fit. I can not imagine a hand worth opening that wouldn't show a four card heart suit.

Not Vulnerable vs. Vulnerable
You hold ♠ A1073   ♡ Q83   ♢ 8   ♣ AKQ83

WEST	NORTH	EAST	SOUTH
—	—	—	1♣
1♦	Double*	1♡	?

* Negative Double

Bid 2♠. The jump to 2♠ shows the approximate equivalent of a hand that would have raised a 1♠ response to 3♠. If opener bids only 1♠ here, North won't know that South has this hand and not a twelve point minimum which would also bid 1♠.

Not Vulnerable vs. Vulnerable
You hold ♠ AJ83 ♡ K73 ♢ 73 ♣ A1094

WEST	NORTH	EAST	SOUTH
—	—	—	1♣
1♢	Double*	1♠	?

* Negative Double

If North has his four spades and you have these pretty good spades too, it is just possible that there is a rat in your auction named EAST. You may not see this situation for a few thousand hands, but if it should occur, you need a way to flush that rat out.

I suggest this. Play that a double shows four spades with 12–15 points. If you have a 16–18 point hand that would have jumped in spades, you bid 2♠. This is a cue bid but on this auction, it is a natural bid showing four spades and a good hand. It is likely that East has diamond support and is intending to get out if doubled. What you need is a way to show that you have spades and also how many points you have.

If by some chance, you have a hand worth bidding 4♠, you double first, showing 12–15 points. On the next round, you will bid strongly which tells partner you have the 19–20 point hand. This works pretty well. Its main objection is lack of frequency. Still, if it happens, it would be nice to be prepared.

Not Vulnerable vs. Vulnerable
You hold ♠ A6　♡ 7　◇ AQ10654　♣ AQ94

WEST	NORTH	EAST	SOUTH
—	—	—	1◇
1♠	Double*	Pass	?

* Negative Double

North promises hearts but does not guarantee clubs. What should South do? 2◇ and 2♣ are both weak bids given this hand. After all, if North has ♣ KJ873 and nothing else, 6♣ will have some sort of play. The right bid is 3♣, highly encouraging, but not forcing. 3♣ is a funny bid. On no other auction can opener jump raise clubs to the three level. Opener has to be cautious about this bid because North doesn't have to have clubs. As long as opener is aware that no fit is promised, using 3♣ as invitational is an adequate way to rebid.

Not Vulnerable vs. Vulnerable

WEST	NORTH	EAST	SOUTH
—	—	—	1♣
1♡	Double*	Pass	?

* Negative Double

You hold ♠ AQ72　♡ 73　◇ K2　♣ AK852

The good spades and nice shape suggest bidding 4♠. You might make a case for bidding 3♠ but I don't know what that would mean. I have never heard that sequence.

You hold ♠ AQ82　♡ 3　◇ AQ5　♣ AKJ63

Bid 3♡! This can only be a splinter in support of spades. This is the only suit North has 'bid' so it is the only suit that South can splinter in support of. This shows enough to bid 4♠, a singleton heart, four spades, and enough left over that South is still interested in a slam if North has some extras.

Not Vulnerable vs. Vulnerable

WEST	NORTH	EAST	SOUTH
—	—	—	1♠
2◇	Double*		

* Negative Double

A quick quiz. What is the fewest number of points North can have? What is the largest number of points North can have? How many hearts does North have? How many clubs does North have? How many spades can North have?

Answers. Since North is at the two level, he ought to have seven or eight high card points along with proper shape. Basically, North needs a point and a half more than he needed for a one level Negative Double. There is no upper limit to North's high card points. North has four hearts and may have five. North's double says nothing about clubs. He may have them, he may not.

North usually denies spade support, but it is possible he has a limit spade raise. NOTE that if South opens with 1♡, it is unlikely that North will make a Negative Double with a limit heart raise.

Not Vulnerable vs. Vulnerable

WEST	NORTH	EAST	SOUTH
—	—	—	1♠
2◇	Double*	Pass	2♠
Pass	3♣		

* Negative Double

What does North have? His original double showed four hearts so that message is not compromised. North ought to have four hearts and enough clubs that he wants to play in clubs and not spades. 3♣ isn't forcing. Negative Doubles do not create forcing auctions unless responder follows with a cue bid. On the auction here, North should have something like:

♠ 3 ♡ AJ63 ◇ 83 ♣ KJ10763

If North had a worse hand or a worse club suit, he should pass 2♠. It is not a good idea to 'save' partner when you have to increase the level to do it.

Not Vulnerable vs. Vulnerable
You hold ♠ 653 ♡ 6 ◇ KQ1085 ♣ AK54

WEST	NORTH	EAST	SOUTH
—	—	—	1◇
1♠	Double*	Pass	2♣
Pass	2♡	Pass	?

* Negative Double

Pass. Leave bad enough alone. What does North have over there? You aren't too sure what he does have but you know some of the things he doesn't have. He doesn't have enough to bid 2♡ the first time. He doesn't have whatever it takes to bid 3♡ assuming you play this as a Weak Jump Shift in Competition. North rates to have a good five card suit with less than ten points or he may have a six card suit that wasn't good enough to jump to 3♡. Whatever he has, we aren't interested. 2♡ is not forcing.

Not Vulnerable vs. Vulnerable
You hold ♠ Q763 ♡ AQ83 ◇ AQ7 ♣ 94

WEST	NORTH	EAST	SOUTH
—	—	—	1◇
1♠	Double*	Pass	2♡
Pass	2♠	Pass	?

* Negative Double

Bid 4♡. When North doubles, he shows four or more hearts but his strength is unknown. The 2♠ cue bid says that he is interested in a heart slam opposite the 12–15 points shown by South's 2♡ rebid. NOTE that North indicates only four hearts at this point in the auction.

308

Remember this rule. South has good quality points for his bidding so far but he has poor shape for a slam. 4♡ says he has a good hand without slam interest. North may do what he likes with this information.

RULE: The Negative Double is intended to make it easy to bid awkward shaped hands. If you have the strength and the shape to make a natural bid, you should make the natural bid.

North obviously has a good enough hand to have bid 2♡ instead of doubling. The reason he didn't bid 2♡ is that he must not have a five card suit. His hand will be in this family:

♠ A8   ♡ KJ104   ◇ KJ83   ♣ KJ8

North should not have less than this. NOTE that this hand has a full sixteen high card points. This is enough to force to game but the shape was wrong for a natural bid over 1♠.

THE RETURN NEGATIVE DOUBLE

Not Vulnerable vs. Vulnerable
You hold ♠ 63   ♡ AJ4   ◇ AQ874   ♣ K108

WEST	NORTH	EAST	SOUTH
—	—	—	1◇
1♠	Double*	2♠	?

* Negative Double

South has a nice hand. It has only fourteen points, but it has a semi–fit for hearts and clubs plus it has a good diamond suit. Values like these would like to bid if a bid was available. I have referred to some funny doubles that you may wish to use. This is one such. If you take the view that there are almost no opportunities for opener to double 2♠ for penalty, you can accept that a double here can be a sort of Return Negative Double. Partner made a Negative Double asking you to bid a suit. Your Return Double says that you have a good hand for partner but that you aren't able to choose a suit. Your double asks him to select one. North will choose from clubs, diamonds, and hearts. It is possible that he will pass for penalty although that would be most unexpected.

Very Important Note !!!

Compare these two auctions carefully. What do South's doubles mean?

Not Vulnerable vs. Vulnerable

WEST	NORTH	EAST	SOUTH
—	—	—	1◇
1♡	1♠	2♡	Double

WEST	NORTH	EAST	SOUTH
—	—	—	1◇
1♡	Double*	2♡	Double

* Negative Double

THE FIRST SEQUENCE—North bid 1♠ over West's overcall and East raised. THE SECOND SEQUENCE—North made a Negative Double and East raised.

On the first sequence, South's double is a Support Double if you play them and it is a PENALTY double otherwise. On the second sequence, South's double is a Return Negative Double asking North to bid something in light of the fact that South didn't know what to bid himself.

Why is the double on the first sequence for penalty and for takeout on the second? The reason is that on the first sequence, the playable suits for North–South are known.

South can raise spades or rebid diamonds if he wishes. There is no need for a takeout double. On the second sequence, there are three possible trump suits. South wants to find the best one. Using double to show some sort of good, but awkward, hand makes more sense than to use it for penalty.

Not Vulnerable vs. Vulnerable
You hold ♠ 63   ♡ AJ4   ◇ AQ874   ♣ K108

WEST	NORTH	EAST	SOUTH
—	—	—	1◇
1♠	Double*	2♠	?

* Negative Double

This is the hand discussed a moment ago. It needs a way to show itself. If left to its own devices, there is no way to proceed. How can South bid so as to get to the best contract opposite each of these possible North hands?

1. ♠ K72	♡ K9852	◇ 93	♣ Q73
2. ♠ 954	♡ Q1062	◇ K102	♣ A52
3. ♠ 982	♡ K762	◇ 3	♣ A9743
4. ♠ 982	♡ K1052	◇ 63	♣ AJ74

Hand One would like to be in 3♡ opposite South's hand. Hand Two should compete to 3◇. Hand Three should compete to 3♣. Hand Four is the hand South is not looking for.

Using the Return Double, North will bid 3♡, 3◇, 3♣, and, I guess, 3♣ on these hands. For the first three hands, the final contract is fine. On the last hand it is so—so. But that is unlucky. North is allowed to have a five card club or heart suit or three cards in diamonds.

There is a funny 2NT bid available to opener also. This is more esoteric yet and I am going to wait on this. I'll give the funny 2NT bids all at once at the end of this section.

Not Vulnerable vs. Vulnerable

WEST	NORTH	EAST	SOUTH
—	—	—	1 ◇
1 ♠	Double*	2 ♠	Pass
Pass	Double	Pass	?

* Negative Double

This is the same sequence yet again, except that it went for another round. What does North have for his second double? Is this double for penalty? Or is it takeout?

The answer is that North has a Negative Double hand but it is more than a minimum and he still wishes to compete in spite of your silence. His typical hand is ten balanced points or so with two or three spades. If he had a singleton spade, he would bid something rather than double. This double is mainly takeout but if South wishes to pass, he may. He knows North has a balanced hand with pretty good values. South has to have some trumps for pass to be right. Here are some possible North hands for this sequence.

1.	♠ 93	♡ AQ76	◇ Q6	♣ K10432
2.	♠ K82	♡ KJ72	◇ 62	♣ QJ62
3.	♠ 72	♡ K654	◇ KJ3	♣ K1063

The first two hands are clear doubles. The third hand is unclear. Double is right on values, but those three diamonds are a little much to have in opener's suit. 3 ◇ might be a better bid.

Not Vulnerable vs. Vulnerable
You hold ♠ 8653 ♡ AJ3 ◇ KJ653 ♣ A

WEST	NORTH	EAST	SOUTH
—	—	—	1 ◇
1 ♡	Double*	2 ♡	?

* Negative Double

Just bid 2♠. Never get involved with science if there is a natural bid available. You've heard that advice a few times already. If you read the rest of this book, you will read that same advice a few more times. Conventions are useful. But they are intended to handle situations where you can not otherwise make the best decision.

Not Vulnerable vs. Vulnerable
You hold ♠ A105 ♡ 53 ◇ AQ8 ♣ KQ652

WEST	NORTH	EAST	SOUTH
—	—	—	1♣
1♡	Double*	3♡	?

* Negative Double

You might have opened this hand with 1NT. Having not done so, you have to decide if this hand is worth a Return Double. But before making that decision, you have to decide how high to play Return Doubles. I think it is reasonable to play them through your Negative Double range. It makes for easy remembering. If you play Negative Doubles through 3♠, you can make a Return Double here. In fact, I would not do so. Here's why. We are at the four level, for starters. Also, North has only four spades. There is no chance that he has five. This means there are only two suits for partner to choose from. With only two suits to pick from and because we are at the four level and because this hand has good defensive values, I would pass and expect to get a plus score.

Not Vulnerable vs. Vulnerable
You hold ♠ AKQ53 ♡ 73 ◇ K3 ♣ J1093

WEST	NORTH	EAST	SOUTH
—	—	—	1♠
2♡	Double*	3♡	?

* Negative Double

Pass. All kinds of reasons. The first reason is that your hand isn't good enough to bid with. You are at the four level if you want to bid clubs. If you feel like bidding 3♠, you'd better be ready to play in a 5–1 or 5–2 fit. Even though North's double promises nine high card points (remember, he is forcing you to the three level), it isn't enough to make up for lack of spade support.

Another less evident reason for not bidding clubs is that North may not have club support. He may have a ten point hand that doubled to keep the bidding open, with the intention of bidding diamonds if you bid clubs. This is a common 'solution' for in–between hands that have length in the higher unbid suit but not the strength to bid the suit. This is a possible North hand:

♠ 82   ♡ J53   ◇ AQJ107   ♣ Q63

North might compromise with a Negative Double over 2♡. NOTE that North does not raise to 2♠ with this hand. Raising a major with a doubleton is asking for trouble. The bidding has a way of continuing and opener rebids his suit expecting real support. Don't raise a suit with a doubleton until it has been rebid. Here is one more example of a hand that makes a Negative Double without correct shape.

What should your partner, South, do with this hand? South holds ♠ A82   ♡ KQ943   ◇ 74   ♣ 963

WEST	NORTH	EAST	SOUTH
—	1♣	1♠	?

Your partner would double. He has no diamond support but still, the hand is too good to pass. This hand can run to hearts if partner bids diamonds so there is no way the bidding can go totally sour.

Not Vulnerable vs. Vulnerable
You hold ♠ QJ763   ♡ Q8   ◇ KJ4   ♣ AJ4

WEST	NORTH	EAST	SOUTH
—	—	—	1♠
2♡	Double*	3♡	Pass
Pass	3♠	Pass	?

* Negative Double

Pass. North shows a limit raise in spades with three trumps. Your queen of hearts is not worth much so in effect you have a minimum twelve point hand with a doubleton.

Not Vulnerable vs. Vulnerable

WEST	NORTH	EAST	SOUTH
—	—	—	1◇
1♠	Double*	Redouble	?

* Negative Double

You should ask what that redouble means. It probably won't affect what you bid but it is better to be informed. It might be something really unusual. There are three common treatments for the redouble. One treatment is for the redouble to show an honor in West's overcall suit. It doesn't promise much in the way of high cards. The second treatment is to play that redouble shows a genuine full–valued raise with a spade honor. The third treatment is to play that the redouble denies support but shows at least ten points. The idea behind this last treatment is that the overcaller may want to double if the opponents bid something he can handle.

From your point of view, most of these redoubles can be ignored. Your bids will be the same as always. One important item is that you do not let yourself be cowed by the redouble. It is relatively nonthreatening. Don't let it intimidate you. If you get involved in a game invite auction, believe your partner. Don't believe the opponents.

LHO OVERCALLS
YOUR MAJOR SUIT OPENING
PARTNER RAISES

Good news. North has a fit. This means that the rest of the auction will be spent deciding how high to go. Finding a fit is good because you save all that bidding space normally spent looking for the proper fit. Since your side is bidding a major suit, you won't have to clutter up your auction with side issues such as playing in notrump. You may of course do so, but notrump will be a rarity.

Not Vulnerable vs. Vulnerable

WEST	NORTH	EAST	SOUTH
—	—	—	1♡
1♠	2♡	Pass	?

* Negative Double

When East doesn't bid, you are no longer obliged to play 3♡ as competitive. You can use it as invitational. Some partnerships like to play that 3♡ is competitive any time the opponents bid so for some a 3♡ bid here could be defined as competitive or preemptive. In the majors, there isn't a lot of reason to do this. It makes sense to play that 3♡ is a normal invitational bid asking for general maximum values. If you normally play that 2NT is some kind of a game try, there is no reason for you not to continue as you always do. The point here is that you know what opener's 3♡ bid means when East hasn't bid anything.

Not Vulnerable vs. Vulnerable
You hold ♠ 8   ♡ KJ763   ◇ KJ4   ♣ A1095

WEST	NORTH	EAST	SOUTH
—	—	—	1♡
1♠	2♡	Pass	?

Questions

1. How many spades do you think East–West can make?
2. Would you bid 3♡ if you played it as preemptive?

Answer to QUESTION ONE. You don't know how many spades they can make. The fact that East passed is a strong hint that East–West can't make many spades. If East had spade support, he would have raised them. If East had values without spade support, he might have made a Responsive Double. The fact that East passed usually means he is broke OR that he has a lot of hearts.

Too many players, holding the South hand, automatically take the view that West can make lots of spades and they bid frantically on that assumption. This is terrible judgment. Here are a few hands that North can have for his 2♡ bid.

1. ♠ AQ954   ♡ 1094   ◇ Q96   ♣ 84
2. ♠ KJ972   ♡ A82   ◇ 10   ♣ J652
3. ♠ Q1073   ♡ Q104   ◇ A1073   ♣ 42

Do you agree that these are all raises to 2♡? I have no trouble with raising on all of these hands. The heart support is adequate, and the high cards are decent. Passing with these hands is poor technique. It is true that you may get to double 1♠ on the first two hands, but there is the possibility that East–West will get together in one of the minor suits. An excellent rule to follow is that you should not be distracted when you have a normal raise of partner's major suit. Go back and look at these three hands for a second. If North has one of these hands, how do you think East–West will do if they bid spades again? The first and second hands will eat West alive in a spade contract and the third hand will do damage to West if he bids spades again. Offhand, 2♠ rates to go down two tricks if North has the third hand.

Answer to QUESTION TWO. The discussion above suggests that South doesn't have to worry about spades. If the opponents bid a suit and nothing happens, it is usually one of the other suits that is dangerous. Go back to the second hand above. The opponents can't make anything in spades, but they can make a couple of diamonds. There is no reason to bid 3♡. If you pass 2♡ and West also passes, you are spared having to play at the three level. If West bids 2♠, you can get an opinion from North about bidding 3♡. North may double 2♠, which you should pass, and he may bid 3♡ which also suits you. If North passes, you can infer that he doesn't have a spade stack in which case you can bid 3♡ yourself. Certainly you don't want to bid 3♡ immediately and be greeted with any of the three hands above.

None Vulnerable
You hold ♠ KJ104   ♡ AQ7642   ◊ K8   ♣ 9

WEST	NORTH	EAST	SOUTH
—	—	—	1♡
2♣	2♡	Pass	?

6–4 hands that have found a fit revalue more than most hands. South has good values in all suits and very few immediate losers. Go directly to 4♡. Do not invite with only 3♡. If you bid 3♡ meaning it to be preemptive or if you passed, go back to GO and wait.

None Vulnerable
You hold ♠ 873   ♡ AQ873   ◊ AQ73   ♣ 8

WEST	NORTH	EAST	SOUTH
—	—	—	1♡
2♣	2♡	2♠	?

With good shape and no apparently wasted values, it is okay to compete to 3♡. There is always the danger that North will put down three spades and the ♣ KQ109. That is the down side. Remember though that the price of silence is not cheap. An easy way to lose matchpoints or IMPS or money is to sell out to low level partscores. If you consistently pass 2♠, you will suffer.

None Vulnerable
You hold ♠ Q83   ♡ AQ873   ◇ AK10   ♣ 83

WEST	NORTH	EAST	SOUTH
—	—	—	1♡
2♣	2♡	2♠	?

This is a better hand in high cards but it is also balanced. You should pass 2♠. Not only do you have more losers, you also have one or two more defensive tricks. There is a good chance 2♠ won't make. NOTE one item which runs throughout these decisions. You don't know if partner has three trumps or four. If he has three, your judgment plus the Law of Total Tricks both suggest you pass. If partner has four trumps, getting to the three level will be more reasonable. When you have modest balanced hands, you should let partner look at his trumps. He will count them more accurately than you can. If he has four trumps, he will stretch to compete. If he has three trumps, he can compete if he wishes, but you won't be unhappy if he passes. Many, many bad decisions have occurred because someone bid to the three level with only eight trumps. That extra trump is the crucial value that makes three level decisions work or fail. It gives you additional playing strength and it diminishes your partnership defensive strength.

None Vulnerable
You hold ♠ J743   ♡ K107632   ◇ AK   ♣ J

WEST	NORTH	EAST	SOUTH
—	—	—	1♡
2♣	2♡	3♣	?

Bid 3♡. This 6–4 won't reach to game but it certainly should compete. North may not bid again except to double if the go on to 4♣.

None Vulnerable
You hold ♠ K1085   ♡ AKQJ5   ◇ 83   ♣ A10

WEST	NORTH	EAST	SOUTH
—	—	—	1♡
2♣	2♡	3♣	?

To make a game try, you have to bid 3◇. In competition, 3♡ is competitive so you can't bid that. The only bid left is 3◇. When you have only one bid to use for your game try, you can't specify what you need. North will not assume you have anything in diamonds. He will look at his entire hand and will try to make a good decision.

None Vulnerable
You hold ♠ A10643   ♡ AKQ   ◇ K106   ♣ 73

WEST	NORTH	EAST	SOUTH
—	—	—	1♠
2♣	2♠	3♣	?

Bid 3◇. This time you have room for two game tries. You would appreciate diamond help and can make your game try where you need help.

You hold ♠ KJ2   ♡ QJ1073   ◇ 3   ♣ AKJ9

WEST	NORTH	EAST	SOUTH
—	—	—	1♡
2◇	2♡	3◇	?

The right bid depends on your understandings. If you play MAXIMAL DOUBLES, you can double, which is your game try. Remember that Maximal Doubles need discussion. Do you play them whenever there is no bidding room or do you play them only when there is no bidding room PLUS the opponents have a fit?

None Vulnerable

WEST	NORTH	EAST	SOUTH
—	—	—	1♡
2♣	2♡	Double*	?

* Responsive Double

East's Responsive Double shows about eight points with 5–5 in the unbid suits. I refuse to guarantee this description, though, because everyone has their own ideas about Responsive Doubles. In any event, you need to know how to handle it. I will start with the observation that this double should be treated as being competition so if you bid 3♡, it should be competitive. The opponents have three suits they can compete in which gives them a pretty good chance of finding a fit.

None Vulnerable
You hold ♠ AK54　♡ A9863　◇ AJ8　♣ 6

WEST	NORTH	EAST	SOUTH
—	—	—	1♡
2♣	2♡	Double*	?

* Responsive Double

As far as the meanings of your bids go, 3♡ would be preemptive and everything else is a game try. Their double gives you one extra bid which you can use. You can redouble. Redouble shows a good hand with defense. You may end up in game but you may also be able to double the opponents if they have misjudged. On this hand, you

321

would be willing to double 2♠ or 3♦. If West rebids 3♣, though, you can't be sure about doubling it. If you redouble, North will know that you have a good hand and he will double 3♣ when he can. In fact, North should be aggressive in his doubles because he knows South will contribute more than normal defensive values.

LHO OVERCALLS OPENER'S MINOR PARTNER RAISES

You aren't going to look for very many five of a minor games so most of your bidding will be in terms of bidding 3NT, competing, or doubling them if possible.

None Vulnerable
You hold ♠ KQ63   ♡ 53   ◇ A7   ♣ QJ853

WEST	NORTH	EAST	SOUTH
—	—	—	1♣
1♠	2♣	Pass	?

Bid 3♣. You know East–West have a heart fit. West has hearts too, but didn't have the shape to make a takeout double or a Michaels Cue Bid. The odds are enormous that West will bid again if you pass. In the major suits, opener's reraise to the three level is invitational if East hasn't bid. In the minor suits, opener's reraise to the three level is preemptive no matter how the bidding has gone.

You hold ♠ A107   ♡ KQJ6   ◇ K32   ♣ J73

Pass. Any bid by opener other than 3♣ is forward going. 2NT shows 18–19 points and 2♡ shows some kind of good hand looking for a game somewhere. There is no such thing as running from a raise.

You hold ♠ 73 ♡ A7 ◇ AJ5 ♣ AQ10832

Make a game try. Almost anything except 2NT will do. I would try 2♠, which will tentatively be interpreted as looking for a spade stopper. These fifteen points have so many potential tricks that game may come home opposite some very weak hands. The fifth and sixth clubs are strong cards now that clubs have been raised.

None Vulnerable
You hold ♠ A7 ♡ 932 ◇ AJ ♣ AQ10875

WEST	NORTH	EAST	SOUTH
—	—	—	1♣
1♠	2♣	Pass	?

You have a spade stopper so you don't need to look for one. Try 3NT. There may be nine tricks if they don't run hearts immediately. Your three little hearts don't look like a stopper, but the fact that you have three of them hints they won't be able to run off a long heart suit.

You hold ♠ Q82 ♡ KQJ7 ◇ AQ8 ♣ KJ3

This is your normal 2NT rebid showing 18–19 balanced points. With some of your 18–19 point hands you can jump to 3NT on the basis of having a source of tricks. This hand has no obvious source of tricks so you will need some high cards to get through. North can pass 2NT, can raise to 3NT, and can go back to 3♣ with a real stinker.

You hold ♠94 ♡ AKJ4 ◇ 94 ♣ AKQJ2

Bid 2♡. This is a game try and is forcing. You will raise 2NT to game and should probably pass if North bids 3♣.

You hold ♠4 ♡ AKJ2 ◇ A9 ♣ AJ9742

Bid 3♠, a splinter bid. This may get you to a slam if North properly evaluates his cards. If 3NT is best, you will get there. Splinters are game forces so you can go slow after your splinter.

None Vulnerable

WEST	NORTH	EAST	SOUTH
—	—	—	1♣
1♠	2♣	2♡	?

When you and North are bidding and raising a minor suit, it brings out the animal in your opponents. Auctions like this one are common with everyone trying to steal something. 3♣ is competitive as always. One question which requires an agreement is the meaning of a cue bid. There are two suits for you to cue–bid. Do you cue–bid the one you have a stopper in or do you cue–bid the one you need a stopper in? NOTE that you can't worry about diamonds if you are aiming for 3NT. You have too many things to worry about without picking on an unbid suit.

None Vulnerable
You hold ♠ K2   ♡ A8   ◊ J72   ♣ KJ9653

WEST	NORTH	EAST	SOUTH
—	—	—	1♣
1♠	2♣	2♡	?

Instead of bidding 3♣, which won't silence anyone, why not bid 3NT? You won't make it but if you don't get doubled, –50 or –100 will be a fine result. You might bid 2NT instead, representing 18–19 points. That could work too. But it leaves West room to bid again at the three level. 3NT is the bid that puts the maximum pressure on the opponents. If West continues with 4♡ and North doubles, you will have it tossed back in your lap. This decision wouldn't please me. I would guess to bid 5♣.

None Vulnerable
You hold ♠ 73 ♡ 974 ◊ AQJ7 ♣ KQ96

WEST	NORTH	EAST	SOUTH
—	—	—	1◊
1♡	2◊	2♡	?

Bid 3◊. This is more preemptive than it looks. West doesn't have a convenient game try and may have to guess. He may have to use a Maximal Double, which is not the most accurate bid in the world. (Yes, the Maximal Double can be used by the overcalling side as well as the opening side.)

None Vulnerable
You hold ♠ Q10 ♡ 92 ◊ AK873 ♣ AKQ4

WEST	NORTH	EAST	SOUTH
—	—	—	1◊
1♡	2◊	3♡*	?

* Preemptive

East's 3♡ bid is preemptive showing very little outside of four card support and a little shape. Not all of your opponents use this convention but if they do, they will alert it. You will be warned. This is a good convention to use. Don't rush to use it though until you are know how to handle the consequences of it. If you use preemptive jump raises, you will have trouble on hands with normal jump raise strength.

Anyway, back to the issue here. You have a good hand. Passing 3♡ is silly. What to bid is not obvious though. 4◊ doesn't get anything done. It will end the auction. 4♣ is possible, but it has the drawback of getting you beyond 3NT. I wouldn't want to double without a heart trick. Which leaves us nowhere. The remaining bid is 3♠. This is a good bid. It is good because it keeps all your options open. If North has a heart stopper, he will bid

3NT. He may return to 4♢. He may jump to 5♢. He won't raise to 4♠ unless he is prepared to play in 5♢ so you don't have to worry about his hanging you.

North should be aware of the lack of room left you by that 3♡ bid. He must cater to the possibility that you have been squished in the auction. This theme comes up in various situations. It is similar to an auction discussed earlier. Here it is again.

None Vulnerable

WEST	NORTH	EAST	SOUTH
—	—	—	1♠
2♢	2♠	3♢	?

The only game try bid South has is 3♡. It is artificial saying only that South is interested in game and not heart values specifically.

None Vulnerable
You hold ♠ J8 ♡ AKJ2 ♢ KJ3 ♣ KQJ4

WEST	NORTH	EAST	SOUTH
—	—	—	1♣
1♠	2♣	3♠*	?

* Preemptive

Some unprintable words come to mind. I don't think we can make a game unless we have 3NT but it still feels like it is our hand. Even if 3NT is cold, there is no way to bid it. I would double 3♠ and hope for 300. You should be aware of just how weak a hand some players will have for this jump raise. East may have something like:

1.	♠ 10765	♡ Q74	♢ 107652	♣ 9
2.	♠ A1073	♡ 743	♢ 9864	♣ 103
3.	♠ Q9762	♡ 9763	♢ 74	♣ 98
4.	♠ K7542	♡ 63	♢ Q1097	♣ 95

The first three hands are all candidates for this jump. The fourth hand is actually on the maximum side of a preemptive jump. You can see that with the exception of the first hand, 3♠ doubled should go down one or two tricks. NOTE that these examples are MY idea of preemptive jump raises. Some players may have more.

None Vulnerable

WEST	NORTH	EAST	SOUTH
—	—	—	1♣
1♠	2♣	4♠	?

You have to use your judgment on this one. East may be saving or he may be serious. It is less likely that he will be saving against a minor suit so the chances are more that East has a goodish hand with real expectations. If you think they can make 4♠, go ahead and save if you know you are safe given the vulnerability. It would be silly to save and go down too many. Some examples:

You hold ♠ 76 ♡ AQ84 ◇ 84 ♣ AQ963

Pass. With equal vulnerability, you should not save. If they were vulnerable, you could consider it. NOTE though that if partner has a singleton or doubleton heart, you might beat 4♠ with a heart ruff.

You hold ♠ Q ♡ KJ104 ◇ A103 ♣ A9763

Pass. For many reasons. 4♠ is running into a poor trump break. You have lots of potential tricks. Either or both of those red tens may be winners. Also, there is a mild chance that your queen of spades will promote partner's jack. When you save, you want to have pure hands with mostly offensive values.

You hold ♠ 83   ♡ 92   ♦ AQ2   ♣ KQJ973

Bid 5♣. This is a clean hand. You have all offensive values and limited defensive values. Your ♦ AQ2 may take two tricks but it isn't likely you can get a diamond ruff. North, remember, is short in spades and he doesn't have four hearts since he didn't make a Negative Double. More importantly, you have a sixth club which means you aren't getting two club tricks on defense.

None Vulnerable

WEST	NORTH	EAST	SOUTH
—	—	—	1♦
1♡	2♦	Double*	?

* Responsive Double showing clubs and spades

This is an ideal moment for some kind of preemptive action. The opponents have two major suits to play with. If you suspect they have a big fit in one of them (usually the unbid major), you can try to hinder them. You can't go hog wild because West now knows if there is a fit. You won't be able to block the fact that there is a fit but you will be able to stop them from discussing their strength.

THE FUNNY 2NT BID

The Funny 2NT convention is commonly used in two specific situations although a creative mind may find more areas where it can apply. The two situations are these.

1. The auction by your side begins by you bidding a suit, partner responding 1NT, and RHO overcalling with two of a suit. For example.

WEST	NORTH	EAST	SOUTH
—	—	—	1♡
Pass	1NT	2♠	?

2. The auction by your side begins by you bidding a suit, LHO overcalling at the one level, your partner making a Negative Double and your RHO raising to the two level. For example.

WEST	NORTH	EAST	SOUTH
—	—	—	1♣
1♠	Double*	2♠	?

* Negative Double

The Funny 2NT Bid
when Partner Responds 1NT

Earlier in this chapter, I alluded to a way for opener to compete without misdescribing his strength. This is one of the example situations from that discussion.

None Vulnerable

WEST	NORTH	EAST	SOUTH
—	—	—	1♡
Pass	1NT	2♠	?

What should South bid with these two hands?

1. ♠ Q7 ♡ A10742 ◊ KQJ82 ♣ 3
2. ♠ 3   ♡ Q7642   ◊ AKJ103 ♣ AQ

On the first hand, bidding 3◊ will be all right if North doesn't get excited. It won't be all right if North decides to bid 3NT. If you feel that South should be able to bid 3◊ and not worry that North will bid again, I ask you what you would bid with the second hand given the same auction. On the second hand, South has good values and would like to hear another bid from North.

The Funny 2NT bid was invented to help opener compete with 3◇ on both of these hands. The way it works is this. If opener bids 3◇, he is showing a good hand. Not a game forcing hand. Just a good hand. If responder wishes to pass, he can. But if he feels like continuing, that's alright too. If opener has the first of the above hands he can bid 3◇ via the Funny 2NT convention. Instead of bidding 3◇, opener bids 2NT. This is conventional and definitely alertable. The 2NT bid tells North to bid 3♣. North will bid 3♣ as requested and South will correct to 3◇, showing the weakish hand that is just pushing. This distinction can be used on all of these hands.

None Vulnerable

WEST	NORTH	EAST	SOUTH
—	—	—	1♡
Pass	1NT	2♠	?

You hold ♠ 72 ♡ AQ10965 ◇ A72 ♣ AJ

With this hand, South bids 3♡. Because he is bidding 3♡ directly, he is showing a good hand. 3♡ shows enough that game is not impossible.

You hold ♠ 74 ♡ KQ109743 ◇ K3 ♣ KJ

South does not want to get higher than 3♡. It doesn't want to pass 2♠ either. The way for South to compete to 3♡ without fear is to start with 2NT. When North bids 3♣, South converts to 3♡ showing a weak competitive hand.

You hold ♠ 542 ♡ AQ872 ◇ A ♣ KQJ3

Bid 3♣. You have a good hand that may make a game or may make only a partscore. 3♣ tells North you have extra values and leaves the decision to him.

You hold ♠ 73 ♡ A8743 ◇ 83 ♣ AKJ3

At matchpoints, South should wish to compete with 3♣. But only if 3♣ is guaranteed to end the auction. The way to achieve this is to bid 2NT, intending to pass when North bids 3♣.

You can see that this convention works nicely on some auctions. It does have some flaws, however. For starters, you can't bid 2NT as an invitational bid any more. If opener has a nice seventeen or eighteen count, he can't bid 2NT because responder will treat it as a transfer to clubs. Another problem is that if opener transfers to 3♣ and then passes, the partnership will be in 3♣ whether responder likes it or not. Because of the possibility that opener is going to pass when responder bids 3♣, responder has to think twice before accepting the transfer. You are North in these examples.

None Vulnerable

WEST	NORTH	EAST	SOUTH
—	—	—	1♡
Pass	1NT	2♠	2NT
Pass	?		

You hold ♠ KJ3 ♡ 8 ◇ K108752 ♣ 1094

Responder should bid 3♣. If opener passes it, it will be as good or bad a spot as any.

You hold ♠ J82 ♡ K7 ◇ QJ10876 ♣ J3

North has a huge preference for diamonds and can show it by bidding 3◇ instead of 3♣. He knows opener is on the weak side so the only goal is to find a safe home. North–South aren't looking for game contracts after this start.

You hold ♠ A72 ♡ 32 ◊ J2 ♣ Q109763

Don't forget that 2NT only tells you to bid clubs. It doesn't promise clubs. North should bid 3♣ and expect to hear South bid 3◊ or 3♡.

There are additional tricks you can use in tandem with the Funny 2NT bid. One of them is the following.

None Vulnerable

WEST	NORTH	EAST	SOUTH
—	—	—	1♡
Pass	1NT	2♠	?

If South has a hand that wants to raise to 3NT, he can get to 3NT in two ways. South can bid 3NT immediately or he can bid 2NT and then bid 3NT over North's 3♣ bid. It is reasonable to play that the direct 3NT bid promises a stopper in spades and that the slower route to 3NT denies a stopper in spades. Believe me, there are tons of things you can do with this convention if you wish to put in the time and effort.

This convention can apply regardless of opener's suit. You can also use the convention when there has been more interference. You may choose to use it on auctions like these too.

WEST	NORTH	EAST	SOUTH
—	—	—	1♡
Pass	1NT	2♠	?

WEST	NORTH	EAST	SOUTH
—	—	—	1♡
1♠	1NT	2♠	?

WEST	NORTH	EAST	SOUTH
—	—	—	1♡
Double	1NT	2♠	?

WEST	NORTH	EAST	SOUTH
—	—	—	1♡
1♠	1NT	2♢	?

It makes sense to use the Funny 2NT bid on all of these sequences. NOTE that I am not recommending you use or do not use this convention. It is not that popular yet, although it seems to be gaining followers.

The Funny 2NT Bid
After Partner Makes A Negative Double

None Vulnerable

WEST	NORTH	EAST	SOUTH
—	—	—	1♢
1♠	Double*	2♠	?

* Negative Double

A second situation which will benefit from the Funny 2NT convention occurs when your LHO overcalls and your RHO raises after North's Negative Double. South is likely to have something to bid since there are three suits open for North–South to compete in. The Funny 2NT bid works exactly the same way here as it did when North responded 1NT and East–West bid. If South has an invitational hand, he shows his suit immediately. If South has a competitive hand, he starts with 2NT, waits for North to bid 3♣, and then shows his intentions. For instance:

None Vulnerable

WEST	NORTH	EAST	SOUTH
—	—	—	1♢
1♠	Double*	2♠	?

* Negative Double

You hold ♠ 73 ♡ Q983 ◊ AKJ8 ♣ K42

South knows there is a heart fit, but it is dangerous to bid 3♡ with this weak a hand because North may bid 4♡. The Funny 2NT lets South bid 2NT and then 3♡ over North's 3♣ bid.

You hold ♠ 83 ♡ AJ83 ◊ AQJ83 ♣ Q10

This hand could make 4♡ opposite some nice nine counts, but it won't make 4♡ opposite a minimum. South can bid 3♡, which is invitational, allowing North to decide.

The Funny 2NT convention is not one you should rush to add to your system. If you do so, you MUST decide the basic parameters and then stick to them. I promise you that you will have some disasters along the way. Your partnership will have at least one of these bad things happen.

1. Opener will have a hand that really wanted to bid 2NT and couldn't because of the convention.

2. Opener will forget he is using the convention and will rebid something on a weak hand. As luck will have it, responder will remember the convention and will alert it. You can imagine the ensuing mess.

3. Opener will remember the convention and will bid 2NT in an effort to compete with some weakish hand. This time, North will forget the convention and will continue to 3NT. Ugh.

4. −10. Fill these in yourself.

Chapter Eleven

EVERYONE BIDS EXCEPT RESPONDER

THE AUCTION STARTS, for example,

WEST	NORTH	EAST	SOUTH
—	—	—	1♣
1♦	Pass	1♥	?

This is a tenuous moment for South. North's pass doesn't mean the end of North–South's chances but it is a warning. It is possible that North–South still own the hand. It might be that South has a big enough hand to outbid East–West and it might be that North has a penalty pass. If South has a singleton or void in West's suit, he may suspect that North is trapping. If South has a balanced hand, he should expect North to be broke until proven otherwise.

AFTER LHO DOUBLES

I am not fond of trapping with the North hand when West makes a takeout double. If I open and West doubles and North passes, I play North for a poor hand which may reach six or seven points but is usually less.

None Vulnerable

WEST	NORTH	EAST	SOUTH
—	—	—	1♣
Double	Pass	1♠	?

You hold ♠ KQ8 ♡ AQ72 ◇ K2 ♣ 10762

Pass. 1NT shows 18–19 high card points with stoppers. This hand is an ace too weak.

You hold ♠ A2 ♡ 832 ◇ K32 ♣ AQJ97

Pass again. You need tricks to compete when your partner is broke.

You hold ♠ 8 ♡ AQ82 ◇ QJ6 ♣ AK1084

Double. Your extra values and good shape allow you to get back into the bidding. Your shape is the primary reason you can bid here. Having sixteen points is not, by itself, a reason to double. The opponents have spades and you are likely to be outbid but you may be able to push them higher than they wish to go.

None Vulnerable

You hold ♠ AQJ5 ♡ 843 ◇ KQJ106 ♣ 7

WEST	NORTH	EAST	SOUTH
—	—	—	1◇
Double	Pass	1♡	?

Bid 1♠. You have good, solid suits. If you catch four spades and a doubleton heart, you can compete to two or three spades. If you pass now, it becomes too dangerous to compete later.

None Vulnerable

WEST	NORTH	EAST	SOUTH
—	—	—	1◇
Double	Pass	2◇	?

You hold ♠ QJ3 ♡ AJ72 ◇ KQ72 ♣ AQ

Pass. Where are you going? East–West have half the deck. You have the other half. There is no future in this hand. Balanced hands should be quiet when the opponents have good hands. A possible bid is double but to what purpose? You don't want partner to compete in diamonds and you don't expect him to have anything else to bid. Passing this hand is just good judgment.

You hold ♠ J853 ♡ A ◇ AQJ97 ♣ K73

Double should mean something. A likely meaning is you have good diamonds and really do welcome a diamond lead. If the opponents end up in a suit contract, North will lead them because he has nothing else to lead. If West ends up in notrump, though, you don't want North talking himself into leading a heart from the Q10643. You want a diamond lead. If you double 2◇, you will get it.

There is a second possible meaning for double. You can play double says you are almost good enough to compete in diamonds but that you need something from partner to make it worthwhile. I don't remember many hands that required judgment as delicate as this. I like double to show good diamonds that want the lead.

You hold ♠ 102 ♡ 8 ◇ KQJ10763 ♣ AQ6

Bid 4◇ with equal vulnerability. Bid 5◇ if they are vulnerable and you aren't. This is one too many if partner is broke. If North has a card in clubs or if he has a useful card somewhere, you have enough tricks. The plus is that East–West are allowed to misjudge. It happens all the time. The keys to this action are:

1. You have a good enough suit to know that no one has a trump stack.

2. You have a pure hand with no slow winners, which means they are likely to have a game.

Bidding as high as you can go is far superior to bidding 3◇ or double and later bidding 5◇ when they bid a game. This gives them time to discuss the best suit and the correct level. Jumping to 4◇ or 5◇ forces East–West to guess on both counts.

LHO OVERCALLS

When West overcalls as opposed to doubling, the bidding doesn't go as quickly. Overcalls offer only one suit to play in. Doubles offer three. If West overcalls and no fit is found, the bidding may stop for a moment unless East can do something on his own. When East passes, South must judge whether to reopen. South may reopen on the basis of a good hand or he may reopen if it looks like North is making a penalty pass.

None Vulnerable

WEST	NORTH	EAST	SOUTH
—	—	—	1♦
1♠	Pass	Pass	?

You hold ♠ 7   ♡ A83   ◇ A10653   ♣ KJ52

Double. It is odds–on that North has spades and is waiting for South to double. South should double with most hands with short spades and does so. There is no suggestion of extra values.

You hold ♠ KJ43   ♡ AQ3   ◇ A1063   ♣ 109

Pass as fast as you can. You have four spades, which says clearly that North does not have a trap pass. Do not bid 1NT. That shows 18–19 points. North is tentatively broke so you will need more points than you have to have a chance in 1NT.

You hold ♠ None   ♡ AJ8   ◇ A109653   ♣ AQ73

Double. It is not at all good to have a void when you reopen with double. A void is a hint that North has good spades but it is also a hint that West has better spades than you may like. If North passes with ♠KJ954 of spades, as he is likely to, you won't have a spade to lead when you get in. That will work badly for the defense.

The reason double is okay with this hand is that you have aces. These will take tricks. Your hand will be a disappointment but it won't be a total loss.

None Vulnerable
You hold ♠ Q6   ♡ KQJ1086   ◊ AK8   ♣ A4

WEST	NORTH	EAST	SOUTH
—	—	—	1♡
1♠	Pass	Pass	?

Bid 3♡, which is a tiny stretch. 3♡ shows more than it would had North responded. North is expected to evaluate his hand in terms of having shown 0–6 points.

None Vulnerable
You hold ♠ 7   ♡ AK   ◊ AKQ9742   ♣ J94

WEST	NORTH	EAST	SOUTH
—	—	—	1◊
1♠	Pass	Pass	?

You do not want to double and hear North pass. Nor do you wish to jump to 3◊ and hear North pass that either. What you want to do is to get North to admit to a spade stopper. There are two ways to do this. You can cue–bid 2♠. Or, if you play the jump to 3♠ asks for a stopper, you can do that. This gets you to 3NT when North has a stopper, but it also gets you to the four level when he doesn't have a stopper. 4◊ may be too high. The alternative I like is to bid 2♠, which shows a huge hand that is afraid to double. It is possible that you can bid 2♠ and get your message across this way. However you define these cue bids, it is necessary to have them available so that you don't have to reopen with a double on hands like the one here.

None Vulnerable
You hold ♠ None ♡ A ◇ KQJ10764 ♣ AQ984

WEST	NORTH	EAST	SOUTH
—	—	—	1◇
1♡	Pass	Pass	?

Bid 2♡. This is another hand type that should not reopen with a double. The last thing you want is to defend against a heart contract. Nor are you interested in hearing about partner's spades.

One possible bid is 3♣. The problem with this is that it might be passed out. Remember, you didn't open with a two bid. If you had a game forcing hand, you would have opened 2♣. If you bid 3♣ here, partner will pass with:

♠ 9763 ♡ 8763 ◇ 2 ♣ J632

You will make eleven or twelve tricks but they won't be worth much when you are in a partscore. You should start with 2♠ and follow with some number of clubs. This will show a huge two suiter which was strong enough in tricks to open with a 2♣ bid but not strong enough in points.

Digressing from the point of this hand, you shouldn't open this hand 2♣ even though it is better, trickwise, than many 2♣ opening bids. You will do better with two suiters if you open them with a one bid. This more or less assures you a chance to show your hand eventually. If you open this hand 2♣, someone out there will bid hearts or spades. You will be at the four level before you can show one of your suits. What will you do if the auction begins 2♣–2♠–Pass–4♠–?. You will probably guess to bid 5◇. Now your partner will have to guess if his king of hearts or clubs is worth anything.

None Vulnerable
You hold ♠ A6　♡ AQ6　◇ 1064　♣ AKJ62

WEST	NORTH	EAST	SOUTH
—	—	—	1♣
1♡	Pass	Pass	?

Bid 1NT. This shows 18–19 points as discussed a few
hands ago. Do not double, jump to 2NT, or rebid clubs.
1NT shows 18–19 balanced points with hearts stopped
and that is exactly what you have.

None Vulnerable
You hold ♠ AQ76　♡ 63　◇ AK62　♣ KQ4

WEST	NORTH	EAST	SOUTH
—	—	—	1◇
1♡	Pass	Pass	Double
2♡	2♠	Pass	?

Pass. Whatever North has, he didn't have enough to bid
the first time. He could have bid 1♠ or made a Negative
Double. His likely hand is something like:

♠ 107542　♡ 853　◇ Q74　♣ J10

If North can count on South to remember the auction, it
is safe for North to bid 2♠ on hands like this.

None Vulnerable
You hold ♠ 8　♡ AQJ6　◇ AKJ43　♣ J104

WEST	NORTH	EAST	SOUTH
—	—	—	1◇
1♠	Pass	2♣	?

Double. This is for takeout showing hearts and
diamonds and a pretty good hand. You suspect that North
has a spade stack but he may have a crummy hand. If he
has the bad hand, you need a good one to make it worth
getting back into the auction. NOTE that double is much

more flexible than bidding 2♦ or 2♡. Double keeps both suits available at a low level. 2♦ loses the hearts and bidding 2♡ forces North to 3♦ if that is his preference.

None Vulnerable
You hold ♠ 83 ♡ AQ874 ◇ K72 ♣ AQJ

WEST	NORTH	EAST	SOUTH
—	—	—	1♡
1♠	Pass	2♦	?

Learn to pass balanced hands like this. Double would be for takeout and you don't have club support. Bidding 2♡ is just awful. If North has heart support, he has a horrible hand. If he has enough that 2♡ will survive, he may be able to bid 2♡ over 2♦.

None Vulnerable

WEST	NORTH	EAST	SOUTH
—	—	—	1♡
1♠	Pass	2♠	?

You hold ♠ 8 ♡ AJ875 ◇ KQ6 ♣ AJ62

Double. With East raising spades, it is unlikely that North has a penalty pass. Still, South should compete when he has the good shape and a king or so more than a minimum. Especially so when you can make a takeout double which gets three suits involved. You should avoid doubling without good shape. The bidding is likely to go higher and you don't want partner bidding a suit you don't have.

You hold ♠ 832 ♡ AKJ32 ◇ 83 ♣ AKQ

Ouch. Something may be right but there is no safe way to bid. If you double and West bids 3♠, North will be within himself to bid 4♦ with:

♠ 96 ♡ 104 ◇ K107652 ♣ 732

It won't be a success. South has to pass. With correct shape, you can stretch by one or two points to double. Without correct shape, pull in by a couple of points.

None Vulnerable
You hold ♠ 6   ♡ A2   ◇ AKJ3   ♣ AQ8763

WEST	NORTH	EAST	SOUTH
—	—	—	1♣
1♠	Pass	2♠	?

What does 2NT mean? If it is natural, South can bid 3♣ which is relatively safe but not productive, or he can reverse to 3◇, which might catch some interest from North. Of course, it may catch North with a crummy hand. If 2NT is unusual, South can bid that, which won't get North–South higher than the three level.

None Vulnerable

WEST	NORTH	EAST	SOUTH
—	—	—	1♡
1♠	Pass	3♠*	?

* Preemptive

You hold ♠ J4   ♡ AKQ82   ◇ AQ7   ♣ QJ4

The preemptive 3♠ bid wins. You have too many losers to double for takeout. North will take a double out and you will go down on a hand that is a favorite to beat 3♠. I have mentioned the preemptive raise of overcalls in earlier chapters. This is one more example of their effectiveness.

You hold ♠ Q3   ♡ KJ743   ◇ AJ   ♣ AKQ3

Pass again. You have points but no tricks and losers all over the place. If you double, North will bid diamonds much of the time and you will hate it. If you bid 4♣, you will get a lot of preferences to 4♡. This is down two tricks if you are lucky and more if you are not.

None Vulnerable
You hold ♠ Q84 ♡ AKQ86 ◇ K73 ♣ 73

WEST	NORTH	EAST	SOUTH
—	—	—	1♡
1♠	Pass	2♡*	?

*Cue bid—usually with support

Double. What does double mean here? I can think of three sensible treatments for a double here.

You can play the double says you want hearts led, just like you do when West makes a takout double and East cue–bids.

You can also play the double as takout, saying you would have doubled if East raised to 2♠. A good hand is needed if you play the double as takeout. You won't have too many of them, but since they are important hands to show, you will be happy to have double available when needed. With a shapely minimum hand , you will pass. If the bidding stops in 2♠, you can come back in later with a belated takeout double.

Finally, you can play the double says you want to compete in your suit, but are afraid to bid higher unless partner has some help. This hand is good enough to compete to 3♡ if partner has heart support and not much else.

♠ A32 ♡ AQJ93 ◇ AKJ ♣ 108

If partner has two small hearts, competing will be wrong. If you play the double to show this kind of hand, you have to pass with your takeout double type hands and hope you can make a later takeout double.

Chapter Twelve

OPENER'S RHO BALANCES

NOT MUCH TO BE SAID HERE except that opener quits bidding unless he has something good to say. The requirements aren't always measured in points. If opener has a very good suit or a second suit to show, he can do so without a big hand. The underlying requirement is that South has enough tricks that opener won't be buried.

RHO REOPENS WITH ONE OF A SUIT

None Vulnerable
You hold ♠ QJ4 ♡ A8 ◇ KJ874 ♣ AQJ

WEST	NORTH	EAST	SOUTH
—	—	—	1◇
Pass	Pass	1♠	?

1NT shows these general values. Even so, I'm not sure I would bid since there is no obvious source of tricks. If North is broke, it won't be easy to get any tricks from this mess.

None Vulnerable
You hold ♠ 7 ♡ 73 ◇ AQJ87 ♣ AQJ83

WEST	NORTH	EAST	SOUTH
—	—	—	1◇
Pass	Pass	1♠	?

Bid 2♣. Your shape protects you from harm. If North can raise clubs, you may end up taking a save against 4♡ or 4♠.

None Vulnerable
You hold ♠ 3 ♡ J8652 ◇ AQ9 ♣ AKJ6

WEST	NORTH	EAST	SOUTH
—	—	—	1♡
Pass	Pass	1♠	?

With good shape, you can double for takeout. You need more than a minimum opening bid but you don't need a huge hand when you have three suits to offer.

None Vulnerable
You hold ♠ J76 ♡ AK763 ◇ AQ7 ♣ KQ

WEST	NORTH	EAST	SOUTH
—	—	—	1♡
Pass	Pass	1♠	?

Pass. All you have is points. You can't rebid hearts and you can't make a takeout double. Pass and beat the players who couldn't resist the lure of nineteen high card points.

None Vulnerable
You hold ♠ 8632 ♡ A ◇ AQJ1075 ♣ K4

WEST	NORTH	EAST	SOUTH
—	—	—	1◇
Pass	Pass	1♠	?

Bid 2◇. Curiously, the better your opponents, the more important it is for you to bid 2◇. Good opponents will have complete methods which will include a 2◇ cue bid. If you bid 2◇, you deprive West of his 2◇ bid. He will have to compensate. NOTE that taking West's 2◇ bid away is a minor issue. You need tricks before you dare risk this liberty. This hand has seven potential tricks so you aren't out of line.

RHO REOPENS
WITH A TAKEOUT DOUBLE

None Vulnerable

WEST	NORTH	EAST	SOUTH
—	—	—	1◊
Pass	Pass	Double	?

When East reopens with a double, you have different considerations. You may have a good hand that wants to keep bidding, but you may also have a hand that doesn't want to play in 1◊ doubled.

None Vulnerable
You hold ♠ A62 ♡ KJ9 ◊ J762 ♣ AJ9

WEST	NORTH	EAST	SOUTH
—	—	—	1◊
Pass	Pass	Double	?

Just pass. You may get passed out in 1◊ doubled. That is the worst thing that can happen. But it doesn't have to happen. North may decide he doesn't like 1◊ doubled either. There is no bid that South can contemplate that doesn't make me shudder.

None Vulnerable
You hold ♠ A762 ♡ AKJ8 ◊ 73 ♣ J92

WEST	NORTH	EAST	SOUTH
—	—	—	1♣
Pass	Pass	Double	?

I would bid 1♡. When you run from a minor suit to a major suit over East's reopening double, it does not promise a good hand. You may have one but very possibly, you are running from 1♣ doubled.

None Vulnerable
You hold ♠ A73 ♡ AQ7 ◇ 72 ♣ AKJ62

WEST	NORTH	EAST	SOUTH
—	—	—	1♣
Pass	Pass	Double	?

Redouble. Redouble shows a hand good enough that your side may still be able to make something. If North has a maximum pass, he can bid or double if it looks right to do so. Your redouble is forward going. It asks North for cooperation. It IS NOT an SOS bid. This applies whether the opening bid is a major or a minor.

None Vulnerable
You hold ♠ Q83 ♡ 9652 ◇ 62 ♣ Q984

WEST	NORTH	EAST	SOUTH
—	1◇	Pass	Pass
Double	Redouble	2♣	?

Double. North showed a big hand and asked for South to do something. South has as many points as can be expected and he has a nice four card club holding. Double shows this hand. North isn't obliged to pass but he will often do so.

None Vulnerable

WEST	NORTH	EAST	SOUTH
—	1♡	Pass	Pass
Double	Redouble	1♠	?

You hold ♠ 843 ♡ 83 ◇ 1042 ♣ KJ863

Bid 2♣. You have something useful given North has invited you to the party.

None Vulnerable
You hold ♠ 9762   ♡ 872   ◇ 2   ♣ Q10653

WEST	NORTH	EAST	SOUTH
—	1♡	Pass	Pass
Double	Redouble	1♠	?

Bid 2♡. You have already passed once. You have four or five support points and North can't expect more. Bid!

None Vulnerable
You hold ♠ 62   ♡ 63   ◇ KJ762   ♣ AKQ10

WEST	NORTH	EAST	SOUTH
—	—	—	1◇
Pass	Pass	Double	?

There are a number of reasons for bidding 2♣. North will have more to think about if he is on lead. Also, 2♣ takes away West's one level responses and it takes away West's jump to the two level. NOTE that 2♣ promises good diamonds. Opener might run from a three card suit into a four card suit at the one level. If opener bids a second suit at the two level over a take-out double, he promises he is prepared for a preference to his first suit.

Chapter Thirteen

MORE UNUSUAL DOUBLES

AT VARIOUS POINTS in this book, I have mentioned some unusual applications of a double. In this final chapter, I will show some of these bids. Since the material in this section is still theoretical, I won't attempt to evaluate it.

THE RETURN NEGATIVE DOUBLE

I talked about this convention in Chapter 10. It is used by the opening bidder on sequences like this one.

South holds ♠ AJ3   ♡ KJ3   ◇ 83   ♣ AJ1074

WEST	NORTH	EAST	SOUTH
—	—	—	1♣
1◇	Double*	2◇	Double**

  * Negative Double
** Return Negative Double

South wants to keep bidding, but doesn't have a clear suit to bid. South wants North to pick a suit. North can bid a major suit which will result in a 4–3 fit or North can raise clubs. North can also pass 2◇ doubled if he wants. If he does pass, he does so knowing that he was asked to bid. South's double was for takeout, not for penalty.

The keys to this auction.

1. South opened the bidding.
2. West overcalled.
3. North made a Negative Double.
4. East made a simple raise.
5. South doubled.

South's double is takeout ONLY if East raises. If East bids a new suit, double by South is for penalty.

Question for your partnership. Does this double by opener apply only at the two level or does it apply if RHO is raising to the three level?

WEST	NORTH	EAST	SOUTH
—	—	—	1◇
2♣	Double*	3♣	Double

*Negative Double

Is South's double penalty or is it for takeout? You must decide.

WEST	NORTH	EAST	SOUTH
—	—	—	1◇
1♡	Double*	3♡	Double

*Negative Double

How about this double? East made a jump raise to the three level as opposed to a simple raise as happened on the previous hand. My view? I suggest you play these doubles on only if RHO raises to the two level.

SECOND DOUBLES
BY THE NEGATIVE DOUBLER

What does it mean when you make a Negative Double and then follow with another double?

WEST	NORTH	EAST	SOUTH
—	1♣	1♡	Double*
2♡	Pass	Pass	Double

*Negative Double

If South doubles 2♡, is it for penalty or does it have a deeper meaning? If this auction occurred at your table presently, do you have a clear definition or are you guessing like a lot of players do? This is the treatment I recommend. If South doubles 2♡, he is showing a balanced good hand that doesn't have a clear natural bid to make. The following hands would all double 2♡ on the sequence above.

You hold ♠ AJ73   ♡ J63   ◇ KQ94   ♣ 93

South can't give up but at the same time, there is nothing sensible for him to bid. Double tells North that South has at least ten high card points and nothing good to bid. NOTE that the original double promised four spades. North may choose to bid a three card spade suit. He may be able to bid clubs or diamonds. It is not likely that he will want to bid 2NT. It is possible that 2NT by North should be some kind of takeout bid asking for South to choose a minor suit. North might have this hand:

♠ K3   ♡ 43   ◇ J1083   ♣ AKJ74

If 2NT were known to be for takeout, it would be the best way to find a minor suit fit.

WEST	NORTH	EAST	SOUTH
—	1♣	1♡	Double*
2♡	Pass	Pass	?

*Negative Double

You hold ♠ J1073　♡ 83　♢ AKJ2　♣ KJ2

South has a better hand now. The answer is still to double. South should not have a singleton heart and he should not have four card support for opener's club suit.

You hold ♠ Q1073　♡ KJ94　♢ KJ4　♣ J3

Bid 2NT. Double would be takeout and North will bid something. He won't pass. It is unlikely you will ever have this good a hand for defense. If it happens, you must not double. It is better to cater to all the hard ten and eleven point hands that come up than the rare hand that really wants to double the opponents.

You hold ♠ K1074　♡ 4　♢ AJ84　♣ K1095

Here is a trick you can use. Bid 2♠. South's Negative Double showed exactly four spades. Nothing has changed that. When South now bids 2♠, the meaning is that in addition to his four spades, he also has club support and likely has a singleton heart PLUS he has too many points to bid only 3♣. In essence, the 2♠ bid says South has a limit raise in clubs along with his four spades.

NOTE that 2♠ is not forcing. North can pass if he wants to. North would do this with a minimum 3–4–3–3 hand.

WEST	NORTH	EAST	SOUTH
—	1♣	1♡	Double*
2♢	Pass	Pass	Double

*Negative Double

This sequence looks similar to the previous one except that West has bid a new suit instead of raising East's hearts. This double needs some extra thought. Since West is bidding a suit South is likely to have, South's double may be thought of as penalty. Still, South's original double does not promise diamonds. It is also possible that a second double could show a good balanced ten point hand which just wants North to bid something. For the sake of consistency, I suggest you play a second double shows a ten point hand that wants North's help in making a decision.

You hold ♠ QJ82 ♡ J83 ◇ K83 ♣ A94

This hand is worth bidding, but it is almost impossible to find a correct bid without help from partner. If double is defined as showing a maximum hand for the earlier Negative Double, you should be able to sort it out.

WEST	NORTH	EAST	SOUTH
—	1♣	1♠	Double*
2♡	Pass	Pass	Double

*Negative Double

This sequence is different from the previous two sequences in that West has bid a new suit which South is known to have. South's double of 1♠ promised four hearts. Given this, I suggest that a second double by South be more penalty oriented.

You hold ♠ J1074 ♡ AJ83 ◇ A109 ♣ 73

South could whack 2♡ with this. NOTE that South is also ready if the opponents run out to spades. Sometimes West bids a new suit intending to run back to partner's suit if he gets doubled. If South had this hand instead:

♠ 103 ♡ AJ873 ◇ A109 ♣ 743

355

passing 2♡ and setting it three or four tricks might be better than doubling and ending up defending against 2♠. Fortunately, you won't see this particular scenario very often.

WEST	NORTH	EAST	SOUTH
—	1♡	2♣	Double*
3♣	Pass	Pass	Double

*Negative Double

South is doubling the same suit he doubled the round before. The same principle should apply here. South is showing a hand with ten or more high card points that needs decision help from North. South won't make this double if he has a natural bid that he could make instead so North will know South doesn't have heart support. Also, South won't have a singleton club.

You hold ♠ KJ83   ♡ 32   ◇ AQ983   ♣ 83

This is the classic example of a second double. South could bid 3◇ too, but that is a little risky. If South had a sixth diamond and one less club, 3◇ would make sense. With the hand he actually has, double will work well if North bids AND ALSO if North chooses to pass.

LATER DOUBLES
BY RESPONDER AFTER HAVING
FIRST RESPONDED IN A SUIT

WEST	NORTH	EAST	SOUTH
—	1◇	1♡	1♠
2♡	Pass	Pass	Double

When responder bids a suit and then doubles on the next round, there are all kinds of reasons for playing double as some sort of Negative Double. Naturally, this situation is cluttered up with different kinds of sequences. On the sequence here, East overcalled 1♡, South bid 1♠, and West raised.

What should South do with this?

♠ KJ873   ♡ 42   ◊ 4   ♣ AJ982

If you agree that South should bid 1♠ on the first round, (that's what I would do) then you will agree that South has a problem on the second round. By all systems that I am familiar with, 3♣ now would be forcing. Be honest now. Could you resist bidding 3♣ here? Or would you rebid 2♠? Or would you pass? I don't think I would pass. But I wouldn't be happy bidding, either. If I bid 3♣, North will have to bid something and I don't really have the values to justify that. For instance, if North bids 3NT, how in the world will it make?

Better is to play that a double now is a belated Negative Double. With this understanding, South will double and North will do something. If North has two spades, he can bid 2♠. It is possible he will pass. South has the ten (almost) points he promises so North won't be unhappy with South's defensive strength. North–South may have to scramble, but the final contract will have a better chance of making than if South bids 3♣, which propels the bidding forward on momentum and not merit.

This situation is not the same as the one where South first made a Negative Double and then made a second double. When South bids a suit first and then comes back in with a double, he is allowed to have a singleton in the opponents' suit. Also you give up something with this double. If South's hand is better suited to defense, he can't double for penalty.

You hold ♠ A7642 ♡ QJ8 ◇ KJ3 ♣ 73

WEST	NORTH	EAST	SOUTH
—	1♣	1♡	1♠
2♡	Pass	Pass	?

If you double, North will usually take it out. You know
North doesn't have spade support (especially true if you
are using Support Doubles) so North will end up bidding
3♣ or 3◇ or will ask you for a minor suit preference by
bidding 2NT. You are better off bidding 2NT, natural, or
passing and taking your two or three trick set. What you
do here is up to your partnership. Do you want to adopt
all kinds of science or do you want to keep your
competitive bidding relatively simple. Simple bidding
has a lot going for it. It is subject to few
misunderstandings and I can't say enough for that.
Unfortunately, simple bidding causes you to miss
opportunities on partscore hands. How badly do you hate
someone stealing a partscore from you? You will have to
decide what you want to do.

None Vulnerable
You hold ♠ 83 ♡ AQ983 ◇ J3 ♣ AJ82

WEST	NORTH	EAST	SOUTH
—	1♠	Pass	2♡
3◇	Pass	Pass	?

Even after you make a two over one response, the belated
Negative Double will be the solution on many hands. On
this hand (used as an aside in my Doubles article in
Bridge Today), the suggested answer was for South to
double. South has a hand that doesn't have a natural bid
so he doubles to tell North that South wants further
bidding. What does North want to do? Even though
South's double isn't strictly for penalty, it is likely that

North will pass it out. Remember, North has already denied heart support so he rates to have one or two hearts and therefore may have some diamond length.

WEST	NORTH	EAST	SOUTH
—	1♡	Pass	1NT
2◇	Pass	Pass	?

As discussed briefly earlier in this chapter, it is possible to play double by South to show a good 1NT bid which wants North to do something.

You hold ♠ A93 ♡ 54 ◇ 1094 ♣ AJ743

South has enough that North–South should own the hand. Double, if used as discussed, says just that. It tells North that South likes his hand but isn't able to make a definitive bid. North, as usual in these cases, is asked to make the correct final decision.

This analogous auction, also mentioned earlier, lets opener do much the same thing.

You hold ♠ Q9873 ♡ AJ3 ◇ 8 ♣ AQJ8

WEST	NORTH	EAST	SOUTH
—	—	—	1♠
Pass	1NT	2◇	?

This discussion applies regardless of whether 1NT can be normal or forcing. South wants North to bid. Unfortunately, there is no call South can make that describes this hand. 2♠ would show a sixth spade. 2♡ would show a fourth heart. 3♣ would be an overbid and might cause North–South to miss a 5–3 heart fit.

The winning bid, once again, is double. But only if it is precisely defined as takeout. Most partnerships, including mine, still play this double is for penalty. If South had the minor suits reversed:

♠ Q9873 ♡ AJ3 ◇ AQJ8 ♣ 8

he would like to double 2♢ for business. It would be a catastrophe if South doubled 2♢ for penalty with this hand only to hear North alert that it was a takeout double and then to take it out to 3♣.

The range of interpretations you can assign to doubles goes far beyond what was shown in this short section. This area of bidding is one of the latest to enter the world of bidding and it is still in the early stages of development. I am not sure yet that I would recommend much of this material at this moment. There is obvious merit to some of the examples, but there is also great danger. Furthermore, in some cases, it is not clear that what you gain is worth more than what you lose.

✳ *The Complete Guide To*
PASSED HAND BIDDING

In this major work, Mike Lawrence presents the first modern and complete guide to Passed Hand Bidding. Questions discussed include: When to open aggressively in third seat? What does a preempt in fourth seat look like? What does a passed hand jump shift look like? How should the auction be continued? How to deal with competition? What useful convbentions are available? Just about every situation that can occur is covered with numerous examples. **YOU WILL DEVELOP THE JUDGEMENT AND METHODS TO SUCCEED.**

Mike Lawrence is a world renowned bridge player and author. As a player, Lawrence has won three world championships besides winning scores of national and regional events. Lawrence is a leading master point holder with the American Contract Bridge League and is a World Bridge Federation Grand Master.

As an author, Lawrence is one of the most prolific wirters on bridge. Not only has he written twelve bridge books but he has also has his own newsletter and is a columnist for the American Contract Bridge League magazine. Two of his books, *How to Read Your Opponents' Cards* and *The Complete Book on Overcalls* were named "book of the year" by Alfred Sheinwold and are recognized as classics.

The Complete Guide To PASSED HAND BIDDING by Mike Lawrence is a 224 page, 5 1/2" by 8 1/2", softcover book which retails for $12.95 . The book can be ordered from Lawrence & Leong Publishing, 10430 Greenview Drive, Oakland, California 94605. For mail orders add $1.50 for shipping & handling. (California residents please add applicable sales tax.)

Mike Lawrence's Bidding Quizzes
THE UNCONTESTED AUCTION

Mike Lawrence's Bidding Quizzes will provide you and your friends with hours of entertainment while also sharpening your bidding skills. Match wits with Mike Lawrence and find out what would have been the best bid and why. Here is a delightful book for bridge players of all strengths. The book deals with uncontested bidding using Standard American Two Over One bidding methods popular among American tournament players today. By challenging each quiz **YOUR UNDERSTANDING OF THE FINER POINTS OF CONSTRUCTIVE BIDDING SHOULD DEFINITELY IMPROVE.**

Mike Lawrence is a world renowned bridge player and author. As a player, Lawrence has won three world championships besides winning scores of national and regional events. Lawrence is a leading master point holder with the American Contract Bridge League and is a World Bridge Federation Grand Master.

As an author, Lawrence is one of the most prolific wirters on bridge. Not only has he written twelve bridge books but he has also has his own newsletter and is a columist for the American Contract Bridge League magazine. Two of his books, *How to Read Your Opponents' Cards* and *The Complete Book on Overcalls* were named "book of the year" by Alfred Sheinwold and are recognized as classics.

BIDDING QUIZZES—THE UNCONTESTED AUCTION by Mike Lawrence is a 280 page, 5 1/2" by 8 1/2", softcover book which retails for $13.95 . The book can be ordered from Lawrence & Leong Publishing, 10430 Greenview Drive, Oakland, California 94605. For mail orders add $1.50 for shipping & handling. (California residents please add applicable sales tax.)

CREATIVE CARD PLAY
The Cure For Unimaginative Bridge

CREATIVE CARD PLAY is no ordinary bridge book. In sixty-one challenging, instructive, and entertaining hands you are invited to explore an expert's thought processes as he masterfully and imaginatively selects his bids and plays. Often his actions will seem surprising but sometimes because of the opponents table actions you will find the reasoning for his actions logical and compelling.

You will learn a whole new perspective in card play by gaining a heightened sensitivity to your opponents confidence or lack of confidence displayed in the bidding or play. You will learn to note and take advantage of an opponents intense interest or obvious lack of interest in the ensuing play. Above all you will become more aware how to create opportunities for the opponents to go wrong more often. **YOUR TABLE PRESENCE CANNOT HELP BUT IMPROVE.**

James Kauder has played bridge for over thirty years professionally and has made money playing in tough rubber bridge games. He has been a frequent contributor to The Bridge World and has been a columnist in the ACBL Bulletin. He has authored the critically acclaimed work The Bridge Philosopher of which this book is a new and improved version. He is the son of Mary Jane Farell a noted bridge teacher and one of the world's leading women players. When not making money playing bridge, poker, or other card games, he is a practicing attorney of law.

CREATIVE CARD PLAY by James S. Kauder is a 240 page, 5 1/2" by 8 1/2", softcover book which retails for $11.95 and contains a Foreword by Mike Lawrence. The book can be ordered from Lawrence & Leong Publishing, 10430 Greenview Drive, Oakland, California 94605. For mail orders add $1.50 for shipping & handling. (California residents please add applicable sales tax.)